BEYOND BIRYANI

BEYOND BIRYANI

The Making of a Globalised Hyderabad

DINESH C. SHARMA

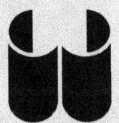

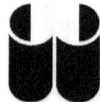

Published by Westland Non-Fiction, an imprint of Westland Books, a division of Nasadiya Technologies Private Limited, in 2024

No. 269/2B, First Floor, 'Irai Arul', Vimalraj Street, Nethaji Nagar, Alapakkam Main Road, Maduravoyal, Chennai 600095

Westland, the Westland logo, Westland Non-Fiction and the Westland Non-Fiction logo are the trademarks of Nasadiya Technologies Private Limited, or its affiliates.

ISBN: 9789371972444

10 9 8 7 6 5 4 3 2 1

Typeset by Mukul

Printed at Manipal Technologies Limited, Manipal

In the fond memory of
Babuji and Mummy

Contents

Section III
A Window to the World (1992–2022)

Abbreviations and Acronyms

AEET	Atomic Energy Establishment Trombay
AP	Andhra Pradesh
API	Active Pharmaceutical Ingredient
ASCI	Administrative Staff College of India
ATA	American Telugu Association
BARC	Bhabha Atomic Research Centre
BEL	Bharat Electronics Limited
BHU	Banaras Hindu University
BPO	Business Process Outsourcing
BSIR	Board of Scientific and Industrial Research
CCMB	Centre for Cellular and Molecular Biology
CDFD	Centre for DNA Fingerprinting and Diagnostics
CIB	City Improvement Board
CID	Commerce and Industries Department
CMC	Computer Maintenance Corporation
CSIR	Council of Scientific and Industrial Research
CLSIR	Central Laboratories for Scientific and Industrial Research

DAE	Department of Atomic Energy
DBT	Department of Biotechnology
DCM	Delhi Cloth Mills Limited
DoE	Department of Electronics
DMRL	Defence Metallurgical Research Laboratory
DRDO	Defence Research and Development Organisation
DRDL	Defence Research and Development Laboratory
DRL	Dr Reddy's Laboratories Limited
DST	Department of Science and Technology
ECIL	Electronics Corporation of India Limited
EFLU	English and Foreign Languages University
EVM	Electronic Voting Machine
GCC	Global Capability Centre
GTS	Great Trigonometrical Survey
HAL	Hindustan Aeronautics Limited
HSS	Hyderabad Science Society
IAS	Indian Administrative Service
IAU	International Astronomical Union
ICRISAT	International Crop Research Institute for the Semi-Arid Tropics
ICS	Indian Civil Service
ICMR	Indian Council of Medical Research
IDPL	Indian Drugs and Pharmaceuticals Limited
IES	Indian Educational Services
IFSC	International Financial Services Centre
IIA	Indian Institute of Astrophysics
IISc	Indian Institute of Science
IIT	Indian Institute of Technology
IICT	Indian Institute of Chemical Technology
IIIT	International Institute of Information Technology
IKP	ICICI Knowledge Park
IL	Industrial Laboratory
IMD	India Meteorological Department
IMS	Indian Medical Service
IRFA	Indian Research Fund Association
ISB	Indian School of Business

ISRO	Indian Space Research Organisation
IT	Information Technology
ITES	Information Technology-Enabled Services
LTC	Low-Temperature Carbonisation
MIDHANI	Mishra Dhatu Nigam
NBL	National Biological Laboratory
NCBS	National Centre for Biological Science
NCL	National Chemical Laboratory
NGRI	National Geophysical Research Institute
NFC	Nuclear Fuel Complex
NII	National Institute of Immunology
NIN	National Institute of Nutrition
NPL	National Physical Laboratory
NRL	Nutritional Research Laboratories
NRSA	National Remote Sensing Agency
NRSC	National Remote Sensing Centre
NRSR	Natural Resources and Scientific Research
NTR	Nandamuri Taraka Rama Rao
OGH	Osmania General Hospital
OU	Osmania University
PWD	Public Works Department
RRL	Regional Research Laboratory
SCCL	Singareni Collieries Company Limited
SRC	States Reorganisation Commission
SOL	Standard Organics Limited
STPI	Software Technology Parks of India
TANA	Telugu Association of North America
TDB	Technology Development Board
TDE	Technical Development Establishment
TDP	Telugu Desam Party
TI	Texas Instruments
TIFR	Tata Institute of Fundamental Research
UCDT	University Department of Chemical Technology
USFDA	United States Food and Drug Administration
VSNL	Videsh Sanchar Nigam Limited
Y2K	Year 2000

Select Glossary

Arzdasht	a detailed memorandum or petition addressed to the ruler
Baoli	a well
Chajja	a protruding, ornamental sun-shade in a building
Diwan	the prime minister of a province
Firman	a written order from Nizam which carried the force of law
Ghair-Mulki	non-domicile
Hakim, Hakeem or Hukeem	a physician practising traditional medicine, especially Unani; it was also the degree in modern medicine awarded by Hyderabad Medical School
Jagirdar	someone given a land grant (with powers for revenue collection) in return for service to the ruler
Mazar	an enshrined tomb
Mulki	domicile

Paigah	premier nobles of Hyderabad; traditionally they maintained troops to protect the Nizam
Peshi	an administrative office attached to the Nizam
Razakar	an armed militia opposed to the merger of Hyderabad with Union of India
Resident or *British Resident*	a representative or ambassador of the Crown in a princely state
Sirf-e-khas	the Crown Lands or the personal estate of the Nizam
Subedar	a provincial governor
Subedari	governorship

A Note on Names

THE NAMES OF SEVERAL CITIES MENTIONED IN THE BOOK have changed over time. To retain the historical flavour, old names (Bombay, Poona, Madras, etc.) have been retained until the time new names were adopted. Many personalities in the Asaf Jahi period were known by multiple names, mainly by their titles. In this book, popular identifiers (either original name or title) have been used. For instance, Salar Jung is more popularly known and recognised than the original name even though it is only a title. Honorifics such as His Excellency, His Exalted Highness and so on have not been used for the sake of uniformity and ease of reading.

The currency in princely Hyderabad was the Osmania Sicca Rupee which was valued at 17 per cent less than the British Government Rupee. Osmania Sicca Rupee has been used in the text wherever applicable.

Too many Reddys, Raos and Rajus figure in the narrative. To avoid any confusion, the first names (or full names without initials) have been used in many places instead of the standard practice of using the full name the first time and the last name subsequently.

Until 1948, Hyderabad was the capital of Nizam's Dominion (the Hyderabad State). From 1948 to 1956, it was the capital of the Hyderabad State in the Union of India. In November 1956, it became the capital of Andhra Pradesh and Hyderabad State ceased to exist. In this book, all references until 1956 make a differentiation between Hyderabad State and the city of Hyderabad. After this, Hyderabad only refers to the city. Telangana was a region of the Hyderabad State till 1956. In all references after 2014, Telangana refers to the state and not the region. After 2014, Andhra Pradesh became a separate state (different from Andhra Pradesh formed in 1956). In this book, unified Andhra Pradesh refers to the state as it existed from 1956 to 2014.

The Industrial Laboratory was established in 1918. It was merged with a new entity—the Central Laboratories for Scientific and Industrial Research (CLSIR)—in 1948 and then renamed Regional Research Laboratory (RRL) in 1956. In 1989, it was renamed once again as the Indian Institute of Chemical Technology (IICT). Another name change occurred when CSIR was added as a prefix—CSIR–IICT. In this book, however, the prefix has not been used.

Introduction: Biryani and Backroom

∽

THE CITY OF NAWABS AND BIRYANI. THAT IS THE COMMON stereotype attached to Hyderabad. Ever since the first low-cost airline appeared in 2003—with no meals provided on board—it has been a running joke that any aircraft taking off from Hyderabad has the enticing aroma of the rice-and-meat dish wafting through it high up in the skies. Afterall, so many passengers bring along packs of biryani to eat on the flight. Even as airlines now serve food on board, for many travellers the biryani wins hands-down in comparison to the add-water-and-wait-to-eat meals.

Hyderabad's diverse cultural past is reflected in its cuisine, and the biryani is an iconic representation of the city's culinary heritage. The rice grains in the biryani absorb the rich flavours of meat and spices as well as the fragrances of saffron, rose and jasmine, making it a dish that appeals to several senses. There are some forty varieties of this dish.[1]

There is, however, much more to Hyderabadi cuisine than the biryani. In fact, in 2019, UNESCO included Hyderabad in the 'network of innovative cities' in the gastronomy category.[2] The rich Hyderabadi food, according to UNESCO, has evolved as 'an unusual combination of native flavours and international recipes'. In a separate development, haleem, another popular meat dish of Hyderabad, was awarded a geographical indication (GI) label for its distinct flavour and variation.[3] However, it is the biryani that has travelled most wide and far, evolving in recent years from being a regional speciality to a pan-Indian gourmet delight.

Let's talk numbers. In 2023, biryani was the most ordered dish on food delivery platforms in India: 3.19 biryanis were ordered every second on Zomato and 2.5 per second on Swiggy. And it was the Hyderabadi biryani that saw the most demand.[4] With daily consumption in hundreds of kilograms, Hyderabad could easily be India's biryani capital. An estimated three lakh dinner plates of biryani are consumed in the city every day. The Hyderabad-based quick-service restaurant chain Paradise has experienced rapid growth, creating a new segment in the multibillion-dollar food industry. In 2018, the restaurant chain served 9 million biryanis, putting it in the record books for the 'most biryanis served in a year' in India.[5] While other types of biryani (Lucknowi, Muradabadi, Kolkata, Malabar, etc.) are popular in many markets, Hyderabadi biryani outsells all of them.

The pan-India popularity of the Hyderabadi biryani is intertwined with the economic liberalisation and globalisation of the Indian economy. On the one hand, people from different parts of India moved into Hyderabad and developed a taste for local cuisine, and on the other, people from Hyderabad travelled all over for work and carried their food habits with them. Both movements created a demand for Hyderabadi food, especially the biryani. New capital and technology helped restaurants to serve this fast-growing demand, thus starting a virtuous cycle of demand and supply with each feeding the other.

The change in the food business is just one of the offshoots of economic liberalisation. Like most urban centres in India, Hyderabad has changed in several ways. Since liberalisation, the city has seen the coming up of shopping malls, multiplexes have replaced single-screen theatres, multistoreyed apartments and swanky condominiums have cropped up across the city, and new public spaces have been developed. The transformation has been so rapid that it caught many people unawares. As a native of Hyderabad who spent the first half of his life in the city and as a journalist covering the science and technology sector since the mid-1980s, I found the metamorphosis fascinating. During my frequent visits to the city in the 1990s and 2000s, I could see and experience the change on every visit. It was palpable everywhere—in my extended family, neighbours, friends and acquaintances as well as in the offices, bazaars and public places. There were noticeable changes in the demography, geography, employment patterns, mobility, spending patterns and culture of the entire city and its suburbs.

In popular imagination, the chief driver of this transformation was the information technology (IT) industry—the poster child of liberalisation. It brought foreign investment, created numerous employment avenues for young professionals and led to the in-migration of skilled workforce from the rest of India. This new generation of Hyderabad residents instantly developed a liking for Hyderabadi cuisine, particularly the biryani, and some cultural symbols like the typical Hyderabadi lingo ('hau' for yes and 'nakko' for no).

Among the early businesses that were established in Hyderabad, taking advantage of the liberalised economic policies and the revolutionary shifts in communication technologies were the backroom operations of multinational corporations. The business grew very fast, earning the city the moniker 'backroom of the world' in the early 2000s. In this phase, multinational and Indian companies chose Hyderabad for the cost advantage as they could hire a large number of people in Hyderabad to do routine and repetitive tasks in what was called IT-enabled services (ITES) and business process outsourcing (BPO). A large number of Indian IT professionals were also recruited to work on-site with clients in America and Europe at low salaries. In what is called 'body shopping', these professionals were sent abroad to work with clients but they remained employees of the Indian vendors who had bagged IT contracts from foreign firms.

By the time the IT industry took roots in Hyderabad in the late 1990s, Bangalore was already home to some of the leading Indian IT firms, such as Wipro and Infosys, as well as several American companies, such as Texas Instruments, Hewlett Packard, Digital Equipment Corporation and Motorola. The city had been crowned with the title of 'Silicon Valley of India' in popular media. Pune, Noida and Gurgaon too had a concentration of software firms. As a late starter, Hyderabad decided to catch up with Bangalore. After the year 2000, a number of political, economic and demand-side factors helped it in the process, which we discuss later in the book.

As a result, corporations started outsourcing high-end work to Hyderabad, for further economic advantage. They realised Indian talent could be used for development work, R&D, engineering and such tasks. This, in recent years, has made Hyderabad one of the most rapidly growing and appealing locations for Indian and global technology firms. The rate of growth of IT exports from Telangana in 2022 was more than double the national rate, with Hyderabad alone accounting for over 95 per cent of the exports. In terms of the number of new technology jobs added in a financial year, according to state government data, Hyderabad surpassed Bangalore in 2021-22 as well as 2022-23. Outside of their headquarters in America, most tech behemoths such as Google, Microsoft, Meta and Amazon have their largest workforce in Hyderabad. The city hosts global capability centres (GCCs) of 250 multinational corporations. These centres are like extended arms of their respective parent companies. They handle core functions, allowing their respective parent corporations to reap the full benefits of outsourcing.

Exports of information technology and ITES from Telangana (with Hyderabad accounting for the most) touched Rs 2,41,275 crore (approximately USD 32 billion) in 2022-23, up from only a few crores in 1991-92. This has created employment opportunities and led to prosperity in the burgeoning middle class. The technology sector directly supported 9,05,715 professional jobs in 2022-23, as per the Telangana government data. In 2021-22, the per capita income of Hyderabad and Ranga Reddy district (which houses the Cyberabad technology area) was Rs 4,03,214 and Rs 8,15,996 respectively as against the national average of Rs 1,72,276, according to the 2023 report of the Directorate of Economics and Statistics, Telangana.[6]

---◆---

This book is an attempt to capture the remarkable story of the rapid transformation of Hyderabad from what was, at best, a proto-colonial city in a quasi-Mughal princely state until the 1940s, to a modern and vibrant metropolis. Fortunately, I have been a witness to almost the entire journey, either directly or through collective family memories. My father, the son of a Marwari businessman from Bombay, did not want to pursue the family business and came to Hyderabad looking for new opportunities. This was in the last week of September 1948, soon after Hyderabad's integration with India. I was born in 1961 at the Victoria Zenana Hospital, a Nizam-era medical facility situated on the Musi riverfront.

In the 1960s, the tales of the last Nizam (he was still alive then) and his rule were fresh in the memory of Hyderabadis. I grew up in an eclectic environment amid social, literary, art and political movements of the 1960s and 1970s. My family lived in the heart of what was called the 'Old City'—first in Begum Bazaar and then in Petla Burj, one of the oldest localities of the city, dating back to the Qutub Shahi era. Several iconic buildings on the riverfront and beyond, like the Osmania General Hospital, High Court, City College, State Central Library, Salar Jung Museum, Khilwat, Chowmahalla Palace, Mecca Masjid and, of course, Charminar and Charkaman, were within walking distance. Over the years, I passed by many of them on my daily trips to school, college and work. No wonder, the first feature I wrote in *Deccan Chronicle* as a budding journalist in 1982 was the story of the four bridges on River Musi, two of which I would use every day.

Even as my lived experience has helped me formulate my ideas and situate them within a historical context, this book is not a nostalgic account of the city. The exercise, though, turned out to be a personal journey of rediscovering people and places in Hyderabad through the lens of history and reviewing the events that occurred over the larger canvas of an Indian princely state. I discovered the meaning and reason for many things that I had heard, seen or experienced as a young Hyderabadi—things that had remained etched in my memory as unconnected childhood observations, or events that I covered as a journalist in Hyderabad in the 1980s.

———◆———

Every book has a purpose and should be able to explore one or several key questions. The purpose of this book is to decode the factors behind Hyderabad's rapid transformation, with all the twists and turns in its journey.

The story of Hyderabad has attracted numerous scholars and academics over time. The city was founded 430 years ago. It was ruled by two dynasties (Qutub Shahi and Asaf Jahi) and has been the capital of four states (Nizam's Dominion, Hyderabad State in independent India, Andhra Pradesh and now Telangana).

Most of the available literature on Hyderabad describes its political history, culture and social dimensions. But they miss out on how these factors interacted and helped shape a modern city and the institutions that contributed to the change. An understanding and appreciation of the role the key institutions, policies and personalities played is critical to understand how Hyderabad achieved its position as a dynamic city-region in the twenty-first century.

Most of this transformation is often attributed solely to the swift economic changes effected in the 1990s. In actuality though, the transition was the result of a series of factors and events spanning almost a century. For instance, the two World Wars, disease outbreaks, the 1908 Musi flood, the Telangana agitations, the rise of regional political parties, all influenced the shaping of the modern Hyderabad we see today. Many city-regions have come to be identified with iconic industries or sectors like manufacturing, finance, fashion, entertainment, education, technology and so on. The most celebrated example is the technology cluster, Silicon Valley, in America. In India, Mumbai is known for finance due to the presence of clusters of banks, stock markets, insurance companies, financial institutions, financial regulators and other associated institutions. Mumbai also houses the entertainment cluster. Other examples of clusters are Surat (diamond cutting), Coimbatore (apparel), Chennai (electronics manufacturing) and Bangalore (software services). In some cases, there could be a set of industries rather than a single sector, like Hyderabad, which has pharmaceuticals, vaccines and technology services. Such connections with specific industries or sectors accrue benefits to the local population, like more employment opportunities, higher wages, higher incomes, higher mobility and a better quality of life, besides impacting other industries beyond the geographical area of the city-region and even the national economy.

How do specialised clusters develop in specific city-regions? What drives specialisation or agglomeration? A general explanation advanced in development economics puts it on the interplay of factors like the availability of skilled workforce or human capital, finance, appropriate policies for regional development and robust institutions (scientific, business, governance, regulatory). To begin with, specialisation may be seeded due to a historical accident or a set of unique factors (for example, locational advantage or natural resources).

A historical factor may sow seeds of specialisation but it does not automatically guarantee the birth of a specialised cluster. For instance, software technology parks (STPs) were opened in several Indian cities—Bangalore, Hyderabad, Pune, Bhubaneswar, Gandhinagar and Thiruvananthapuram—around the same time, but only Bangalore and Hyderabad emerged as major clusters. In the same manner, the founding of institutions is critical but not a sufficient condition for growth.

The availability of skilled workforce through research universities and academic institutions is another necessary but not a sufficient precondition for clusters to develop. For example, the mere presence of an Indian Institute of Technology (IIT) in Kanpur—modelled after the Massachusetts Institute of Technology (MIT)—did not make Kanpur a technology hub. In the 1990s, specialised IT training institutes, known as Indian Institutes of Information Technology (IIITs), were founded in Gwalior, Allahabad and Hyderabad (the IIIT in Hyderabad is now known as International Institute of Information Technology) but they did not lead to an IT industry in Gwalior or Allahabad. So, the seeding of institutions and industries needs sustained nurturing for a city-region to become a cluster. Besides creating local talent pools, the workforce can also be developed through inter-region migration. And pooling of skilled workers is driven by factors like amenities, weather, social infrastructure, a culture of diversity, government policies and so on.

Such existing theoretical frameworks of cluster development cannot fully explain the rise of Hyderabad as a technology cluster. To understand this, we have to go to the early years of the last century. Hyderabad was not under direct British rule, but British officers were appointed to high posts and they shaped developments in education, industrial research and city improvement (we discuss this in Chapters 1 to 4). The establishment of Osmania University, which was India's first vernacular university, was an indigenous project but was formulated and executed by intellectuals who came from outside Hyderabad, as detailed in Chapter 5. The university became an important centre of knowledge creation and dissemination.

At the time of its integration with India in 1948, Hyderabad had some important educational and scientific institutions, in addition to several colonial artefacts (railways, postal system, paper currency, etc.). But it lacked a research university like the Indian Institute of Science in Bangalore. Its industrial base was relatively weak compared with the neighbouring Mysore State and Baroda State in Western India. Industrial undertakings like Praga Tools, which were established to support the War efforts, faced a downturn after the War ended. Hence Hyderabad received special attention in the post-Independence period with the establishment of public sector enterprises, defence units and research laboratories. Hyderabad stood to gain as India embarked upon new areas like nuclear energy, electronics and missile development in the 1960s. This part of the journey has been discussed in Section II (Chapters 6 to 9). The book stays away from covering agriculture research and the emergence of Hyderabad as India's seed capital, as that is a vast story and merits an independent book.

By the end of the 1980s, the city had a large number of research laboratories, public sector companies, small and medium ancillaries in the private sector, entrepreneurial firms and several technical colleges. It possessed a large pool of workforce with scientific and technical skills in the public and private sectors. This workforce became an important asset in the period of the economic liberalisation ushered in by the Central government and state-level reforms initiated by a young and ambitious chief minister. There was an exponential growth in the areas of IT, pharmaceuticals and vaccine manufacturing. Greenfield projects like Cyberabad and Genome Valley gave a new identity to Hyderabad globally. This exciting phase has been presented in Section III (Chapters 10 to 14). With fast-paced development came adverse impacts on the city's ecological, geological and heritage buildings, and even on the city's culture (Chapter 15).

The regional efforts for development were supplemented a great deal by the Central government's policies and initiatives (new patent law, STP scheme). In this book, I have described how the role of the state at every stage was central, even after the economic liberalisation in the 1990s.

Being at the confluence of the North and South, the city's geographical location was a great advantage. (Political leaders like Chandrababu Naidu and K.T. Rama Rao often quote a marketing line when talking about Hyderabad: 'it is the North of South India and the South of North India'.) And so was its inclusive culture. The city's tolerant culture and linguistic plurality played a major role in attracting professionals with diverse backgrounds. As they say, *Hyderabad ka paani* (Hyderabad's environment) makes people from different parts of the country feel at home.

In Hyderabad's journey of becoming a technology cluster, besides geographical advantage and tolerant culture, several other factors came together at different points in time: historical accidents (in terms of locational decisions), sustained efforts to build a pool of skilled workforce, conducive industrial promotion policies, fortuitous political alignments, external factors like proactive diaspora, skill shortage in the West, technological changes (Y2K—Year 2000—problem, the internet boom, etc.). This book pieces together parts of this jigsaw puzzle through the lens of key institutions to answer the question: how did Hyderabad become a technology city in the twenty-first century?

Before getting into the specifics, let's familiarise ourselves with a brief political history of Hyderabad.

The Four Centuries of Hyderabad

The story of Hyderabad begins with the Qutub Shahi kings. After the dissolution of the Bahmani empire, the Persian nobleman named Sultan Quli established the Qutub Shahi sultanate in Golconda in 1518. The sultanate, which covered the region of Krishna and Godavari deltas, was abundant in raw materials, including minerals and diamonds. The Koh-i-Noor, one of the largest cut diamonds in the world, was among the numerous precious stones mined in this kingdom. The Qutub Shahi capital was located in Golconda, which developed into a significant trading hub in the sixteenth and seventeenth centuries, drawing visitors and merchants from countries in Central Asia and Europe. A road was constructed to link Golconda to the port city of Machilipatnam (Masuliptnam) on the Coromandel Coast to facilitate trade.

However, traders and travellers coming from Machilipatnam had to wade through River Musi to reach Golconda during the monsoon months when the river would be overflowing. Ibrahim Quli, who ascended the throne of Golconda in 1550, decided to solve this problem by building a bridge over Musi in 1578. The 600-feet-long bridge was made of twenty-two granite stone arches, and it was constructed 54 feet above the riverbed at a point where the river's width was narrow and the banks were deep. It was named Ibrahim Bridge. Later, as more bridges were built across the Musi, it became popular as Purana Pul (old bridge). The old bridge, which continues to remain in use, was an engineering marvel of its time and found notable mentions in the accounts of foreign travellers. Jean-Baptiste Tavernier compared its beauty to the Pont Neuf of Paris.[7] The connectivity to the port town provided by the bridge may have contributed to boosting Golconda's global trade. Between 1580 and 1640, as much as 14 per cent of the cargo arriving in Lisbon was from Golconda.[8]

Hyderabad's history revolves around the tale of this bridge. Ibrahim's son, Mohammed Quli, was in love with a dancing girl from Chichlam, a sleepy village on the road connecting Golconda to Machilipatnam. According to folklore, Ibrahim Quli commissioned the bridge after learning that his son was putting his life in danger by riding his horse during the monsoon across a swollen Musi to meet his paramour. Mohammed Quli succeeded Ibrahim Quli in 1580. Subsequently, in 1589, he wed the dancing girl. A poet at heart, Mohammed Quli refers to his partner as Telangan, Bhagmati and Hayder Piyaari (Hyder's beloved) in his poetry.[9] Some historians believe that her original name was Bagamma.

After marrying Bhagmati, Mohammed Quli decided to build a new city near Chichlam and relocate his court there. This decision was not solely motivated by Bhagmati's relationship with Chichlam. Historians attribute Mohammed Quli's decision to build a new city to two factors. First, Golconda had become overcrowded, resulting in unsanitary conditions and epidemic outbreaks. The nobility of the kingdom petitioned the king to build 'a new and beautiful' capital for Golconda.[10] As a result, a large area south of Musi was chosen to build the new capital, which included seven villages, including Chichlam.

The second story is also related to an epidemic. When a plague outbreak killed hundreds of people, the people of Chichlam planted a tazia[11] at a highway crossing. One day, Mohammed Quli happened to notice it. He stopped there and prayed to the Almighty, vowing to erect a 'magnificent monument' to 'remember and respect your wondrous powers and inestimable kindness forever'.[12]

Whatever the motivation, the construction on the new capital began soon after the epidemic ended. The foundation of the new city was laid on an auspicious day, the first day of the new millennium on the Hijri calendar (1/1/1000 AH). The date in the Gregorian calendar was 19 October 1591. Mohammed Quli desired that the new city should be a 'replica of heaven on the earth and unequalled in the world'.[13] He assigned the job to his trusted prime minister, Mir Momin Astarabadi, who was a descendant of the family that traced itself to the Prophet. Momin, who was born in Iran, was a great scholar, fluent in Arabic and Persian as well as other subjects such as architecture, town planning and metrology.[14]

Mir Momin drew up a plan, with the centre of the proposed city being the spot where Mohammed Quli had prayed in front of the tazia. The central piazza was designed as a massive double cross. A grand central structure was built on one cross, with four archways pointing to the four quarters of the city and one minaret at each of the four corners of a central court. As a result, it was given the name Charminar (four minarets). The second cross, the Charkaman, was built a little further ahead on the road to Musi. It had four distinct arched gateways with an ornamented fountain in the centre. Each arch was 375 feet from the centre and was designed to serve a specific purpose. Palaces, gardens, serais, shops and other structures were built on the four roads leading from the Charminar. On the banks of Musi, Mohammed Quli also established Darush-Shifa (meaning house of cure), a general hospital and medical school.

Mir Momin was assisted by Abu Talib, Kamaluddin Shirazi and Shahr Yar Jahan. Together they 'designed the monuments, the inlay and stucco work with vegetal and geometric patterns' as well as symmetrical landscapes, gardens and calligraphy on religious structures.[15] The Charminar was not conceived just as a magnificent building but as the civic centre of a new medieval city that was carefully planned around it.

Qutub Shahis being Shia by faith, Mohammed Quli named the city 'Haiderabad' (the city of Haider) after the title of the fourth Caliph of Islam, Hazrat Ali.[16] All around the Charminar and Charkaman were gardens, waterways, fountains and tree-lined boulevards. This made European travellers and historians describe the city as Bagh Nagar or the city of gardens.[17] This part of history has become contentious in the twenty-first century amidst the frenzy to change the names of cities and roads. Some political groups want Hyderabad to be renamed Bhagyanagar since they say its original name was Bhag Nagar. However, the jury is still out if the city's name was Haiderabad from its very inception or Bhag Nagar/Bhagyanagar (the city of fortune) as claimed by some.

The new city became a bustling hub for trade in diamonds, pearls, spices, silk, aromatic substances and many other goods, attracting businessmen from Persia, Europe and other places. The city had a cosmopolitan culture, with traders, bankers and jewellers from Persia and Armenia doing business along with local businessmen.[18] The Charkaman area continues to be famous for pearls even now.

The Qutub Shahi kings had a deep interest in art, literature, science, engineering, town planning and architecture. Many of them wrote poetry in Dakhani and Telugu and patronised scholars in their courts. By faith the kings were Shia Muslims, but this did not limit them from appointing Sunnis and Hindus as generals and ministers. Ibrahim Quli was married to a Hindu woman, Bhagirathi, and Mohammed Quli was born to her. Mohammed Quli too married a Hindu, Bhagmati. Moharrum used to be observed on a grand scale in Golconda. In the hinterland, even the Hindu populace hoisted tazias during the month of mourning observing it as pirula panduga (Telugu, meaning the festival of pirs or saints). The practice is prevalent in some Telangana villages even now.

The Charminar represents the design, architecture, engineering and scientific prowess nurtured during the Qutub Shahi period. This is also reflected in the intricate geometrical patterns in the construction of the tombs of the rulers during the sixteenth and seventeenth centuries. The tombs of the Qutub Shahi rulers, the members of the royal family and those associated with it, are laid out in an elegant garden of fruit trees. The well-planned garden has water channels, causeways, cascades, water cisterns and fountains.

Among the surviving water bodies in Hyderabad that were developed during the Qutub Shahi period are the Durgam Cheruvu and Hussain Sagar. The Durgam Cheruvu, around which the present-day infotech city is laid out, had an elaborate hydrological system for supplying water to Golconda.[19] A new extradosed cable bridge constructed in 2020 has made the forgotten lake a new tourist attraction in the city.

The Asaf Jahs

The Mughal emperor Aurangzeb conquered Golconda in 1687, making the Deccan one of the six provinces of his empire, and moved its capital from Hyderabad to Aurangabad. When Aurangzeb's grandson, Farrukhsiyar, became the emperor in 1713, he appointed Qamar-ud-din as the new Subedar for Deccan and gave him the title of Nizam-ul-Mulk. Qamar-ud-din had served the empire in high posts and was appointed as wazir in 1722. Following court intrigues in Delhi to upstage him, he reverted to his position in the Deccan and re-acquired the subedari in 1724. The reigning emperor in Delhi, Mohammad Shah, confirmed his position as the Subedar of six provinces of the Deccan and conferred upon him the title of Asaf Jah.[20] Nizam-ul-Mulk (Asaf Jah I) was an independent ruler for all practical purposes but maintained staunch loyalty to the throne in Delhi.

Nizam Ali Khan (Asaf Jah II), who ascended to power with help from the forces of the East India Company, decided in 1763 to shift the capital back to Hyderabad. The reason was strategic. Aurangabad was too close to the Maratha territory and prone to attacks.[21] After being under the French protectorate for some years, Nizam Ali Khan entered into a 'subsidiary alliance' with the British and became a protected state under them.[22] The British further consolidated their hold over Hyderabad during the rule of Sikandar Jah (Asaf Jah III) and Nasir-ud-Daula (Asaf Jah IV) through the formation of the Hyderabad Contingent in 1798 and cession of the cotton-producing region, Berar. A new cantonment town, Sikanderabad (Secunderabad), was built to house British military contingents. It came to be known as the twin city of Hyderabad, though the two differed culturally—one was a medieval, walled city and the other was a multicultural military and business town.[23]

In May 1853, during the reign of Afzal-ud-daula (Asaf Jah V), the twenty-four-year-old Mir Turab Ali Khan was named the Diwan. Khan later became famous by his title of Salar Jung and, over the next three decades, played a pivotal role in Hyderabad. After the premature death of the Nizam, his infant son, Mir Mahbub Ali Khan, was anointed the sixth Nizam and Salar Jung was made a co-regent (along with Paigah noble, Shamsul Umra III). In the feudal hierarchy, Paigah nobility ranked next only to the Nizams and the two were related by marriage. During the period of the regency of the child Nizam from 1869 to 1883, Salar Jung became the de facto ruler. His tenure as Diwan was marked by the further cementing of Hyderabad's ties with the British and the introduction of administrative, judicial, educational and financial reforms.[24] These changes paved the way for Hyderabad's transition from medievalism to modernity.

Mahbub Ali Khan (Asaf Jah VI) assumed the sovereign rights of the state in 1886 after he turned eighteen. Among the governance reforms that he introduced was the proclamation of a constitutional edict, Qanunche-i-Mubarak, which facilitated the formation of a legislative council. It was more a committee of heads of departments to frame rules, and not a legislature with elected members or with powers to make new laws. Mahbub Ali Khan was a benevolent ruler, fondly known as Mahbub Pasha (the beloved leader). He generously supported scientific and medical research and sponsored young men and women for studies abroad. He handled the devastating floods of 1908 with kindness and deftness.

Like many princes of his time, Mahbub Ali Khan cherished wine, women and the good life. His penchant for clothes was legendary; he never wore a dress twice. The Purani Haveli, one of his primary residences, had the longest wardrobe in the world. Mahbub Pasha passed away in August 1911 at the Falaknuma Palace following a drinking binge. He was only forty-five.[25]

The palace and the nobles were disturbed by the untimely death of Mahbub Pasha, even though a succession plan had been in place since 1887. Under this plan, Osman Ali Khan, the eldest son of Mahbub Pasha and Amat-uz-Zehra Begum, would become the next Nizam. Before his death, Ujala Begum, another wife of Mahbub Pasha, had been pressuring him to change the succession plan and make her toddler son, Salabat Jah, the heir apparent.[26] After Mahbub Pasha's death, the matter of succession was deliberated upon by senior courtiers who decided to adhere to the original arrangement, which Lord Curzon had confirmed during his 1902 visit to Hyderabad.[27] Mir Osman Ali Khan was crowned as the seventh Nizam (Asaf Jah VII) on 1 September 1911, at the age of twenty-four.

The tenure of the seventh Nizam lasted from 1911 to 1948. It was eventful. It witnessed two World Wars that presented an opportunity for the young Nizam to boost Hyderabad's ties with the British. During the First World War, the Nizam sided with the British and the Allies in their war with the Ottomans and opposed the Khilafat movement in India. In Hyderabad, he separated the judiciary from the executive and constituted a civil services cadre. On the cultural front, he funded the Department of Archaeology and supported the conservation of paintings in Ajanta Caves. Above all, he initiated large-scale development work and provided a boost to education, scientific research and industrialisation.

As colonial rule ended and India was partitioned in August 1947, the paramountcy of the Crown also lapsed. Most princely states decided to merge with the new Dominion of India and accepted its constitutional and democratic structure. But the Nizam opposed Hyderabad's accession to India. He argued that Hyderabad was organised as a 'country' and hence it would remain independent.

However, 'Azad Hyderabad' turned out to be a short-lived dream, as India finally decided to use force and launched a military operation (euphemistically called 'Police Action') under the codename 'Operation Polo' in September 1948. The Nizam's troops, along with the radical militia known as Razakars, surrendered within a week, facilitating the state's integration with India. The Police Action was a traumatic event causing widespread displacement and bloodshed, which some historians compare with the Partition.

After two years of Indian military rule, a popular government was elected with Burgula Ramakrishna Rao as the chief minister. Osman Ali Khan was appointed the Raj Pramukh (a titular post that was abolished in 1956) like deposed princes in other large provinces. The former Nizam passed away on 24 February 1967 at his King Kothi Palace, and was buried next to the grave of his mother in the family mosque, Masjid-i-Judi, across the road from the palace.

The Telugu States

As the Nizam's dominion, Hyderabad comprised three distinct geographical and linguistic regions: Telangana, Marathwada and Kannada-speaking areas adjoining the Mysore State. This multicultural and multilingual character of Hyderabad was retained even after the state merged with India. The political boundaries were not altered after the integration with India in 1948. On the other hand, the Madras Presidency had some Telugu-speaking districts and leaders there demanded the creation of a separate Telugu state. Potti Sriramulu, a freedom fighter and a Gandhian, went on an indefinite fast in support of the demand and died while fasting. In the aftermath of his death, the Telugu-speaking districts were carved out of Madras Presidency and made into a new state, Andhra, in 1953, with Kurnool as its capital. This was the first state to be formed based on language, prompting similar demands from other regions of the country.

Soon there was an outcry for a larger Telugu state by merging Andhra with the Telugu-speaking parts of Hyderabad State. This and all such demands were referred to the States Reorganisation Commission (SRC). Leaders of Telangana opposed a merger with Andhra because Telangana's relatively lower economic development would make it difficult for the two Telugu-speaking areas to assimilate with the richer Andhra. Telangana's hinterland under the Nizam had remained largely underdeveloped because of the feudal system and the autocratic nature of the Nizam's rule; the Andhra region had significantly advanced economically and educationally under the British.

The SRC left it to the state assemblies to take a call on the idea of a unified Telugu state. Yet, Union home minister Gobind Ballabh Pant got the two sides to agree to a merger and hammered out a 'Gentlemen's Agreement' that promised proper representation to Telangana in the state cabinet, a regional development council to look after its special interests and reservation for Mulkis (domiciles of the former Hyderabad State) in educational institutions under the Mulki Rules framed in 1919. The result of this compromise took the shape of a unified Andhra Pradesh, which was formed in 1956 with the merger of Andhra and Telangana, with Hyderabad as its capital. Marathi- and Kannada-speaking districts of Hyderabad became a part of Maharashtra and Mysore (later Karnataka) states respectively.

As promised, Hyderabad experienced a flurry of development during its first ten years as the capital of Andhra Pradesh. The Central government under Prime Minister Jawaharlal Nehru embarked upon an industrial development strategy aimed at import substitution and gave primacy to the public sector. Keeping the imperatives of regional development in view, many public sector enterprises, research centres and defence facilities were allocated to Hyderabad in the 1960s. Still, there was resentment about Telangana's neglect and the violation of the Gentlemen's Agreement because the political power was in the hands of Andhra leaders. M. Channa Reddy, a prominent Telangana leader and a minister in the cabinet of Indira Gandhi, gave vent to these feelings and launched a regional party in 1969 to press for a separate Telangana state. The Mulki Rules became a bone of contention between the

Andhra and Telangana regions. The state witnessed one crisis after another in the 1970s, with leaders from Andhra, too, demanding a separate state, Vishalandhra.

The state's politics took a dramatic turn in 1982 when the charismatic superstar of Telugu films, N.T. Rama Rao (popularly known as NTR), launched Telugu Desam Party (TDP). NTR combined his enormous screen appeal with the emotive issue of Telugu pride and disenchantment over the Congress party's rule. He won a formidable majority in the state assembly elections and became the chief minister in 1983. His government soon plunged into a crisis when a senior minister, N. Bhaskar Rao, revolted while NTR was in America for a heart surgery. Though he was reinstated, NTR dissolved the state assembly and sought a fresh mandate in 1985, which he received with an overwhelming majority. In the next elections in 1989, the Congress party returned to power. NTR bounced back in December 1994, but his term as the chief minister was once again cut short, this time by his son-in-law N. Chandrababu Naidu. Naidu remained the chief minister for the next ten years.

The demand for a separate Telangana resurfaced strongly after the death of chief minister Y.S. Rajasekhara Reddy in a helicopter crash in September 2009. The movement this time was led by K. Chandrasekhar Rao (KCR) who had formed his party, Telangana Rashtra Samithi (TRS), in 2001. He later joined hands with the Congress and served as a minister under Prime Minister Manmohan Singh. Following KCR's sudden move to go on an indefinite fast in 2009, the Central government hurriedly accepted the demand for a separate Telangana. After a pitched political battle in the state assembly and the Parliament, and violence in both Telangana and Andhra regions, a new state was born on 2 June 2014. In effect, the Telangana region of the pre-1948 Hyderabad State which was merged with Andhra in 1956 was demerged in 2014. It was agreed that Hyderabad would serve as the common capital for the new Andhra Pradesh and Telangana for ten years.

———•———

In its 430-plus-year long journey, the city has witnessed tumultuous political changes as well as social, economic and cultural transformation. In this journey, the interconnected changes that Hyderabad has undergone in the past hundred years are particularly crucial to understand its current positioning as a global technology city. This book is an attempt to do so.

SECTION I

Science and Modernity in a Princely State (1908–1948)

1

Chloroform, Malaria and Stargazing

∽

The completion of a scientific investigation of such magnitude, and with the aid of the refinements of a modern physiological laboratory in the capital of the largest native Indian state, is an event of historical importance, and may be regarded as an earnest of the time when East and West will cooperate for the advancement of science.

—*British Medical Journal*
(on the animal experiments in Hyderabad to test
the efficacy of chloroform, 1890)[1]

ONE OF THE BYPRODUCTS OF COLONISATION WAS THE introduction of modern science in India. The seventeenth century saw the coming of medical practitioners, naturalists, adventurers and missionaries from Europe to India, who brought with them scientific ideas. This took a more formal shape with the emergence of scientific disciplines and specialised societies in Europe in the late eighteenth century.

The beginnings of modern science in India can be traced to the Asiatic Society of Bengal. Founded by William Jones in 1784 to advance scientific pursuits, the activities of the Society ranged from map-making to the documentation of unique flora and fauna. Over time, it came to include the Great Surveys, such as the Botanical Survey, Trigonometric Survey, Geological Survey and so on. As the imperial power grew in India, these surveys evolved into independent scientific organisations.[2]

In fact, Hyderabad's earliest contact with Western science was through one of the Great Surveys. James Achilles Kirkpatrick, who succeeded his brother, Col. William Kirkpatrick, as the Resident of Hyderabad in 1796, facilitated Hyderabad becoming a part of the Great Trigonometrical Survey (GTS) that was launched in 1800 to map the subcontinent. The Nizam's territory formed a large part of the area that was surveyed under GTS after special permission was granted for the survey teams to operate in the region. The third Nizam, Sikandar Jah, lent his troops to protect and assist the survey teams led by Col. William Lambton.[3]

It was in Hyderabad that Lt George Everest, who would eventually lead the survey after the death of Lambton, joined it in 1818. Everest spread the web of triangulation, which began at Cape Comorin at the tip of the Indian peninsula, to the whole of the Krishna–Godavari region, which formed a part of the Hyderabad State then.[4] Lambton and Everest used the Great Theodolite, a measuring instrument that weighed 500 kilograms. In 2017, the Great Theodolite was on display at the Survey of India at Hyderabad.[5]

James Kirkpatrick, more famous as the 'White Moghul' who married Khair-un-nissa, the grand-niece of Mir Alam (Diwan of Sikandar Jah), was a man with scientific ideas. He is also known for building a palatial building—the Residency—in Hyderabad. In the process of designing and constructing this magnificent mansion, he ordered expensive fitments, including scientific instruments, from England and elsewhere. Kirkpatrick requested his brother, then in England, 'to lay out 500 pounds on a reflecting telescope, 12 or 14 feet in length, as an ornament to his terrace, in the use of which he expects to be sufficiently instructed by one of his staff who was the son of the Professor of Astronomy in Edinburgh.'[6] The Residency building represented the growing presence of the British in Hyderabad. The area around it had bazaars and residences of civil servants, bankers and missionaries. As the number of Europeans grew in the area, churches and schools were built. The first public school was established by the Church of England in 1834. Named Hyderabad Residency School, it was meant to educate the children of Europeans. Subsequently, it was moved to the Gun Foundry area and renamed St. George's Grammar School. It prepared children for the 'overseas school certificate examination' conducted by the University of Cambridge.

A few miles away from the Residency was the cantonment town of Secunderabad where the Subsidiary Force and the Hyderabad Contingent were stationed. This town had all the necessary facilities, including dedicated medical infrastructure, that the British officers and their families needed. Surgeons and medical officers—all of them British—were employed as regular army personnel. The subordinate staff members, such as dressers, on the other hand, were recruited from the locals. For training the subordinate staff, Assistant Surgeon Thomas Key and Staff Surgeon Simon Young organised a small medical school at Bolarum in 1835. Though meant only to serve the needs of the British troops, the medical school was the first institution of higher education in Hyderabad. In Bengal the same year, a full-fledged medical school, the Medical College of Bengal, became functional for training Indians who would serve in military and civil establishments.[7]

Unlike other medical schools in British India, the one in princely Hyderabad was not properly organised. British Resident Maj. Gen. Stuart Fraser decided to shut it down when the officer-incharge was transferred to another station in 1846. The decision attracted criticism in the press, forcing Fraser to clarify that he had abolished the Bolarum school 'merely to afford him the means of establishing one with wider aims'.[8] He then sought the permission of the Nizam and the governor general for a new medical school to train hakims for government service and to take up a private practice. Although 'hakim' refers to a practitioner of the Unani system of medicine, the medical school decided to retain the title even for those trained in modern medicine. The Hyderabad Medical School, established in 1846, was supposed to be 'the most beneficial to the people, rendering them independent of European aid, and in time, removing their prejudices against European practice'.[9] Dr William Campbell Maclean, posted earlier as Residency Surgeon in 1844, was made the superintendent of the school.

The idea of a Western medicine school got ready approval of Nizam Nasir-ud-daula (Asaf Jah IV). The Nizam had likely been suffering from diabetes. He had been under the treatment of Unani hakims but showed no signs of improvement. Sometime in 1845, he decided to consult the Residency Surgeon. But, he had one condition—he would not consume any medicine in any form, including smelling it. Maclean carefully analysed the Nizam's symptoms and his diet. Seeing that the Nizam's diet was loaded with animal fat and sweets, Maclean recommended certain modifications to it, which led to the Nizam's condition improving within a few weeks. Based on this experience, the Nizam was convinced of the efficacy of modern medicine. He approved the opening of the school while observing that 'if this science is taught to the people of our kingdom, our dear subjects will be greatly benefited'.[10]

The Diwan, Mir Alam, who suffered from Bright's disease, was also under Maclean's treatment. He too supported the idea of the medical school. Yet another patron of the school was the Paigah noble Shamsul Umrah, who was 'a good mathematician, and gave much of his time to the study of mechanical philosophy as well as electrical science, in which he took the deepest interest, following closely the latest discoveries of Faraday'.[11] Mir Alam's nephew, Nawab Turab Ali Khan (Salar Jung I), who became the Diwan in 1853, patronised the medical school in later years.

The school started functioning from a large semi-circular bungalow (belonging to one Mr Ogilvie) in the Gun Foundry area.[12] In 1848, it was shifted to the premises of the Residency Hospital (now the Sultan Bazaar Government Hospital) where it had 'a convenient room for practical anatomy, medical store rooms and a cutler's workshop,' in addition to classrooms, a small museum with apparatus for conducting demonstrations and a few useful books.[13]

Western medicine was introduced in Hyderabad at a time when it was steeped in obscurantism and medieval healing practices. Hakims mostly served the rich and the nobles, and survived on state grants and jagirs (land grants). They neither had dispensaries nor hospitals and believed in the 'existence of occult drugs of wonderful power'. They estimated the value of medicines (like tonics and aphrodisiacs) by their rarity and the cost to procure them.[14] The poor had to depend on quacks who were 'dealers in cures for impotence' and talismans, while hujams (barbers) acted as surgeons who 'let blood and operate, sew up wounds, arrest haemorrhage, and perform all minor as well as some of the major operations of surgery'.[15]

The absence of formal school education made it difficult to attract pupils to learn medicine. Only four students showed up in the beginning, so teaching could not start for almost a year. A school run by Shamsul Umra taught courses in Urdu and Arabic. He asked teachers to select some bright students and from among them he shortlisted ten. He gave each of these students 'a knife, scissors, ink pot and 5 quires of paper' and sent them to Maclean.[16] That was how the Hyderabad Medical School got its first batch of students.

The lack of knowledge of English—an outcome of schools attached to religious and theological institutions teaching only Persian, Arabic and Sanskrit and not English—posed as a challenge. The medical school, therefore, opted for instruction in Hindustani. Lectures were compiled from English medical texts and translated by a Munshi (Shaik Ali) with the help of an assistant surgeon (one Mr Murray) who was well-versed in Urdu and Persian.[17] Lectures delivered on different subjects over a period of time were printed as textbooks in Hindustani. Classroom lectures were followed by practical experience in the dispensary, including dissecting dead bodies and performing surgeries on patients.

While the teaching of medicine in Hindustani posed difficulties for teachers, it created a desire among students to learn English. They wanted 'to master that language which contains all the stores from which his teachers have derived their science and information.'[18] Diwan Salar Jung I was a great advocate of the 'necessity of acquiring a fair knowledge of the English language'. As a child, he learnt English from Henry Brown, a British tutor whom he later appointed as his private secretary. His leaning towards the English language reflects in the advice he gave to medical students in 1859. He said, 'You cannot advance in your profession, you cannot retain even what you have learned, without mastering the English language, sufficient at least, to read it freely. You do not require to speak it or to write it, but you do require to be able to read it with advantage; so that, with this key, the storehouse of Western science may be within your power.'[19]

He patronised English in Darul-Uloom, which he established in 1854 as the first state-supported educational institution. The syllabus included the sciences—physics and chemistry—as well as mathematics and astronomy.[20] English was one of the subjects taught at Madrassa Aliya, which Salar Jung had established in 1873 for his children and those of other nobles.

During his visit to England in 1876, Salar Jung met Aghorenath Chattopadhyay, who was pursuing DSc in chemistry at the University of Edinburgh. He persuaded Chattopadhyay to settle down in Hyderabad. The following year, Chattopadhyay founded the Chaderghat High School (also known as Gloria High School) in Hyderabad. Three years later, the school was affiliated with Madras University as a second-grade college. Then, in 1881, it merged with another small school, City English High School, and was raised to the rank of a first-grade college and renamed as Nizam College.

The medical school not only generated an appetite for learning English but also firmly anchored Western science in Hyderabad. Salar Jung argued that while ancient knowledge was important, it should not remain static because medical science had developed since then. He explained:

What did the ancient hukeems know of anatomy? Very little indeed. They called the arteries air carriers and they knew nothing of the circulation of blood. ... Their knowledge of physiology was so imperfect that our first-year students have more accurate views of the important science than they could have had. ... In *Material Medica*, they indeed knew many drugs; but could prove the real action and value of very few. What they knew of diseases of the heart and lungs, what of vaccination or the endless variety of nervous and skin diseases?[21]

In effect, Salar Jung was advocating scientific methods of observation and evidence. This also reflected his knowledge of modern medicine and the importance he attached to it.

The medical school served as a nucleus for the development of modern medicine in Hyderabad. In 1866, a public hospital was constructed on the northern bank of Musi. It was named Afzalgunj Hospital after the reigning Nizam. It served as a teaching hospital for the medical school. A separate government cadre for medical service was created and government medical officers were posted in districts. By 1866, the Hyderabad State had a medical school, a general hospital-cum-teaching hospital, a state-run medical department and a state medical service.

Chloroform Commissions

The medical officers posted in the cantonment and the Residency were drawn from the ranks of the Indian Medical Service (IMS) and were mostly trained in Britain. Dr Edward Lawrie, who became the Residency Surgeon in 1885, had worked in England and in IMS at Madras and Lahore. A seminal contribution of Dr Lawrie was the introduction of medical research in Hyderabad, with experiments conducted to establish the efficacy and safety of chloroform as anaesthesia. At that time, the use of chloroform as anaesthesia was the subject of a major controversy in medical circles of Britain and Europe. Dr Lawrie led the formation of Hyderabad Chloroform Commissions to investigate chloroform and developed the 'Hyderabad technique' of administering it safely, earning the city a permanent place in the annals of medical history.

From 1846, the use of anaesthesia—first ether and then chloroform—went through experimentation by many leading physicians and surgeons such as James Young Simpson, John Snow and James Syme. The safe dosage and method of its administration were contentious among surgeons and doctors. When deaths occurred due to the administration of chloroform, probable causes for it stirred more controversies. Leading surgeons in England and Europe reported the cause of chloroform-related deaths as its adverse impact on the functioning of the heart.

Lawrie had been a student of Syme in Edinburgh. Upon his arrival in Hyderabad, he introduced the use of chloroform in clinical practice. He also initiated animal experiments with the help of his students, to establish the cause of death in the event of overdosing. In the first set of experiments, he anaesthetised 128 'full-grown pariah dogs' with chloroform and analysed the death, concluding that 'in no case did the heart become dangerously affected by chloroform until after the breathing had stopped'.[22] The experiments were conducted under the aegis of a panel called the Hyderabad Chloroform Commission headed by Patrick Hehir. The commission was appointed by the Nizam.

In January 1889, Lawrie announced the findings of the Commission at the annual award ceremony of the Hyderabad Medical School where the chief guests were the Duke and Duchess of Connaught. The event was covered in the 23 February 1889 issue of *The Lancet*. The report quoted Lawrie as saying, 'no doubt deaths would go on occurring until London schools which, of course, influence the whole world, either entirely changed their principles and ignored the heart in chloroform administration, or else confined themselves exclusively to the use of an anaesthetic like ether, which with all its disadvantages, they know how to manage'.[23]

The challenge to the British medical community on a highly controversial issue, coming from a fellow British officer serving in a princely state, was bound to attract attention. The editors at *The Lancet* observed, 'We should require more than the scanty statements of experiments performed upon dogs, notoriously non-susceptible to chloroform syncope before we could accept the conclusions of the Hyderabad Commission.'[24] Lawrie replied to the criticism in the columns of the medical journal, saying that the heart could show signs of danger only when 'the limits of safety have already been exceeded'. The matter was brought to the notice of Nizam Mir Mahbub Ali Khan and Lawrie sought his help to challenge *The Lancet* and others opposed to his findings. The Nizam agreed to fund a visit by experts nominated by the medical journal to witness and participate in another round of animal experiments. He sanctioned an amount of 1,000 Pound Sterling from his personal purse for this. Thus was born the Second Hyderabad Chloroform Commission in 1889.

A group photo of the Second Hyderabad Chloroform Commission, 1890
(courtesy: Osmania Medical College Alumni Association)

The decision to address a question that concerned 'the welfare and the happiness of the whole mankind' wrote *The Pioneer*. The newspaper noted, 'Nothing can show better the beneficent nature of the solid and friendly tie that binds together the British and the Nizam's Governments than the remarkable and cosmopolitan interest which H.H. the Nizam and his officials, one and all, have taken in bringing the question of safety of chloroform to the proof.'[25] *The Lancet* thanked the Nizam and the Diwan, Asman Jah, for their generosity in appointing the Commission, paying for its expenses and for agreeing to present a copy of 'the complete work to all principal medical libraries throughout the world'.[26]

The Lancet deputed Sir Thomas Lauder Brunton, a Fellow of the Royal Society and reputed pharmacologist, to head the Second Chloroform Commission. Brunton arrived in Hyderabad on 4 October 1889. The Commission had Gerald Bomford, Hehir and Chamarette as members and was assisted by a sub-committee consisting of Dr Rustomji D. Hakim, Kelly and Dr Gay. The Commission carried out fresh animal experiments, besides repeating the ones done by the first Commission. The animals had chloroform administered in 'every possible way and under every conceivable condition'. It was found that 'in every case where chloroform was pushed, respiration stopped before the heart'.[27] In the issue dated 7 December 1889, the journal published a telegram from Brunton about the animal experiments which were conducted at the Afzalgunj Hospital. It read: 'Four hundred and ninety dogs, horses, monkeys, goats, cats and rabbits used. One hundred and ninety with manometer. All records photographed. Numerous observations on every individual animal. Results most instructive. Danger from chloroform is asphyxia or overdose: none whatever heart direct.'[28]

The Nizam witnessed experiments in the laboratory on two 'special and memorable occasions'—11 November and 29 November 1889 when chloroform was administered to a goat, a small horse and a monkey in his presence.[29] The full report of the Second Chloroform Commission was serialised in The Lancet in 1890, with the conclusions supporting Lawrie fully.

This, however, did not settle the controversial respiration versus heart question. There were more rebuttals and rejoinders in the columns of The Lancet, British Medical Journal and Nature as well as popular press, with Lawrie continuing to defend his position. In 1901, the British Medical Association formed the Special Chloroform Committee to further investigate the matter. Lawrie retired the same year and returned to England. He died four years later.

Medical historians look at Lawrie's contribution to the science of anaesthesia in different ways. K. Bryn Thomas observed, 'To some extent, Lawrie is both villain and hero. Villain for adhering to a biased idea in defiance of the evidence of others; a hero in stimulating others by persuading a rich prince to pay. On the whole, he was more a villain since many must have been comforted by the honeyed words from Hyderabad, while chloroform continued to kill.'[30]

Chloroform was not the only obsession of Lawrie while in Hyderabad. He also dabbled in malaria, which was among the tropical diseases engaging the attention of British researchers and doctors posted in India, including Ronald Ross.

Hyderabadi Mosquitoes and a Nobel Discovery

In 1880, the French scientist Alphonse Laveran found the plasmodium parasite in the blood of malaria patients, but it was still not known how humans got infected. Sir Patrick Manson, considered the father of modern tropical medicine, established the relationship between mosquitoes and filariasis infection. He postulated that malaria too was transmitted by mosquitoes but the mode of transmission of malaria was still a subject of research. In 1895, Edward Lawrie made an astounding claim in telegrams sent to the editors of *The Lancet* and the *Times of India* denying the existence of plasmodium in the blood of malarial patients and stating that the Laveran bodies were ordinary pus cells.[31] In public lectures, he lambasted the *British Medical Journal* for advocating that the cause of malarial fever was an animal parasite living in the blood.

Lawrie got into a spat with Ronald Ross, who was a fellow officer of IMS and his contemporary, and other malaria researchers through articles and comments in the *British Medical Journal*. Lawrie experimented with pigeons to disprove Ross who had cultivated a parasite of birds (*Proteosoma*) in gnats and showed that healthy birds get infected when bitten by these gnats. Lawrie kept a set of young pigeons in a mosquito net for a long time and reported that *Proteosoma* was present in pigeons even though they had not been bitten by any insect. So the presence of *Proteosoma* in the birds had nothing to do with insect bites. Ross wrote back to the journal that the whole experiment was flawed since the parasite Lawrie had found in pigeons was not *Proteosoma* at all but another parasite which was commonly found in pigeons, crows and so on. Ross called Lawrie 'a violent anti-plasmodist' and a victim of the fixed idea that 'scientific men have wickedly conspired to pass off an altered blood corpuscle as the parasite of malaria; he accuses us all of manufacturing evidence and so on.'[32]

Ross was born in Almora in 1857. At the age of eight, he was sent to England for education. He joined IMS in 1881 and was posted in Madras. Being the son of a high-ranking military officer, he had typical prejudices against 'native Indians' whom he found 'hard-working as any, faithful, docile and intelligent.'[33] After postings in Quetta, Port Blair and Burma, Ross was shunted to Bangalore. It was in Bangalore, where he was posted as acting garrison surgeon, that he became aware of the nuisance caused by mosquitoes. He began devoting time to read medical books and developing research ideas. After three years in Bangalore, he moved to serve in the 20th Madras Infantry in Secunderabad.

In 1894, when Ross was in England on leave, he happened to meet Sir Patrick Manson who encouraged him to work on malaria. Manson's work had shown the possibility that mosquitoes had a role in the transmission of malaria, just as they did in filariasis. On his return, Ross got engrossed in malaria research, which mainly involved dissecting different species of mosquitoes, fed on patients infected with malaria, to see if any traces of parasites could be found. It was a laborious and painstaking experiment—breed different species of mosquitoes from larvae, make newly bred mosquitoes to bite malaria patients, and then hunt for the parasite in the guts of mosquitoes. Since it meant keeping malaria patients in mosquito nets for long hours to let mosquitoes bred by Ross bite them, he would pay one anna for each engorgement caused due to a mosquito bite. Many would still refuse, thinking Ross was indulging in some kind of witchcraft.[34] Ross does not mention in his memoir nor do his biographers, but other accounts mention that patients for these blood-sucking experiments in Begumpet Hospital were recruited from the Afzalgunj Hospital, among others.[35]

The prevalent hypothesis was that malaria was transmitted when someone swallowed an infected mosquito. To test this hypothesis, Ross got a mosquito infected from a patient named Abdul Qadir and tried to infect a healthy person, Laxman, by making him swallow the infected mosquito. Laxman did not get infected. Sceptics like Lawrie did not believe that the blood of those infected could harbour the malaria parasite.

To disprove critics, Ross agreed to hold a lecture–demonstration with a malaria patient at the Hyderabad Medical School, in the presence of Dr Lawrie and Dr Abdul Husain, who was the superintendent of the Afzalgunj Hospital. On 11 July 1897, the day of the demonstration, Ross got a fever patient in the Begumpet Hospital, drew blood from his finger, put it on a slide and found the parasite when the slide was examined under the microscope. He sent away the patient, along with an attendant, to the medical school in Gun Foundry. In the afternoon, he went to the lecture and made his presentation. At the end of it, he called the patient, pricked his finger, prepared a slide and put it under the microscope. To his surprise, he did not find any parasite. As a subsequent discovery would later reveal, the parasite could not be detected in the infected patient's blood because of its complex life-cycle in the human host.

Ross was dejected but he soon renewed his research efforts by procuring some dappled-wing *Anopheles* mosquitoes for his experiments. Unlike other mosquito species, Ross had noticed that dappled-wing mosquitoes rested on human skin, positioning themselves at an angle that allowed efficient feeding on human blood. He started breeding this species in his laboratory. On 16 August 1897, an assistant informed him that several adult insects had emerged in the colony. A malaria patient, Husein Khan, who had agreed to participate in the experiment, was ushered into the mosquito net, ready to be bitten by the newly bred dappled-wing mosquitoes. A bunch of them were released in the net to feed on Khan's blood, after which the patient was allowed to leave. Meanwhile, Ross started dissecting the mosquitoes that had fed on

Khan's blood. For a couple of days, Ross did not find anything in the guts of the mosquitoes he dissected.

On 20 August 1897, Ross noticed something peculiar. He found pigmented cells in the gut of Mosquito 39, a female *Anopheles* mosquito. Further work on mosquitoes fed on malaria patients showed that the parasite grew to a point where it reached the salivary glands of the mosquito ready to get transmitted through a bite. On 22 August, Ross wrote a detailed letter, he to Manson. A few days later, he sent a report titled 'On Some Peculiar Pigmented Cells Found in Two Mosquitoes Fed on Malaria Blood' to *British Medical Journal*.[36]

In effect, Ross had discovered how the malaria parasite got transmitted from one infected person to another through a mosquito. The report was published on 18 December 1897. By the time it was published, Ross was in Kherwara in Rajputana where he was transferred in September 1897. He could not continue his research in Kherwara as it had no malaria patients. A few months later, Ross was posted to Calcutta where he resumed malaria research at the Cunningham Laboratory, soon demonstrating the presence of the parasite in the salivary gland of mosquitoes. This, along with the discovery made in Secuderabad, fully explained the cycle of malaria transmission. In 1899, Ross returned to England and joined the Liverpool School of Tropical Medicine as a lecturer. In 1902, he was awarded the Nobel Prize for his discovery. Though Ross was born in India, he was not a Hyderabadi. However, the city can bask in the Nobel glory as the prize-winning discovery was made on its soil and through experiments conducted on its residents.

Ross was forgotten in Hyderabad after he moved to England. His first official recognition came in 1935 with the installation of a memorial tablet in the building where he made his path-breaking discovery. The tablet was erected by the Secunderabad Cantonment authorities in the building that previously housed the military hospital.

How Hyderabad 'rediscovered' Ross is an interesting tale. It so happened that Lt Col. A.F. Morton, a British officer from Hyderabad, who was on a holiday in Ceylon in 1933, came across an article about Ross. *The Ceylon Times* mentioned that Ross had made the discovery using a microscope at the Indian Military Hospital (IMH) in Begumpet in Hyderabad. Upon his return, the officer asked his colleague Maj. H.B. Marcoolyn about the location of IMH but he was told that no such facility existed in Hyderabad.

'I realised that IMH must have been re-appropriated for some other purpose. With the aid of the records in the Garrison Engineer's office, I was able to discover that it had been turned into an Officer's Mess,' recalled Marcoolyn.[37] Marcoolyn then requested Col. Sandeeman, president of the Cantonment Board, to erect a tablet in the mess building in the memory of Ross. The building subsequently became the office of Deccan Airways. It is now in a state of neglect.

The episode was recalled by Maj. Gen. S.L. Bhatia, head of medical services, in May 1953 when the Government of Hyderabad decided to set up the Ross Memorial Institute in the same building, to honour Ross for conducting research and taking 'effective measures for the control of malaria, especially in Hyderabad state'. The institute was later renamed Ronald Ross Institute of Parasitology and placed under Osmania University.

Another centre that commemorates the memory of the scientist is the Sir Ronald Ross Institute of Tropical and Communicable Diseases, popularly known as Fever Hospital.

Photographing the Heavens

If modern medicine made its debut in Hyderabad via the cantonment, another scientific discipline—astronomy—was introduced under different circumstances. While theoretical astronomy was taught in Darul-Uloom along with geography, mathematics and sciences, Hyderabad did not have an astronomical observatory. The credit for introducing modern observational astronomy in Hyderabad goes to Zafar Jung, son of the Paigah noble Khursheed Jah Bahadur. Jung was home-tutored in Persian and Arabic. He and the Nizam, Mahbub Ali Khan, as children, grew up under the watchful eyes of Salar Jung I. Zafar Jung was chosen as Mahbub's companion when Captain John Clerk was appointed to teach English to the Sovereign.[38] In 1884, Zafar Jung was sent to England for higher education with two tutors in tow—Mr Stevens and Moulvai Sayed Mahmood. He was in

England for a year. During this period, he also visited Paris. Upon his return, he completed his military training and was given the task of holding the ceremonial morchal behind the Nizam.[39]

Zafar Jung developed an interest in astronomy while studying in England. He acquired two equatorial telescopes—a 15-inch Grubb refractor and an 8-inch Cooke astrograph—and three others of 'minor importance' with lenses of 12, 10 and 7 inches, with an idea to establish an observatory in Hyderabad. The telescopes were mounted on portable stands at his estate in Phisalbanda. Subsequently, he acquired chronometers, clocks, barometers and thermometers for collecting meteorological data. In September 1901, he informed the Nizam of his intention to establish an observatory in Hyderabad: 'When this observatory building is constructed it will be one of the greatest observatories in India. If your Highness approves, I will designate it as the Nizamiah or H.H. Nizam's Observatory. My great desire is that after my death, the observatory should belong to the government.'[40]

Zafar Jung appointed Rudolf Grubb, the son of Sir Howard Grubb, a leading supplier of astronomical instruments globally, as the superintendent of the proposed observatory. The appointment was for three years at a monthly salary of Rs 1,000. This became controversial as Zafar Jung began using Grubb's services for secretarial work as well. Seeing letters signed by Grubb as Jung's private secretary, the Resident complained to the Diwan, Maharaja Kishen Pershad, that the Government of India had only permitted Grubb to work as superintendent of the telescope.[41] Zafar Jung clarified that Grubb was handling secretarial work only during his spare time. The Resident eventually agreed to let Grubb work as Jung's secretary provided his salary was 'restricted to the amount already sanctioned'.

To make the telescopes operational, Zafar Jung got in touch with Kodaikanal and Madras observatories. In 1903, he hired Subba Rao, a first assistant in Madras Observatory, at a salary of Rs 100 a month and living quarters in the Paigah estates. In 1904, at Jung's request, Michie Smith, director of Kodaikanal and Madras observatories, visited Phisalbanda to examine the telescopes. Smith found that 'the situation of the (Grubb) telescope, in the heart of the city, and the defective housing arrangements, render it impossible to make very stringent tests as to the quality of the object glass.'[42] Smith suggested 'both telescopes are well worth erecting in a good house and on a suitable site' outside the city.

But before a site for the observatory could be found, Jung died in 1907 at the age of forty-three. According to his Will, the observatory was taken over by Nizam's government and placed under the administration of the Finance department, which also looked after education. George Casson Walker, who headed the Finance department, recommended that, as suggested by Smith, a site 'at considerable elevation lying at some distance from any habitation and with a clear view should be found.'[43]

A site on high ground in Begumpet was selected for the construction of an astrograph building, a workshop and other buildings. In March 1907, Arthur Brunel Chatwood, an astronomer from Oxford, was appointed the first director of the Nizamiah Observatory. Besides taking up astronomical observations, the new facility was supposed to 'carry on complete meteorological observations and to collaborate if desired, with the Director General of Indian Observatories'.

At this time, several observatories around the globe were engaged in an international programme to map the sky. An astrographic catalogue or *carte du Ciel* was initiated at the International Congress of Astronomy held in Paris in 1887. The task of recording photographic measurements of the positions of stars was divided among eighteen observatories in both hemispheres. The Santiago Observatory in Chile, which was assigned to map the zones between 17 degrees and 23 degrees, could not carry out the work. Herbert Hall Turner, professor of astronomy at the University of Oxford, suggested that Nizamiah should seize this opportunity. Turner tried to convince the Nizam of the advantages of participating in the prestigious project. 'You would earn the gratitude of other nations by completing this great scheme,' he wrote to the Nizam in February 1908.[44]

The building to house the 8-inch Cooke astrograph was completed in 1909. The revolving dome, 25 feet in diameter, was made by T. Cooke and Sons of York and was brought to Hyderabad in parts. But observations could not begin due to some glitches with the telescope. Parts of it were sent back to England for repairs and a 10-inch 'follower' telescope was mounted in place of the original 8-inch finder.[45] The import of equipment and parts from England got delayed with the Nizam's government seeking exemption from customs duty as the equipment was meant for educational purposes.

The astrographic work finally began when the first photographic plate was exposed on 9 December 1914. The period coincided with the First World War and it became difficult to get photographic plates from England. A large number of them were lost when *SS Persia* sank in the Mediterranean.[46] Some pages of the catalogue sent for printing to Edinburgh were lost in transit and some got burnt in a serious fire at Neil and Company, the printing press. Even before the observations started at Begumpet, Chatwood passed away and Robert John Pocock, a protégé of Turner, was appointed in his place.

The Santiago observatory was a different story. It was managed by German astronomers who tried to forestall work given to Hyderabad. 'The Germans created a ridiculous fuss and said the whole was theirs and they will do it. But I encouraged Pocock to go ahead all the same, with the result that his share will be soon complete while Santiago has only measured a very few plates in 23 and of course, published nothing. I fear they are a broken reed. They are even sending us poor plates in 22 until we made a fuss. So much for German efficiency,' Turner later observed.[47]

Despite disruptions caused in supplies due to the War, the Nizamiah Observatory completed the mapping of stars in zones 17, 18, 19 and 20 by 1919. Two volumes of the Hyderabad section of the astrographic catalogue covering zones 17 and 18 were published in 1918, followed by another on zone 19 the next year. At this point, Turner wrote to the Nizam suggesting that Hyderabad should take up the mapping of zone 22 (already photographed by Santiago) to ascertain if some anomalies noticed were due to stars themselves or a change in the observatory. Turner wrote a personal letter to Amin

Jung Bahadur, peshi minister, explaining the technical reasons for doing so as Amin Jung himself was an astronomer and a Fellow of the Royal Astronomical Society.[48]

After Pocock died in 1918, T.P. Bhaskaran Shastri, a Madras University graduate who joined the observatory in 1912, succeeded him but was formally confirmed only four years later.[49] The observatory was also tasked with timekeeping and meteorological observations (temperature, humidity, wind speed, rainfall, etc.). It collaborated with India Meteorological Department (IMD) to study the upper atmosphere with balloons carrying instruments. It also acquired instruments for seismographic observations. In 1935, an elementary course in astrophysics was introduced for BA and BSc students at Osmania University.

A Culture of Science in a Princely State

Indian princely states in the nineteenth century were not directly under British rule but were strongly influenced by the British presence. Their engagement with new ideas of science and modernity was facilitated by progressive Diwans like Salar Jung in Hyderabad and Madhav Rao in Travancore and Baroda. As a result, these states became a part of global scientific pursuits like the *carte du Ciel* and the international geomagnetic survey (this was initiated by the British Association for the Advancement of Science and resulted in the publication of *Trivandrum Magnetical Observations*). With such investments in science, the princely states sought to keep pace with advances in science in Europe and narrow the 'knowledge gap'.[50] In addition, such engagement accrued benefits locally.

The Hyderabad Medical School helped develop a culture of science and inquiry. It catalysed the formation of the Hyderabad Medical and Physical Society in March 1853, the first scientific society in the state. The society published a journal *Proceedings of the Hyderabad Medical and Physical Society*. Dr George Smith launched another journal in 1855 intending to connect students of the medical school and practitioners. Hakims posted in government dispensaries were encouraged to write articles and report case studies. *Risala-e-Tibabat-i-Hyderabad* (Hyderabad Medical Journal) was the first medical journal in Hindustani.

Residency Surgeon Dr Edward Lawrie trained several of his students in the administration of chloroform. One of them was Roopa Bai Furdoonji, the first Indian woman to be trained as an anaesthetist and arguably the first woman anaesthetist in the world.[51] In one of his clinical lectures, Lawrie described Furdoonji's work: 'In the case of operation for the removal of the uterus and its appendages for sarcoma, which you witnessed yesterday, chloroform was administered, and the patient was fully kept anaesthetised for one hour and a half by Miss R. Furdoonji, a fifth-year Parsi lady student, without assistance or interference from anybody.'[52]

Furdoonji was among the earliest women in India to study medicine. She was admitted to Hyderabad Medical School in 1885, just two years after Kadambini Ganguly joined Calcutta Medical College. Anandi Bai Joshi was the first Indian woman to be trained as a doctor, but she could not practise as she passed away in 1887, a year after her return from America.

Significantly, not many contemporary medical schools in Europe and America admitted women candidates at that time. The presence of women in a medical school in a princely state, therefore, did not go unnoticed in the West. A report on Hyderabad Medical School, published in the *British Medical Journal* on 4 May 1895, noted that the students of 'this interesting little school' included both men and women who were 'Mohammedans, Hindus, Parsees, Eurasians, and English'. Women were given the same opportunities of administering chloroform and performing surgeries as men, it said.

Roopa Bai later went to Edinburgh University for higher studies and was in the Nizam's government service till 1919.

Lawrie innovated a medical device for the administration of chloroform to patients. It was a conical inhaler made of cloth to allow free admixture of air with chloroform close to the nose without interfering with the patient's breathing. It was named 'Hyderabad Cap', the first medical device invented in and named after Hyderabad. The cloth cone had a small piece of absorbent cotton stitched to its apex, into which a drachm of chloroform was poured every three-quarters of a minute. The cone was supposed to be held loosely but closely over the mouth and nose.[53]

Among the anaesthetists trained by Lawrie in the administration of chloroform were Krishtiah, Mahomed Abdul Ghani, Shivram Balkristna, Ms E.A. Lawrie, Ms Williams, Ismail Khan, A.V. Raja Gopal, Narain Gobind and Yusuf Baig. Dr (Maj.) Mutyala Govindarajulu Naidu—later to marry Sarojini Chattopadhyay—accompanied Lawrie in May 1895 to England to demonstrate the Hyderabad technique of administration of chloroform.

Though Lawrie's claims relating to chloroform were, in the end, rejected by his peers, he was successful in introducing modern medical research, particularly large-scale animal studies, in Hyderabad. Unlike Ross who carried out malaria research on his own and did not involve local students or doctors, Lawrie's research was carried out under state patronage at the state-run Afzalgunj Hospital and the Hyderabad Medical School. His work placed Hyderabad on the global map, connected Hyderabad medical graduates to the world of European medicine and higher learning and, above all, built the confidence of the rulers and elite in modern medicine and research.

In the same way, Nizamiah Observatory spurred the development of astronomical, meteorological and seismic observations as well as research and education. It was positioned as a full-scale institution to spread scientific ideas in Hyderabad. Its objective was to 'stimulate a general taste for scientific pursuit', conduct 'illustrated lectures on scientific subjects, particularly astronomy' and extend 'every reasonable assistance to amateurs in carrying on serious scientific work.'[54]

The observatory introduced astronomy in Hyderabad at a time when the discipline was about to take a new direction globally with the advent of spectroscopy. It became a nursery for the first set of indigenous astronomers. They had the advantage of immersing in an emerging branch of astronomy due to Nizamiah's participation in an international project. They recorded observations, developed photographic plates and did mathematical calculations to determine the coordinates of stars observed according to the accuracy parameters laid down in Paris. Those who participated in the exercise included C. Hanmant Rao, F.B. Shroff, D.R. Sripati Rao, Syed Ahmed, M. Anantanarayanan, Manali Kakuzhi Bappu, U.S. Raghavendra Rao and M. Ahmadullah. T.P. Bhaskaran was co-opted as a member of the *carte du Ciel* Commission of the International Astronomical Union (IAU) and made a Fellow of the Royal Astronomical Society.[55]

The observatory inspired a young boy who would not only become the father of modern astronomy in India but lead IAU in the second half of the twentieth century.

Manali Kakuzhi Bappu was among the first set of recruits of the observatory. While he was engaged in the work on astrographic catalogues in the 1920s and 1930s, he got married and settled down in Hyderabad. His son, Vainu, would accompany him to the telescope rooms at night. This introduced the young boy to the mysteries of the sky and 'he developed a deep familiarity with the sky and the instruments'—an experience that would remain an important asset all through his life.[56] Vainu Bappu became interested in building instruments while studying at Nizam College. He built a spectrograph and used it to obtain the spectrum of the night sky airglow, turning his bedroom into a makeshift observatory. He published his first paper in a standard scientific journal in 1946 when he was only nineteen.

The young Bappu's career in science took a decisive shift when Professor Harlow Shapely, director of the Harvard College Observatory, visited Hyderabad in early 1947. Shapely was among the large number of foreign scientists invited to attend the thirty-fourth session of the Indian Science Congress which was held in Delhi and had Jawaharlal Nehru as its general president. Many of the foreign scientists toured universities and scientific institutions in different cities. In Hyderabad, they delivered public lectures at Nizam College and Osmania University.

Shapely, along with Astronomer Royal of England Sir Harold Spencer Jones, visited the Nizamiah Observatory on 14 January 1947, and 'discussed with its staff schemes of further development'.[57] It was during this visit that Shapely met M.K. Bappu and his son

Vainu Bappu, who was already a budding astronomer. Shapely encouraged the young Bappu to pursue a doctorate at Harvard once he finished MSc. Bappu had already obtained a Nizam's Government scholarship of 400 Pound Sterling for four years to pursue a course in electrical engineering at Battersea Polytechnic of the University of London. After meeting Shapely, Bappu changed his mind and decided to pursue astronomy at Harvard. Meanwhile, Hyderabad was integrated with the Union of India and the administration changed.

Bappu found himself in a difficult situation—a scholarship to go to the UK but an offer to study astronomy in the US. 'He approached the scholarship committee to get the subject changed. At that time, my father-in-law, Hadi Bilgrami (grandson of Syed Husain Bilgrami), was the secretary of the committee. He took up the matter with Chief Civil Administrator Bakhle appointed by the Government of India. Bilgrami explained that Bappu already had an offer from Harvard and changing the subject of scholarship was within the executive powers of the civil administrator. That's how Bappu could proceed to the US to pursue astronomy,' recalled Sanjar Ali Khan, a friend of Bappu at Nizam College where both were mentored by physics professor J.C. Kameswara Rav.[58]

Just a few months after he arrived at Harvard, Bappu became a part of an 'accidental' comet discovery while scanning photographic plates at the Harvard College Observatory. He noticed an unusual object in one of the plates, and over the next few days observed the same region of the sky along with colleague Gordon Newkirk and Professor Bart J. Bok. The unusual object turned out to be a new comet. It was subsequently named Bappu–Bok–Newkirk Comet. But the bureaucracy in Hyderabad got upset and reprimanded Bappu for deviating from the subject of his PhD ('photoelectric photometry of eclipsing variables').[59] Fred L. Whipple, chairman of the Department of Astronomy, wrote back saying, if Bappu had failed to note this unusual object on the photographic plate, 'it would have been a sin of scientific omission' and 'to have failed to announce the discovery would have been a serious neglect of his duty to the scientific world.'[60]

Bappu's troubles with the bureaucracy continued even after he returned to India in 1953 with a doctorate from Harvard and having conducted postdoctoral research at Princeton, Palomar and Lick observatories. According to the scholarship conditions, Bappu was to serve in the government for ten years. He was offered the post of a lecturer in physics at Osmania University, which he turned down. Bappu was freed from the bond conditions only after interventions by Sir C.V. Raman and Akbar Ali, the director of Nizamiah Observatory.[61] Bappu joined the Uttar Pradesh State Observatory in Varanasi (which he got shifted to Nainital), became the director of the Kodaikanal Observatory, established a new observatory at Kavlur and finally founded the Indian Institute of Astrophysics (IIA) in Bangalore. Today, IIA operates some of the finest telescopes in the world, including the space telescope Astrosat launched in 2015. It developed scientific payloads for *Aditya* L1, the first space-based Indian mission to study the Sun, which was launched by the Indian Space Research Organisation (ISRO) in 2023.

2

Mahua Flowers and the World Wars

∽

My ultimate object is to set up demonstrational factories at state expense, taking up one or two promising products at a time, and by that means proving in a practical way to our capitalists the utility and profitable nature of each enterprise. An ounce of practice in this country is worth any amount of preaching.

—G.E.C. Wakefield,
founder of Industrial Laboratory, Hyderabad, 1916[1]

THE FIRST WORLD WAR JOLTED BRITAIN AND ITS COLONIES in many ways. The shortage of artillery shells during the War made Britain realise the vital gaps in scientific and industrial research. Colonies were thrown in disarray as they were told to supply men and materials for the War. This spurred activities to boost industrial production and war supplies. Industrial research laboratories were organised to work on weaponry and associated systems, while the Ministry of Munitions coordinated supplies from the colonies. The Indian Munitions Board was created to coordinate the manufacturing of shells and other war materials at workshops of Railways and Public Works Department (PWD) as well as government mints. The overall target was to produce 11,000 shells per month in India. In 1915, the Hyderabad Mint was assigned to produce 13-pounders.[2]

The War made the import of finished goods difficult. This led to the colonies feeling the need to establish manufacturing industries based on locally available raw materials. Even before the War, progressive princely states like Mysore and Baroda had formulated policies to encourage economic growth based on industrialisation. They patronised local industries for the manufacture of alcohol-based products, essential oils, soaps and pharmaceuticals. All industrial enterprises in Mysore were State-owned. Meanwhile, Baroda encouraged private industries, by offering incentives like free land and tax breaks. As a result, companies like Alembic Chemical Works moved their factories from Bombay to Baroda. Before the War, Hyderabad had a very rudimentary industrial activity that included a State-run distillery and some cottage industries.

At the beginning of the twentieth century, the Nizam was under pressure to set right the state's finances. All top posts in the administration were in the hands of British officers. George Casson Walker was the finance secretary, while G.E.C. Wakefield was appointed the director general of Revenue. As part of the exercise to shore up Hyderabad's revenues, Wakefield noticed that the state was spending a lot on importing finished products like sugar, salt, paper, dyes, edible oil, cigarettes, glue, leather, buttons and so on, despite possessing raw materials needed to make them.[3] For instance, sugar worth Rs 30 lakh was being imported annually despite the abundant availability of sugarcane, mahua and palmyra, which could be used to produce sugar. Flowers of the fast-growing mahua tree were being utilised only to make country liquor. Hyderabad imported leather goods but exported animal hides worth Rs 45 lakh a year because it lacked a tanning and leather industry.

Wakefield brought this up with the Nizam, emphasising that if Hyderabad wanted to industrialise, it should invest in research aimed at utilising the numerous raw materials available in the state. 'Industrial development is nowadays impossible without the help of the laboratory,' he wrote to Nizam while requesting him to permit the setting up of an industrial laboratory so that raw materials found in the state could be exploited on an industrial scale.[4] The plan was approved and, to begin with, the industrial laboratory was established on the campus of the Government Distillery at Narayanguda.

In the summer of 1915, Wakefield was holidaying in Ootacamund in the Nilgiri hills along with Resident Alexander Pinhey. He decided to take advantage of the opportunity to visit a cordite factory in Aruvankadu to acquaint himself with the industrial processes being followed there. He discovered that the factory was importing the acetone needed to make the explosive from Canada.

The acetone imported from Canada was expensive. The Canadians were making it from wood using a laborious process. Chemists in Hyderabad had told Wakefield that mahua flowers could yield not only sugar but also acetic acid and some acetone. Dr Mc Ewen, a professor of science at Nizam College, was engaged in research on mahua flowers, along with chemists at the Government Distillery. Previously, mahua's ability to produce acetone had received little attention because scientists were primarily concerned about making sugar. That mahua flowers could be a cheap source for producing acetone, a substance vital for boosting the firepower of Allied forces, was a Eureka moment for Wakefield.

On his return to Hyderabad, as Wakefield recalled later, 'We continued to experiment; a chemist from Bombay was retained and (he) spent a few days in Hyderabad advising us; an experimental factory was set up in the Mint because of workshops and power facilities; certain microbes necessary for the process were imported from England and eventually, with the help of Mr Gamlen (Master of the Mint) and under the superintendence of Dr Mutyala, Distillery Chemist, acetone was produced from mahua flowers.'[5]

Owing to ill-health, Wakefield proceeded on leave to England in the winter of 1915 but the mahua discovery continued to obsess him. He briefed Thomas Holderness, head of the India office, about the advantages of producing acetone from mahua compared to the prevalent process that used wood. He also interacted with Dr Gilbert J. Fowler, a professor of chemistry at Manchester University. Fowler informed him about a new process of extracting acetone from starch and sugar that his colleague Dr Charles Weizmann (Chaim Weizmann) had developed. At that time Weizmann was on deputation to Admiralty Laboratories as its director. His process involved using a bacterium (*clostridium acetobutylicum*) to ferment a starch-rich substance like maize to produce acetone. The organism was isolated in his lab so it came to be known as the Weizmann bacillus. Weizmann is widely regarded as the father of biochemistry because of his large contribution to industrial fermentation. He renounced British nationality in 1948 to become the President of Israel.

Wakefield was convinced that the Weizmann process could be applied to mahua flowers, which were full of sugar, and that other sources of starch and sugar 'were bound to be very much more expensive than mahua flower'.[6] At his request, Holderness convened a meeting where Wakefield explained the Hyderabad experiments with mahua to Fowler and Weizmann. Weizmann asked Wakefield to get samples of the flower for testing with the Weizmann bacillus. The consignment arrived in a few weeks and the flowers were tested at the Admiralty lab. The results were so favourable that the India office wrote to the Government of India to plan an acetone factory in India to extract acetone from mahua flowers using the Weizmann process. Wakefield wrote to the India office that 'the Government of His Highness the Nizam had been very glad to make the discovery over to the Imperial Government, and except, with the object of helping the Imperial Government, had no desire to manufacture acetone'.[7]

Fowler was chosen to supervise the project in India where he was appointed a professor of applied chemistry at the Indian Institute of Science (IISc) in Bangalore. The institute, established with a generous endowment from Jamsetji Nusserwanji Tata and a land grant from the Maharaja of Mysore, was in its formative stage and the academic programme was yet to take shape fully. There were just two departments at that time—General and Applied Chemistry and Electro-technology.

Wakefield and Fowler sailed to India in the same ship, with Fowler carrying test tubes containing spores of the Weizmann bacillus required for the fermentation of mahua flowers. The basic equipment for erecting an industrial-scale facility to make acetone was also on the same ship. The objective was to quickly assemble a factory on the institute campus till a permanent site was found.

Fowler arrived in Hyderabad in June 1916 at the request of Wakefield to assess the potential of research and industrialisation in the state. He was impressed with the work underway in Hyderabad. The motor cars that ferried Fowler around in Hyderabad were run entirely on motor spirit made from mahua flowers, providing him with further proof of the potential of this plant resource.[8] At this time, alcohol was finding new industrial applications in pharmaceuticals and as 'power alcohol' for use in motor cars. British provinces and princely states seeking to promote industrialisation saw a huge potential in power alcohol.

Fowler offered to train the first set of chemists for the Narayanguda Industrial Laboratory at IISc Bangalore.[9] Four chemistry graduates—S. Mahdi Hassan, S.R. Bhate, K. Habib Hassan and N.N. Inuganti—were selected from candidates who had applied for a job in the laboratory. All of them were sent for training to IISc, along with Dr N. Mutyala, a chemist working in the Government Distillery, who was to lead the team. The Nizam government paid full salary to the five during their stay in Bangalore between July 1917 and April 1918. The group worked extensively on morphological, biochemical and other aspects of mahua, particularly factors that determined the yield of alcohol from the flower. Habib Hassan worked on converting mahua decoction into syrup which could be used to make jams. The researchers could also extract essential oils from the flowers. Parcels of flowers were sent from Nizamabad every week as they ripened on the trees.[10] In addition, the Hyderabad government sent many samples of minor forest produce and minerals for investigations by the group.[11] Fowler eventually established the acetone factory in Nasik and used jawari (sorghum) for the fermentation process.

The chemists, upon their return from Bangalore, continued to work on problems like alcohol fermentation, utilisation of mahua flowers, preparation of cultured yeast, extraction of alkaloids from plants, making paper pulp from forest produce and so on. In later years, the Industrial Laboratory prepared techno-commercial reports aimed at helping new industries. These included reports on using tannery waste to make glue as a byproduct, manufacturing sugar from date palms, power alcohol from mahua flowers, boot polish from locally made methylated spirit, paper from bamboos, salt and katha from backwaters of Raichur and Gulbarga, and various products from oilseeds.[12] The laboratory maintained a well-stocked library of technical books, textbooks and scientific journals.

The scientists at Hyderabad maintained close ties with IISc. Mehdi Hassan was deputed again to IISc in 1921 to work on the natural history of the lac parasites—characterisation of species and their life history.[13] He worked out the sex ratio of the insects which varied under different conditions. Habib Hassan was sent to IISc to work on the hydrogenation of oils and later to the University of Leeds for training in leather manufacturing.[14]

In 1927, the functioning of the laboratory was reviewed to assess if the various government departments were making use of its testing and analytical services. Ms Roland V. Norris, a Reader of biochemistry in IISc who was deputed for the purpose, suggested that a central laboratory could be formed 'to provide in the most economical way the staff and equipment for such assistance.'[15] To set its research agenda, she said that a scientific advisory board with experts from the Nizam College and Osmania University should be constituted. The recommendations of Norris led to the upgradation of the Industrial Laboratory into a Central Laboratory. In IISc, Norris worked on the spike disease of sandalwood before moving to the Tea Research Institute of Ceylon as its director in July 1929.

It took another war—the Second World War (1939–45)—to give a fresh impetus to manufacturing activity and usher in the second wave of industrial research in British India and Hyderabad. In the inter-War period, British provinces took some steps for industrial reorganisation but made little headway. The War, once again, caused shortages of commodities as imports were disrupted. In Hyderabad, new units that were developed with state funding were Allwyn Metal Works, Praga Tools, Hyderabad Starch Products and Hyderabad Chemicals and Fertilisers—all for the War effort.

The War made Britain and the Allies realise the importance of scientific knowledge and research to enhance the speed and efficiency of their response on the battlefield. There were several scientific, medical and technical missions to do with weapons, equipment and methods of war, and to address issues related to food, health, transport, communication, vector control and so on. The Royal Society joined the campaign by forming the British Commonwealth Science Committee to explore collaboration between the Commonwealth and the Empire on scientific matters during the War period as well as post-War reconstruction.

An industrial workshop established by Nizam's government to contribute to the Allied Forces during the Second World War, 1940 (courtesy: Telangana State Archives and Research Centre)

The Government of India formed the Board of Scientific and Industrial Research (BSIR) 'to mobilise the scientific and industrial talent of the country for research and production of war materials'.[16] Some twenty research committees were formed on subjects like glass and ceramics, vegetable oil, fuel, leather, pharmaceuticals and drugs, metals, dye-stuff, building research and so on. In 1942, the Council of Scientific and Industrial Research (CSIR) was established and BSIR was brought under its purview with Shanti Swarup Bhatnagar, a chemist from Punjab University Chemical Laboratories, as director of Scientific and Industrial Research.

As an ally of the British, Hyderabad contributed handsomely to the War effort, sponsoring two squadrons of the Royal Air Force, sending 12,000 soldiers to fight and investing 40 million Pound Sterling in Government of India loans meant for the War. It established a Scientific and Industrial Research Board for the 'promotion and development of industries in the state using industrial research', which would also coordinate with the central BSIR. The Board, headed by Aqueel Jung Bahadur, Member of Commerce and Industries in the Executive Council, was allocated a modest grant of Rs 25,000. Eight research committees— industrial fermentation, pharmaceuticals and drugs, fuel, forest products, ceramics, fibre, vegetable oils and heavy chemicals— were formed.

Urdu & English

Telugu & English

Marathi & English

Canarese & English

War seals issued by the Nizam's government, 1940
(courtesy: Telangana State Archives and Research Centre)

As the War drew to an end, the Viceroy requested the Royal Society to depute Scientific secretary Archibald Vivian Hill to India for advice on the organisation of scientific research in India as a part of the post-War reconstruction plan. Hill had received the 1922 Nobel Prize in Physiology or Medicine (jointly with Otto Fritz Meyerhof) for elucidation of the production of heat and mechanical work in muscles. In India, Hill visited several scientific institutions, universities and research stations in provinces and princely states, including Hyderabad. Ghulam Mohammed,[17] who had participated in the formation of CSIR, was now in Hyderabad working as finance member in the Nizam's Executive Council. He hosted Hill in Hyderabad and facilitated closer coordination between CSIR and Hyderabad BSIR. In these discussions, it emerged that India needed regional laboratories to work on local problems, in addition to national laboratories being built under CSIR. Since Hyderabad was rich in raw materials—edible oil seeds, coal, clays, minerals and so on—it was suggested it should have a full-fledged industrial research programme.

Following up on the suggestion, the departments of Commerce and Industries, Finance and Post-War Planning of Hyderabad prepared a joint note in February 1944 proposing formation of new Central Laboratories for Scientific and Industrial Research (CLSIR). The objectives of CLSIR were much wider, going beyond the original goal of utilising local raw materials for industrial production. The new approach recognised that 'to raise the standard of living of the people, it is not only necessary to aid industries but also to provide additional power, agricultural assistance, chemical fertilizers and modern agricultural implements'. For agricultural and industrial progress, appropriate utilisation of natural resources was critical—a goal that could be achieved 'only through scientific and industrial research conducted on a continuous basis'.[18] Four key areas identified for the work at CLSIR were industrial development, agricultural chemicals, forest products and drugs. The Industrial Laboratory was merged with CLSIR.

Through a firman issued on 5 August 1944, the Nizam appointed Dr Muzaffaruddin Qureshi, head of the Department of Chemistry at

Osmania University, as the first director of CLSIR. A postgraduate in science from Punjab University and DPhil from Berlin University, Qureshi was an important figure in the Indian scientific community. He was a 'Foundation Fellow' of the National Institute of Sciences in India (NISI, which later became the Indian National Science Academy). CLSIR started functioning from a few rooms allocated in the Department of Applied Chemistry of Osmania University, in addition to the Industrial Laboratory office in the Government Distillery.

The Slow Pace of Industrial Development

The Industrial Laboratory, a byproduct of the First World War (1914–18), was Hyderabad's first scientific research organisation. The first industrial process it developed made useful products with mahua flowers, with direct inputs from Weizmann and Fowler, the global leader in industrial fermentation. A review of the functioning of the laboratory in 1927 found that government departments were not taking full advantage of the facilities available at the laboratory though some of them needed assistance in testing and analytical services.

Along with Industrial Laboratory, the Nizam's government formed a new Commerce and Industries Department (CID) called Sanat-o-Hirafat, to boost industrial production. The constitution of these two bodies spurred the first wave of industrialisation in the state. The Commerce and Industries Department promoted 'pioneering industries' based on research on raw materials done at Industrial Laboratory. Deccan Glass Work, Power Alcohol Factory and Government Soap Factory were a result of research-led industrialisation. Small tanneries, units making handmade paper, clay tiles and so on also came up.[19] The Commerce and Industries Department formed an Industrial Engineering section to make blueprints for factories and the Industrial Trust Fund (ITF) to provide financial assistance. The department would send personnel abroad for training in specific industries. Upon their return, these people were designated as State Technical Scholars and given the responsibility to help local industries like dyeing, glass, tiles, alcohol and so on.

However, princely states like Mysore and Baroda, which set up similar industrial laboratories at the same time as Hyderabad, raced ahead in industrialisation. Most large princely states provided some form of protection to indigenous capital as well as access to technology, market and finance. By the time of the Second World War, Mysore had an impressive array of large state enterprises and private industries. The British helped in setting up Hindustan Aeronautics Limited (HAL) as a joint sector company with Walchand Hirachand. Baroda became a hub of chemical and pharmaceutical industries.

Such industrialisation evaded Hyderabad. The Hyderabad units set up during the War became sick as the demand for their products fell once the War ended. When Wakefield planned Industrial Laboratory, his vision was to develop industrial processes, demonstrate them at a pilot scale and then hand them over to private parties to run. The industrial policies pursued by the Nizam were aimed at developing industries in the state sector. Moreover, Hyderabad did not have any mercantile community or an identifiable business class or a class of capitalists. Private industries, if any, were in the hands of the nobility, which lacked business acumen. The state control of ownership, finance and technology overshdowed the possibility of a real capitalist class emerging in Hyderabad, as C.V. Subba Rao has pointed out in his landmark study.[20] The feudal social structure, marked by the pre-capitaist forms of extraction of resources, was a constraint for industrial growth. Therefore, according to Rao, the state's efforts to boost industrialisation made little difference. Yet, the institutions founded for industrial research and technology promotion proved useful in the state's development after the political situation changed in 1948, as discussed in later chapters.

3

A Beautiful, Healthy and Efficient City

~~

When the improvement schemes now suggested are carried out and the city equips herself with clean houses, flush-down lavatories, dustless roads, paved footpaths, wider bridges and a plentiful supply of open spaces, parks and gardens and public monuments, she will be able to hold her head high among her sister cities in India ... (if) the remodelling and modernization will proceed apace, and Hyderabad of the future will become a beautiful, healthy and efficient city.

—M. Visvesvaraya,
on his vision of a future Hyderabad, 1930[1]

RIVER MUSI IS BARELY NOTICEABLE IN MODERN-DAY Hyderabad. There is little water running through it and construction has taken over much of the riverside. The floodplains have been encroached upon, and untreated waste flows into the river at many points. Its bridges, both old and new, are no longer the architectural marvels they once were but are now sites of traffic jams.

38

During the monsoons, the river periodically comes up in public discourse when rising water levels can lead to local flooding, as had happened in October 2020, July 2022 and July 2023. Yet, the story of Hyderabad remains inextricably linked with the fortunes of this river, particularly with the 1908 flood and its aftermath.

Today, River Musi is a pale shadow of its past. At the beginning of the twentieth century, it flowed through the middle of the city, bisecting it. On its south bank was the walled city housing the palaces of the Nizam as well as residences of principal nobles, while on the north bank was the British enclave with the imposing Residency building, British administrative offices and the Residency Bazaar surrounding it. A few miles away further north was the cantonment in Secunderabad. Between the Residency and the cantonment was the sparsely inhabited Chaderghat suburb. The total population of Hyderabad and the suburb was less than half a million at the beginning of the twentieth century.[2] The 1908 flood changed the urban geography, the centre of political power and the face of the city for ever.

It was not uncommon for River Musi to be in flood, but the most devastating of floods occurred on 28 September 1908. The river originates in the Anantagiri Hills, flows eastwards to pass through the city and then moves into Nalgonda where it joins River Krishna. River Musi has its tributary, Isi or Esi, which is near the Golconda Fort. On the fateful night, the water level rose so dramatically that it submerged the high arches of the Purana Pul and washed away a part of the Afzal Gunj bridge (Naya Pul). The south bank of the river had been artificially raised to prevent flooding while the north bank was generally low-lying. This resulted in the inundation of several areas on the north bank—Begum Bazaar, Kolsawadi, Dhoolpet, Dal Mandi, Chudi Bazaar, Osman Shahi, Muktair Pura and so on.[3] Among the south bank areas that were affected were Char Mahal, Petla Burj, Ghasimiya Bazaar, Mehboob Shahi, Anjeer Bagh and so on.

Hundreds of houses either collapsed or got damaged, and thousands of people were swept away by the gushing waters or got buried under collapsing structures. Some two thousand people were washed away in Kolsawadi alone. Water also breached the Residency area. All one could see on either side of the river were 'fallen houses, collapsed roofs, bare walls and a tangled mass of trees, logs, rafters and shrubbery' while human corpses and carcasses of animals were strewn everywhere.[4] People climbed atop trees and high buildings to save themselves. One such tree still stands in Kolsawadi with a plaque commemorating its life-saving role. Boats were requisitioned from the Boat Club and rafts were made by fastening empty cans to cots.

Mir Mahbub Ali Khan (Mahbub Pasha), who was the reigning Nizam at that time, supervised rescue and relief operations. The acting British Resident Michael O'Dwyer—who was later to gain notoriety for endorsing the Jallianwala Bagh massacre as the governor of Punjab—sought an audience with the Nizam to offer help. Religious saints and astrologers were consulted. Mahbub Pasha was known to patronise many of them, providing monthly bursaries and supporting the performance of religious rituals of Hindu priests.[5] According to one account, a word was sent to a priest-astrologer, Jhoomar Lal Tiwari, on how to 'tame' the river in this hour of calamity. Tiwari advised the Nizam to appease Muchkunda (another name for Musi) which, according to Hindu beliefs, is an incarnation of the goddess Bhawani.[6] A Marwari priest who had migrated from Kuchera (Jodhpur State) to Hyderabad around 1875, Tiwari lived in a haveli of a banker-merchant in Mahbub Ganj, the grain market named after the Nizam.

The river banks had religious and spiritual connections for both Hindus and Muslims. They were dotted with temples, maths, mosques, mazaars and cremation grounds. Many turned to prayers after the flood because they believed it was an 'act of god'. Mahbub Pasha, eager to alleviate the sufferings of his people, heeded the advice of the Hindu priest and reached the banks of the swollen river near the Purana Pul to perform the puja. He entered the river waters and worshipped the 'angry goddess', pleading with her with folded hands to retreat. A golden tray was prepared with 'a sari, pearls, yellow rice, condiments, red kumkum powder, two coconuts encased in gold and silver and a small oil lamp' for the special prayers.[7] According to several accounts, the floodwater began to recede after the Nizam made the offering to the river goddess.

The flood may have been an act of god, as believed by people in Hyderabad, or a combined effect of meteorological and hydrological factors, but the story of a Muslim ruler following the Hindu tradition of worshipping a holy river has remained ingrained in the collective memory of generations of Hyderabadis. It is an eloquent expression of syncretic culture—often called the Ganga–Jamuni tehzeeb— which is considered the soul of Hyderabad. The episode is cited as an example of goodwill between the Hindus and Muslims prevailing in Hyderabad over centuries, in general, and during the rule of Mahbub Pasha, in particular.

An emergency meeting of high officials was convened on 29 September by Faridoon Jung Bahadur, the Nizam's political secretary, at his palace in Saifabad. In attendance were Akbar Hydari, Maj. Mahir-ud-Dowla Bahadur, Fazil Mooraj, Aziz Mirza, Sohrabji Jamsehdji and Col. Shore who was deputed by O'Dwyer. Since the flood had caused damage to Afzal Gunj Hospital, medical relief was organised at Public Gardens for men and at Fateh Maidan Pavilion for women. Kitchen committees were formed to set up separate community kitchens for Mohammedans and Hindus, and given a budget of Rs 5,000 each.[8] The Military Secretary and City Kotwal were told to make arrangements for the removal of corpses from the debris and to shift the injured to hospitals. Col. Shore was tasked with arranging the distribution of 'quinine pills of five grains each' through the city police. A Ladies' Committee was constituted to provide relief to distressed pardanashin (veiled) women, with Ameena Hydari as secretary and Sarojini Naidu as joint secretary.[9]

Along with relief operations, the administration moved swiftly to plan the reconstruction of the flood-ravaged city and take long-term measures on scientific lines for protection from future floods. The Finance department decided to 'obtain the services of a competent engineer either in India or in England' for this purpose.[10] George Casson Walker, a British civil servant heading the Finance department, was proceeding to England on leave. Walker, along with his deputy Akbar Hydari, began scouting for an engineer suitable for the assignment. They chose Mokshgundam Visvesvaraya, superintending engineer of the Public Works Department (PWD) of the Bombay Presidency, who was then on a six-month tour of Europe and North America, preparatory to early retirement.

The request from the Hyderabad administration was sent to the governor of Bombay who cabled it to the India office, which in turn, reached out to Visvesvaraya in Milan. The cable reached him on 29 October 1908. The speed at which the Hyderabad and Bombay officials moved was remarkable, given the layers of bureaucracy and hierarchy involved. Visvesvaraya, however, was not in a hurry to accept the assignment as he wished to continue with the remaining five months of his tour. He used the interim period to negotiate the terms of engagement with the Hyderabad government, finally agreeing to join with effect from 15 April 1909, for a consulting fee equivalent to the salary of a commissioner of a revenue division.[11]

Visvesvaraya, a product of British India, appeared the best choice, acceptable to both the Nizam and the British. Still, the selection of an Indian engineer, and not a European, for a prestigious and lucrative assignment in the largest princely state of the country did not go unnoticed. Visvesvaraya's friends kept him abreast of reports in the Bombay press about the appointment. He was a familiar name in the engineering circles for having executed challenging projects in British India but was yet to gain the fame he would as the Diwan of Mysore State in the decade to follow. Hyderabad was his first major assignment outside British India and it presented an opportunity to implement new ideas in planning and urban development.

Blueprint of a Modern City

Soon after he arrived in Hyderabad on 15 April 1909, Visvesvaraya began collecting field data and information, spending 'several mornings inspecting the ruins along the banks of Musi'. Among the local officials assisting him were PWD secretary Fazil Mooraj, special relief commissioner Maj. E. St. Wake, municipal commissioner A.H. Stevens, assistant superintending engineer Ahmed Ali and assistant engineer A.C. McLeish.[12] He identified the primary cause for the flood to be the intense rainfall owing to a cyclonic storm in the Bay of Bengal. The rain gauge at Shamashabad recorded 12.8 inches of rainfall in 24 hours and 18.90 inches in 48 hours.[13]

The catchment area of Musi had a vast network of rainfed tanks that served the irrigation needs of farmers in the semi-arid areas and also stored excess water from the river and streams. The system had existed since the Deccan kingdom of Kakatiyas. The heavy rainfall had a cascading effect in Musi's upper catchment where as many as 788 irrigation tanks existed. 'Small tanks intercepted what they could at first but when water came too fast for them they gave way one after another and poured their accumulated water into the river,' Visvesvaraya's investigation found. In all, 221 tanks breached. Some of them were very large, like the Palmakul and Parti tanks. The two tanks had a combined storage of 390 million cubic feet but probably had 800 million cubic feet of water when they breached. 'The bursting of these two large tanks made a very serious addition to the river flow and proved to be the last straw on the back of the riparian camel,' Visvesvaraya noted in his report.[14]

Mahbub Pasha, who in deference to the sentiments of his subjects had publicly worshipped the river goddess a few months earlier as if the flood was an act of god, now had a scientific explanation for the deluge.

Visvesvaraya was given a comprehensive task. He was 'to prepare a complete scheme of drainage for the Hyderabad city and Chadarghat'; 'to plan the reconstruction of the riverfront and the adjoining areas damaged by the flood'; and suggest 'general improvements in the city in harmony with the riverfront'.[15] The terms of his engagement showed that Hyderabad was not just looking at measures to protect it from floods but was seeking to become a modern city through new ideas like riverfront development.

Since the discharge in Musi during the flood was about four times the river channel's capacity, Visvesvaraya suggested increasing the capacity of the channel, construction of embankments on both sides and clearing obstructions to flow of water in the riverbed. Floods could still occur if discharges were like those in September 1908. Therefore, the engineer proposed the construction of two storage reservoirs for storing the excess discharge—one on each branch of the river, at distances of 6.5 and 8.5 miles respectively above the city.[16] The reservoirs, he argued, could also serve the drinking water needs of Hyderabad and help improve irrigation.

Visvesvaraya cited the examples of the flood prevention measures proposed in the Passaic Valley near New York after River Passaic faced floods like those in River Musi. He quoted an article published in the *North American Review*, which said, 'Prevention of floods and irrigation are twin ideas. They should be developed together.'[17] Though Visvesvaraya had spent his entire engineering career in British India, he drew new ideas from America for his first major project in princely India.

The total cost for building flood protection reservoirs, drainage systems and development of the riverfront was pegged at Rs 153 lakh. This was not much since it was said that 'many of the cities smaller than Hyderabad, both in British India and the Native States, have gone in for far expensive drainage schemes'. Relatively smaller cities like Karachi and Benares too had opted for a modern sewerage system based on the 'water carriage principle'.[18] As reconstruction on such a large scale would 'involve sacrifices on the part of both the Government and the residents', Visvesvaraya suggested the constitution of 'a small but influential consultative committee' to deal with possible conflicts.

After submitting his report to Mahbub Pasha, Visvesvaraya went over to the neighbouring princely state of Mysore, to take over as its chief engineer. Subsequently, he was appointed the Diwan. In August 1911, his royal patron in Hyderabad, Mahbub Pasha, passed away at the young age of forty-five. On 1 September, the twenty-four-year-old Mir Osman Ali Khan was crowned the seventh Nizam of Hyderabad.

The first major project that the new Nizam sanctioned was the building of a reservoir on River Musi as suggested by Visvesvaraya. On 23 March 1913, the Nizam laid the foundation stone for the first reservoir at Gundipett. It was hailed as 'the biggest thing ever done in Hyderabad'. A.T. Mackenzie, the superintending engineer of PWD, pointed out during the foundation-laying ceremony, 'In no part of the world would it be a small matter to dam up a river draining nearly 300 square miles of country and subject to violent floods, with a wall 125 feet high, to transform it into a placid lake three or four times the area of the Husain Sagar, and capable of containing ten times the quantity of water, to construct a covered conduit 12 miles long, and a pipe system for one million people.'[19] The new reservoir was named Osman Sagar.

While Osman Sagar was Hyderabad's first such project, the region had seen bigger irrigation projects in the mid-nineteenth century. British engineer Arthur Thomas Cotton executed a massive barrage on Godavari and developed a canal network in the northern districts of Madras Presidency, adjoining the Hyderabad State. The project converted the region suffering from the cycle of famines and floods into a grain bowl. It helped irrigate nearly a million acres of land where rice and sugarcane were cultivated, resulting in the prosperity of the coastal districts. Kammas, the largest landowning and cultivating caste group in the region, benefited the most. That is why Arthur Thomas Cotton is revered as a demi-god in this region till today.

The first development project of twentieth-century Hyderabad began with a bang, literally. After the ceremonial stone was lowered into the ground, '101 dynamite blasts were fired by electricity on the rocky side of the gorge beyond and great pieces of granite were blown into the air and fell in showers of stone and dust.'[20] The reservoir, with the twin objectives of preventing floods and supplying drinking water to Hyderabad and Secunderabad, was completed in 1918 at a cost of Rs 54.5 lakh. Osman Sagar became a favourite picnic spot for Hyderabadis through most of the twentieth century.

The work on the reservoir on Esi got delayed due to a controversy about its need. Ahmed Ali, the chief engineer of PWD who had assisted Visvesvaraya, contended that the 'calculations were exaggerated and flood propensities of the river had been overestimated.'[21] The matter was referred to Michael Northersole, former inspector general of Irrigation in Bombay State. He opined that Hyderabad would not be entirely immune from the dangers of flood 'considering that Esi had a bigger catchment area and a larger number of tanks within its basin'. The large masonry dam and reservoir on Esi, work on which began in 1919, was inaugurated in July 1927. It was named Himayat Sagar after Osman Ali's son and the future prince of Berar, Mir Himayat Ali Khan Azam Jah.

Though Hyderabad was the fourth largest city in India and 'the first in native states', it lacked a proper system of waste disposal and drainage. The sewerage from larger drains and masonry side gutters found its way into Musi, while used water seeped into the ground 'poisoning the wells' and 'polluting the air with its noxious exhalations'.[22] Manual scavengers were licensed to collect human excreta. The municipality charged Rs 2 per month for 'the privilege of depositing nightsoil in the municipal filth carts'. The waste was mixed with earth, loaded into buffalo carts, taken to fields and utilised in agriculture.[23] Settlements around the river banks used pit toilets, which would often overflow.

As the city was built on undulating ground with rapid slopes towards the river and most of the populated areas on both sides of the river were on slopes, Visvesvaraya proposed an underground drainage scheme based on the gravitational principle. The plan was to ensure that sewerage flowed smoothly in open drains and to prevent its mixing with stormwater, through a 142.5 mile-long sewer system. The system was designed such that it would serve the needs of the existing population (4,23,579) and be able to accomodate 30 per cent increase in the future.[24] PWD's Ahmed Ali (assistant superintending engineer), M.V. Lele (assistant engineer) and P. Bhoj Raj (sub-engineer) assisted Visvesvaraya in preparing this plan.

It took almost fifteen years for both the reservoirs to be functional, while the drainage system took even longer due to differences of opinion over cost and technical details. The original scheme for the construction of an underground drainage system costing Rs 52 lakh was designed to prevent rainwater from entering sewers and excluded certain parts of the city that had no water supply. In 1921, A.W. Stonebridge, a sanitary engineer of Hyderabad, submitted a new proposal costing Rs 163 lakh for the disposal of sewage and rainwater. Since the cost difference was too much, Visvesvaraya was consulted. He slashed the cost down to Rs 100 lakh by reducing the size of sewers and suggested that separate stormwater drains be constructed by the City Improvement Board (CIB).[25] A major challenge was the 'construction of the inverted siphon across the Musi river which connects the intercepting sewer on the right bank of the river with the outfall sewer which runs along the left bank to the septic tanks.' The work was also hampered in 1928 due to the plague 'scattering the labour hands that had been mustered.'[26]

Getting Rid of Nurseries of Plague and Pestilence

The work on building the dams and the underground drainage was just the beginning of the modernisation project. More work was needed to rebuild the city, not just to protect it from floods in the future but also from epidemics. The unhealthy sanitation and waste disposal practices in the city often resulted in outbreaks of cholera, malaria, plague and other diseases. Within a couple of years of the flood, an outbreak of plague followed.

The primary reasons for the Qutub Shahi kings deciding to shift their capital from Golconda to Hyderabad at the end of the sixteenth century were congestion, unsanitary conditions and the frequent outbreak of epidemics. The layout of the new city was carefully planned with the Charminar at its centre and four trunk roads leading out in four directions. Each quarter was laid out with tree-lined streets, open spaces and gardens. However, the growth of the city in the later centuries did not conform to any plan. Irregular streets and lanes were built and housing clusters grew haphazardly. All this left the city administrators with the same problems of insanitation and diseases that Golconda had faced three centuries earlier.

When Visvesvaraya visited the city in 1909, he found the conditions pathetic. 'A stranger visiting the city for the first time and insufficiently acquainted with the habits of the people might suspect that mosquito breeding was one of the industries of the city,' he observed.[27] An official report described the condition of Hyderabad in 1914 as: 'The city is undeveloped in point of sanitary dwellings for the poor, whose huts and hovels are made up of mud walls, tile roofs and mud floors. The narrow lanes and dark alleys reeking of filth complete the drab scene. Here are nurseries for plague and pestilence.'[28]

A lack of hygiene and sanitation could result in plague, which was a major killer. The city of Hyderabad witnessed an outbreak of the epidemic in August 1911, which subsided only in April 1912. Officials recorded 18,478 cases and 16,901 deaths in a population estimated at 3,87,000. For seven weeks, at the height of the epidemic, there were a thousand deaths per week. Some thirty health camps were established and a special drive was launched to kill rats. Non-venomous Dhaman snakes were deployed to kill rats and bandicoots.

Following the epidemic, Lt Col. H.E. Drake Brockman, the first whole-time director of the Medical department, recommended organising a separate Public Health department and Central Sanitary Board with sanitary officers and inspectors at the village level.[29] The only measures available for protection against plague were inoculating the feet and legs of people to protect them from fleas, unroofing huts so that they got exposed to the rays of the sun, evacuating people from infected houses and localities, and disinfection.

To find a more durable solution, Hyderabad scientists conducted experiments of a pioneering nature. Dr Shrinagesh Mallannah, who had graduated from the Hyderabad Medical School and accompanied Lawrie in 1895 to England on a lecture tour, was the chief bacteriologist to the government at that time. He had been working on plague since 1900 and conducted studies at the Hygienic Institute, Hamburg, in Germany, during 1905-06. These studies involved infecting animals (rats and rabbits) with the plague bacillus, extracting glands of immunised animals and preparing from them a solution that could be used to treat plague infection. Based on the clinical observation that 'recovery was faster in cases where the glandular reaction was the most marked', Mallannah hypothesised that 'organs in which the plague poison exercises its concentrated effect may probably be the centres where the antibodies are manufactured in great quantity in case of recovery.'[30]

Mallannah had an illustrious medical career. The government sponsored him to pursue Maintenance of Certificate (MoC) in psychology in England. A few years later, he obtained more degrees: a Diploma in Public Health from the University of Cambridge and Doctor of Medicine from the University of Edinburgh. Back in Hyderabad, he joined the medical school as a lecturer in pathology and physiology and was the superintendent of the pathology laboratory. His son, Satyawant, studied at the University of Cambridge and then went to Royal Military College at Sandhurst before joining the Indian Army in 1923. After a remarkable career under the British and in free India, Gen. Satyawant Mallannah Shrinagesh was appointed the Chief of Army Staff in 1955. After he retired from the Army, the government made him the first principal of the Administrative Staff College of India in Hyderabad.

In an interesting study, Mallannah used tobacco leaves to control fleas that spread the plague. He believed that the destruction of fleas was critical to ending plague epidemics since 'it is only through the agency of fleas that the diseases are communicated from rat to rat, from rat to man, from man to man and from the man back to the rat'.[31] The prevailing control strategies focused on disinfection, killing rats and evacuating people from affected localities. Instead, Mallannah suggested, fleas should be targeted using tobacco leaves. He found that tobacco could kill fleas instantaneously and suggested disinfecting plague-infected houses with tobacco leaves as a preventive measure.[32]

Mallannah designed an elaborate field experiment that involved 'tobaccoing' a set of fifty-two houses in highly infected areas (Mogalpura, Kamel Khadeem, Philkhana, Imlibund, Fateh Darwaza, Yacootpura, Hussaini Alam). Another set of fifty-two houses in nearby areas was used as a 'control'. Tobacco leaves were stitched on cloth and spread in rooms and rat holes were plugged with tobacco paste. At the end of the experiment, the number of plague cases in houses treated with tobacco were found to be zero.

In a second experiment in the Second Lancers area in Golconda, Mallannah introduced guinea pigs in newly infected houses, the occupants of which had been shifted out. After a few days, the pigs died due to the plague. The same houses were then tobaccoed and guinea pigs were re-introduced. Pigs did not die this time.

Together, the two experiments made Mallannah conclude that
tobacco leaves were efficacious in killing fleas that spread the plague.
He argued that it was a cost-effective solution compared with
evacuation and disinfection practised in Hyderabad and Bombay.[33]

While scientists tried different public health measures,
Visvesvaraya's plan proposed improvement in overall sanitary
conditions in the city to prevent the outbreak of diseases. To
translate this vision into action, a new institution, theHyderabad
City Improvement Board (CIB), was created in 1912.[34] The Board
was tasked with developing the sanitation system and building
healthy dwellings. It decided to prioritise clearing of slums and
housing the displaced people 'in model colonies to safeguard
their health and indirectly the health of the whole population of
Hyderabad'.[35] It planned playgrounds for the poor children and
parks to act as the lungs of the city. The first slum clearance scheme
was rolled out in Nampally, which 'had been a centre of plague,
cholera and other epidemics'. Old houses were pulled down and new
rat-proof sanitary dwellings were built for different classes. The area
eventually became free of plague, prompting the Nizam to issue an
order making Nampally a model for slum clearance in other parts of
the city.

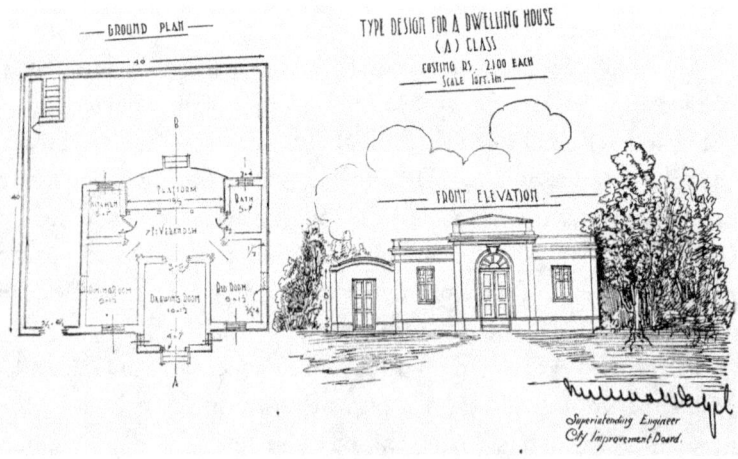

*The plan of a model house developed by the City Improvement Board,
1930 (courtesy: Telangana State Archives and Research Centre)*

New housing complexes were developed with four types of houses (A, B, C and D) for different economic classes. The houses were equipped with flush latrines and bathrooms, and had courtyards. The occupants had to pay a small rent to the government. Later, loans were extended for 'hire purchase'. Model houses were built in Mallapally, Aghapura, Khairatabad, Bhoiguda, Azampura, Malakpet, Moghalpura, Bazar-e-Noorum Oomra, Sultanshahi, Amberpet, Dabirpura, Red Hills and Yadgar Husain Kunta.

Rat-proof godowns were built in the city's grain markets, while separate markets were constructed for selling fish, meat, vegetables and fruits. Pathergatti and Moazzamjahi shopping arcades were designed on the lines of 'Universal Stores' found in Europe and America where people could buy everything they needed in one place. The 'sanitary' houses 'saved the cost and trouble of evacuation during epidemics (and) the sufferings due to the dislocation of business and the misery caused by the loss of life' for their occupants.[36]

The overall progress, however, was slow. In twenty-five years, the Hyderabad CIB could construct just 2,500 model houses in eleven localities, accommodating 10,000 people at a total cost of Rs 30 lakh.[37] The focus on improving water supply, drainage and sewerage systems, and building sanitary dwellings for the poor was meant to make Hyderabad healthy and hygienic, but the health gains of these projects remained uncertain even after two decades. This was due to the delay in executing the drainage scheme, particularly connections from main line to individual houses. 'The introduction of copious water supply within the past 10–15 years, without simultaneously making provisions for drainage, has resulted in increased unhealthiness,' Visvesvaraya pointed out in 1930.[38] Manual removal of human excreta was still in practice in many areas, while progress was slow in making the grain markets rat-proof.

Another review by Visvesvaraya in 1932 pointed to significant gaps in the drainage system. 'Out of 40,000 houses to be connected, only 100 have had water closets installed till now,' he reported.[39] This was despite the municipality making a connection with sewer compulsory for houses with a rental value of Rs 30 or more. To educate people, the Hyderabad CIB opened a 'Drainage Show Room' at the Osmania General Hospital to showcase sanitary appliances and fittings, with exhibits on how to use them.

The problem appeared to be much deeper than just a lack of education among people. There were six agencies or government departments engaged in executing works or administering public utilities. They functioned under three different members of the Executive Council and three secretaries with 'no clear policies or understanding and coordination of their activities'.[40] The municipality had 'no statutory position and no power of execute' and bore 'no resemblance to institutions that go by this name in British India'. New members of the body were elected by older members, and it had, the report noted, 'a President who never presides and a Municipal Commissioner who is only responsible to the Government'.[41]

Visvesvaraya suggested enactment of a Municipal Act to make the Hyderabad municipality a 'real local self-governing authority on the lines of large municipalities in British India' as well as restructuring of CIB to make it a representative body with engineering and sanitary experts as members. He advocated for an engineer to be its president or vice president, and enlist the services of town planners from London, Berlin or Boston.[42] Without governance reforms, he warned, the money being spent would not yield 'dividends in the shape of better health or improved living conditions'. He was hinting at the democratisation of governance—an issue that Nizam's government was grappling with on the political front.

Steps Towards Modernity

The 1908 flood is considered a turning point in the journey of Hyderabad. It attempted to change it from being a late-medieval city to becoming a modern metropolis. The flood was a natural and ecological disaster but it triggered a project of modernisation of the city. In the late nineteenth century, Hyderabad witnessed technological development in the form of the railways, telegraph system and so on, typical symbols of colonial modernity. The railways propelled the city's expansion to the areas north of the river, and away from the walled city. The flood marked the beginning of the next stage—'modern and metropolitan'—during which the city expanded further on the other side of the river.[43]

In the years preceding the flood, the Chaderghat and Residency areas witnessed changes as a larger number of British officers were posted in the Hyderabad administration. The nobility also moved northwards. The flood further accentuated this shift, with Osman Ali Khan making the King Kothi—not far from the Residency—his primary residence. Senior officials followed suit. The power centre of the city thus shifted away from the walled city, which later came to be called the 'Old City'. Many new official buildings and business centres were developed in the newer parts of the city.

These changes, however, were not a part of any structured urban development plan. There was no organised effort to develop the road infrastructure or drainage system. Urban historians have argued that the Asaf Jahi capital, till the beginning of the twentieth century, developed primarily around buildings—ornamental devadis, Palladian hilltop palaces, elaborately carved personal tombs—that symbolised the power of the elite.[44] In contrast, the medieval Hyderabad as built and developed earlier during the Qutub Shahi period was a planned city.

Therefore, the idea of rebuilding the city in modern ways after the floods was a departure from the immediate past. The reconstruction that followed the floods—dams, flood-protection river walls, drainage and sewerage systems, new housing colonies, business marts and so on—brought contemporary ideas and concepts of urban planning and renewal. Land acquisition for the construction of new buildings, slum clearance, payment of compensation and development of public spaces like parks and playgrounds were all new for Hyderabad. It ruffled the high and mighty. The Residency had to retract its boundary from the river bank to make way for a new road along the banks. On the other side, parts of the Salar Jung estate were acquired for a similar road.

The second major driver for the redevelopment of Hyderabad after the flood was the need for plague control and protection from other communicable diseases resulting from unsanitary conditions and rat-infested houses. The justification for huge investments in underground drainage systems, new markets, gardens and housing projects was to ensure healthy living and working spaces for people. It was a great public health measure, along with the opening of new medical facilities and health centres.

The third factor that pushed Hyderabad towards modernity at the beginning of the twentieth century was the growing British influence in the state's administration. All top posts in key departments like finance, revenue, education, general administration, commerce and industries, and public works were occupied by British service officers. They not only streamlined the administration but also introduced new ideas. Though Hyderabad was not directly under British rule, its rulers, being 'faithful allies', were open to British influence. They also encouraged the import of non-British talent from the rest of India.

Most importantly, the floods and disease outbreaks coincided with a change in the regime. Mahbub Pasha was succeeded by his son Osman Ali Khan, who wanted to assert his own authority by distancing himself from traditional nobility. He did away with the age-old system of the Diwan being the head of the administration and took over its direct control. Later, he passed on the powers to an Executive Council. In his initial years in power, Osman Ali Khan wished to be recognised as a modern ruler. In his speech at the foundation-laying ceremony of the first reservoir on Musi in 1913, Osman Ali Khan said, 'Last Sunday I saw in the papers that His Imperial Majesty the King-Emperor personally laid the foundation stone of a reservoir in his capital, London. For this reason, I am very glad that I have also the opportunity of performing a similar function here in Hyderabad.'[45]

By invoking the King Emperor and drawing parallels with the construction of a new reservoir in London, the young Nizam was seeking to place Hyderabad on par with contemporary developments in Britain. And by accepting the naming of the new project as Osman Sagar (and not making it a memorial for Mahbub Pasha who had commissioned Visvesvaraya to prepare a blueprint), Osman Ali Khan took a decisive step to position himself as the architect of a modern Hyderabad. All major development projects subsequently bore his name.

4

New Skyline on the Riverfront

∽

A new quarter would be brought into existence with magnificent roads and stately buildings, striking vistas and agreeable views which must prove a permanent source of pride and pleasure to the teeming population of this city ... the boulevards (along the riverfront) will be the lungs of the city benefiting all classes of people.

–M. Visvesvaraya,
on his vision of the Musi riverfront, 1909[1]

THE SITUATION IN WHICH ONE-FOURTH OF THE DWELLINGS in the city were destroyed due to the 1908 flood presented an opportunity—rebuilding a part of the city in new ways. Along with the construction of a river wall for flood protection, Visvesvaraya envisaged a riverfront with 'boulevards or broad avenues with suitable sidewalks and trees', with new buildings, gardens and public places alongside. Two river roads were conceived to serve as 'promenades and pleasure resorts' for the people residing on the adjoining narrow and crowded streets. The boulevards would be 'the lungs of the city' benefiting all classes of people. They were planned to be broad enough to accommodate electric tramways which would come 'sooner or later' for communication between the city and the suburbs, according to the blueprint.[2] At that time, tramways had already been introduced in four large cities in British India, and even in smaller ones like Baroda.

To give a new look to the riverfront, Visvesvaraya proposed that the front views of buildings to be constructed on these roads 'should be substantial edifices calculated to give distinction to the riverfront'. And 'no mud hovels or mean looking buildings should be permitted here if the new locality is to be rendered healthy and picturesque'.[3] To ensure this, he suggested that 'only substantial houses costing not less than, say rupees 10,000 each should be allowed along the boulevards'. Visvesvaraya felt that the government's plan of locating certain large public offices along the south bank of the river was 'a good beginning'. He also argued that if wide boulevards were proposed along the river banks, other parts of the city too should be improved and brought into harmony with them.[4]

To translate this vision into reality, a new implementation agency—the City Improvement Board (CIB)—was created as no existing government body could handle the task. The idea of CIB was based on Western notions of modernising urban spaces. Till then, all construction activities were undertaken by the Public Works Department (PWD) and the concept of urban planning was new to Hyderabad. Visvesvaraya believed that 'each city and large town in India should have a separate improvement board (in addition to) the municipal council to prepare schemes for expanding the areas under its jurisdiction and for the construction of houses on good models'.[5] City planning was to ensure the development of 'parks, playgrounds, theatres, museums, art galleries and other means of public recreation and instruction' with readily accessible railway and tramway facilities, boulevards and other means of transit and communication. In addition, Visvesvaraya emphasised planned dwellings for different classes of citizens, with sanitation and drainage facilities.[6] The vision matched the ambitions of the young ruler of Hyderabad who wished to create a distinct identity for himself.

Along with slum clearance and the construction of modern housing facilities, CIB undertook the construction of a river wall from the Afzal Gunj Bridge to the Musallam Jung Bridge and the other stretch from the Afzal Gunj Bridge to the Oliphant Bridge. On the north bank, a park of about 16 acres was developed, while on the south bank a 40-feet wide road was constructed. The upper portion of the stone wall resembled a fort boundary. Along the road were constructed gazebos with rounded domes and stone benches for people to sit and relax facing the river. Wide footpaths were constructed along the wall on both banks. Overall, it gave the effect of a majestic river boulevard with a green riverbed and rocks jutting out here and there.

A series of magnificent structures built as a part of the riverfront, constructed between 1914 and 1930, gave Hyderabad a new skyline. These included the High Court of Hyderabad, City High School for Boys (which later became the City College), Osmania General Hospital, Osmania Park and Asafia State Library. A new building for the Hyderabad Railway Station at Errannagunta (Kacheguda) was built in 1914.

The remnants of the boulevard along the River Musi, 2024
(photograph: author)

The 1908 flood damaged many old buildings that housed government offices, courts, hospitals and schools. Several of these institutions had to function from multiple locations and in rented premises. The High Court of Hyderabad was one such institution. When Mahbub Pasha introduced legislative reforms by setting up the Legislative Council in 1892, he made the chief justice of the High Court one its members. He desired a separate building to house the High Court and wanted it to be located not far from Charminar and Chowmahalla Palace. When Osman Ali Khan became the Nizam, he ordered a place to be found on the riverfront for the construction of the High Court, as desired by his late father.

The riverfront became the site for new and old institutions that were not just grand architecturally but represented a change in administration. The new building of the High Court signified the culmination of judicial reforms initiated in the mid-nineteenth century. In 1855, Salar Jung I had established the Adalat-e-Badshahi, which functioned under his supervision and had a chief justice and four other judges. In 1861, he separated civil and criminal jurisdiction and fixed regular salaries for judges instead of land grants which they used to receive for their services.[7] The High Court of Hyderabad worked under a charter granted by the Nizam based on statutes under which High Courts functioned in British India. Subsequently, the functioning of the judiciary was separated from the executive.

As the area on the river banks was devastated by the floods, chief engineer Mackenzie was asked to find a site that was both suitable and safe. He identified a site on the southern bank, next to the place where the City High School building was under construction. The site had some private residences and temples which needed to be acquired and razed. A large temple situated next to the City High School was spared as the Marwari community managing it appealed for its protection.[8] The Diwan, Maharaja Kishen Pershad, constituted a committee for the supervision of the construction work, and a budget of Rs 10 lakh was approved. In 1916, the budget was revised to Rs 17.42 lakh and finally to Rs 21 lakh.

Speaking at the inauguration of the High Court building on 20 April 1920, the Nizam described it as 'a veritable palace of justice'.[9]

He said, 'Even as the Court will be so superbly located, it will, in the discharge of its duties, build up its traditions on the impregnable rock of justice, equity and good conscience. It is my earnest desire that the administration of justice in my Dominions may be so carried out that the rich and the poor alike may have an abiding faith in its righteousness.'

In the judicial system of the Nizam's government, the final power of reviewing a court order rested with the Nizam. Such petitions had to be made to the Nizam, who then referred them to the Judicial Committee of His Exalted Highness the Nizam. In September 1948, when Hyderabad was integrated with India, hundreds of such appeals were pending with the committee. As the High Court of Hyderabad became a part of the judiciary of India, these pending appeals were transferred to the Supreme Court of India. This posed a problem as court papers in Hyderabad were in Urdu and it would have taken a lot of time and resources to get them translated into English. The Chief Justice of India, Justice H.J. Kania constituted a bench of judges conversant with Urdu and created an ad hoc bench of the Supreme Court of India in the High Court of Hyderabad. The bench consisted of Supreme Court judge Mehar Chand Mahajan, chief justice of Hyderabad High Court C.R.S Naik and the senior most judge of High Court Khalil-uz-Zama Siddiqui. About 500 appeals were disposed in six months.

The Nizam, who was once head of the judiciary in Hyderabad and whose firmans carried the force of law, had to seek justice from the same High Court that he had inaugurated in 1920. This happened in the case relating to the suspension of payment of the Privy Purse of Rs 50 lakh to the Nizam based on a petition filed by someone claiming to be a relative of Asaf Jah III. Ironically, the case came up in the court of chief justice of the Andhra Pradesh High Court, Pingle Jaganmohan Reddy who was appointed a judge of the Hyderabad High Court by Osman Ali Khan in February 1948.

Reddy insisted on a personal undertaking from the Nizam that he would repay the amount if he lost the case. The lawyers agreed but Reddy wanted the undertaking to be signed by the Nizam. In the afternoon, the paper signed by Mir Osman Ali Khan was presented in the court. 'Time had completed a full circle. Here in this court, I took a seat as a judge under the royal edict, firman, issued by the Nizam and now here I was sitting as Chief Justice dealing with a petition filed by the same Nizam and receiving an undertaking signed by him,' Reddy recalled in his autobiography.[10]

Just as the building of the High Court began a new chapter in the judicial history of Hyderabad, the grand building of the City High School was a step towards reforming an archaic educational system. Until that point, physical infrastructure in most state-run schools was rudimentary and they were running in buildings either gifted by nobles or in their former palaces. The newly founded Osmania University too functioned from private buildings in the Gun Foundry initially.

A dedicated, grand building for a state-run school was a new idea in Hyderabad which was trying to catch up with other states in the field of education. Other leading princely states already had royal schools—Raja's Free School (Mysore, established in 1833), Mayo College (Ajmer, 1875) and Scindia School (Gwalior, 1887). Some of them were meant for children of nobles and others for commoners. All of them were housed in magnificent buildings. In Hyderabad, the work on planning and construction of the City High School began in 1917 and was completed by 1920. The Jagirdar's College, meant for sons of jagirdars, was established in 1923. It exists as the present-day Hyderabad Public School.

Yet another landmark institution constructed on the riverfront, across the river on the northern bank, was the Osmania General Hospital (OGH). Though built in the early twentieth century as part of riverfront development, it stands today as a great symbol of state-funded medical education, clinical research and public health in the mid-nineteenth century.

OGH succeeded the Afzal Gunj Hospital which was closely connected with the two landmark events in global medical history discussed in the Chapter 1. The flood had badly damaged the hospital and its working deteriorated since then, as reflected in this description by a visiting observer: 'The drains seem to overflow with disinfectants, dressings were being carried away, and a foul smell met me at every turn of the overcrowded wards, and the whole place depressed me past words. . . . The underpaid and overworked nurses, the dirty blankets, the herding of children with grown-up people—well it all cried loudly for Florence Nightingale.'[11]

In 1915, it was proposed to build a bigger and more modern general hospital. A site at Gosha Mahal Kunta was identified for it, but in a firman dated 8 September 1917, the Nizam desired that the hospital should be constructed on the riverbank and named after him. A site was selected close to the northern bank but it had about 300 'huts, kutcha tiled roof buildings with winding lanes' which were constructed after the flood.[12] The land, therefore, had to be acquired at a considerable cost and Rs 5.25 lakh paid as compensation. Two temples and a graveyard in the area were left untouched and provided with 'independent entrances leading to public roads'.

The building plan submitted in June 1918 involved the construction of the main building, quarters for nurses and doctors, fittings and furniture and so on, at a total cost of Rs 18.5 lakh. The building committee, consisting of Akbar Hydari, Syed Mehdi Hasan Bilgrami, F.E. Gwyther, A. Lancaster, M. Karamatullah and Mehr Ali Fazil, approved the blueprint with minor changes on 24 April 1918. Three tenders were received for the construction— from S. Pahlow & Co., Baboo Khan and Sons and Narotham Dass. The lowest quote of 0.2 per cent below the estimated rates came from Dass who had just completed the High Court building.[13] Dass signed the 'agreement bond' on 24 June 1920.

The United Trading Corporation, whose managing partner was G.K. Nambiar, was contracted to supply and install the X-ray unit and other equipment. The Government Mint supplied furniture but a later inspection found that its finish was very rough and 'not well suited for hospital use'. The Mint was later involved in a controversy over the supply of electric fans. It teamed up with an English firm, Wardle Engineering Company, but its tender was rejected in favour of K.R. Chari and Company who represented a German firm. The

Mint officials lobbied through the Finance department and got the orders placed with Chari quashed.

'Whatever may be the objection, personal or racial predilections of individual officers of the Government, we are sure that the policy of Your Exalted Highness Government is not to condemn the German products although they fulfil all the requirements of efficiency coupled with cheapness,' Rajagopala Chari petitioned to the Nizam in March 1926.[14] He pointed out that even the English Government was allowing German goods to be imported into India.

The budget of the hospital project was eventually increased to Rs 21.22 lakh. Lt Col. B. Jeewan Singh, who succeeded Lancaster as the director of the Medical department, suggested the addition of a separate building for the out-patients dispensary. To do so within the sanctioned amount, Singh suggested 'reducing the height of domes on the main block and curtailing ornamental mouldings'.[15] Among the facilities the hospital had was 'an electric lift' which could carry a stretcher. The hospital had eighteen wards for non-paying patients, each containing twenty-four beds, making a total of 432 beds. There were thirty-six beds spread over twenty rooms for 'paying' patients. In 1926, the revenue from paying wards was Rs 22 per day.

The hospital complex was spread over an area of 12.25 acres on the north bank of Musi and faced the river gardens developed by CIB. The park, covering an area of 16 acres, was an elegant public space that afforded a beautiful view of the High Court and the City High School buildings across the river. 'The proximity of an extensive public garden is a decided advantage to the hospital as it presents a bright outlook to the patients from the hospital and a refreshing walk to the invalids,' noted the planners.

The hospital boosted the primacy of Western medicine in Hyderabad and also became an icon of progress and modernity. Hyderabad's Western medical institutions attracted publicity and visits from high-profile dignitaries in British India. For instance, the foundation of the Victoria Zenana Hospital in the city was laid by the Princess of Wales. The hospital edifice is crumbling in the present time and was facing the threat of demolition in 2023.

The Imprint of Vincent Esch

Three major iconic buildings on the riverfront—City College, High Court and Osmania General Hospital—were designed by the British architect Vincent Jerome Esch. In addition, he designed the Hyderabad Railway Station (Kacheguda) and the Jagirdar's College at Begumpet.

When he arrived in Hyderabad, Esch was already a leading architect in British India and was assisting William Emerson, the chief architect of Victoria Memorial Hall in Calcutta. The style popular in those days of combining Western architecture with Indian motifs or elements was known as the Indo-Saracenic style. Esch deployed Deccani motifs extensively in the buildings and chose to describe the style as 'Moghul-Saracenic' in his writings. While the design elements were drawn from grand buildings like the Golconda Fort and the Mecca Masjid, Esch pioneered the use of new construction techniques and materials like steel and concrete in all the buildings he designed.

The hospital building reflected Indian architectural heritage and combined elements from different styles. The main building was three-storeyed with coloured rubble stone masonry covered with plaster. The completion report of the building stated, 'To bring out the effect of shallow setback and offsets, slate-coloured plaster has been applied except in panels and decorations which are picked out in white. The skyline is broken by 17 domes of various sizes. Of these, eight are at the eight ends of the front and the rear blocks, two over the two intermediate features and seven in the central feature.'[16]

The main dome had a diameter of 25 feet at the base and 27 feet at the bulged portion. For lighting the dome, eight circular glass discs, 4 feet in diameter, were provided and 'a pattern of five pointed stars with coloured glass' was fitted in the discs. The octagon below the dome had 15-feet-high arched openings in each bay, filled in with glazed windows. The openings in the square below the dome were filled with lime mortar jaali (trellis) work. The flooring was of polished stone, except in the operation theatres and the central hall where marble was laid. The doors and windows were of Rangoon teak panelled and glazed with ground glass. To offset the length of the building, there was a vertical emphasis on the detailing. Domes, chajjas and merlons gave it a distinctly Indian look while massing and internal plans followed Western norms.

The High Court building was made from granite stone and cusped domes. While the verandahs were an Indian element, the overall form and internal organisation of the building followed Western methods.[17] The building interior had a grand staircase, ornamented with arched jaalis and stained glass.

The City High School was constructed mostly using granite, but the stone was not lavishly dressed as it was in the High Court. Its base was 'cyclopean rustication' and the upper storeys were plastered. The building had an arched plinth of 11 feet height of roughly dressed granite. The two floors above were built of stone and faced in shell plaster. The jaalis and brackets were made using marble but, again, less ornamental than the High Court. Separate entrances were planned for senior boys and junior boys, and both sides had tiffin rooms and other facilities for students. There was a huge central hall at the main level, with a gallery on three sides on the second floor meant for use by junior students.[18] Esch described the style he deployed in this building as 'perpendicular Mogul Saracenic' with Gothic influence.

Though Esch executed three major projects on the riverfront, his services were terminated in December 1921 following differences with the PWD of Hyderabad and a dispute over payment of dues. Esch was not invited to the opening ceremony of the High Court where Viceroy Lord Chelmsford was present though he was 'more than satisfied to learn that H.E. the Viceroy was entirely cognizant of the fact that we designed the High Courts.'[19]

Esch's firm blamed some PWD officials for an adverse opinion of his work and pointed out that 'our professional abilities and practice is too well known and appreciated and widespread to be affected by the loss of future work in Hyderabad'. At the same time,

Henry Marshall, superintending architect of the Queen Victoria Memorial, wrote to the Nizam on behalf of Esch that 'we will be prepared to tender our professional services if called upon to do so' because the Nizam's state had proved itself 'worthy of our admiration in the manner in which it has helped the British national cause in the late war'.[20]

Though Esch exited Hyderabad under acrimony, his architectural style left an imprint on buildings designed by architects of CIB and PWD, with minor differences. The Asafia Library (which later became the State Central Library), Jubilee Pavilion and Unani Hospital were among such buildings. The style was subsequently referred by Hyderabadi scholars as 'CIB architecture' and 'Osmanshahi style'.

The Asafia Library (State Central Library), the last major building constructed on the riverfront in 1936 (photograph: author)

The Kutub-Khana Asafia building was the last major structure to be constructed on the riverfront. The Asafia Library was established in 1891 through the efforts of Syed Hussain Bilgrami, who was

the director of public instruction and had also been a tutor to two
Nizams (Mahbub Pasha and Osman Ali Khan). He would procure
rare books in Arabic that were in danger of extinction and republish
them. He established the library with 'a view to collect and retain in
the country most of the manuscript books about the Islamic Culture
and the Hindu Period that were passing out of the Dominions for
trifling sums'.[21] The library purchased such manuscripts and books
from private collections. It operated from a small building in the
Gun Foundry area until it was shifted to the riverfront. At the end
of 1940, in its oriental and occidental sections, it had over 52,000
books including 11,000 manuscripts.

Riverfront: Ornamental or Useful?

At the opening of the High Court building, the first major structure
on the riverfront, Nizam Mir Osman Ali Khan described it as a
'great architectural beauty' and 'an ornament of my capital' in
which 'the very best engineering talent has been requisitioned to
give it a solid foundation and structural elegance'. The High Court
building, and other magnificent structures on the riverfront, were
ornamental in terms of their grandeur and were designed to give a
new identity to the capital city of India's largest princely state.

Architecturally grand structures were the norm in all major
princely states that sought to emulate the Presidency cities of
Bombay, Calcutta and Madras in their efforts to embrace modernity.
Rulers of the princely states used the size and style of these
structures to make a statement and represent their powers. So even
buildings to house schools, colleges, hospitals and administrative
offices, all had to give the look and feel of monuments. At times,
little attention was paid to the functional aspects of these grand
buildings.

The princely states hired leading British, European and American
architects to design the new monuments. The presence of Vincent
Esch in Hyderabad in the early twentieth century was a part of this
trend. The architects and designers found work in princely states due

to Diwans or high officials having connections with or experience in British India. Some princes themselves had knowledge of the new trends in architecture and town planning.

The degree to which ornamental buildings proved to be functional were reflective of deeper reforms which varied from state to state. For instance, Baroda built attractive buildings for educational institutions in the late nineteenth century (State Library, Anglo Vernacular Boys School, Baroda College, female training school/ girls school, zenana school, etc.) as a part of well-planned efforts to spread education to all. Baroda had an active library movement. While the Nizams discouraged any library movement, a large state library building was constructed in Hyderabad, mainly to house oriental books and manuscripts.

While the grand Osmania General Hospital was constructed, the older Hyderabad Medical School (later Osmania Medical College) did not get a permanent building for a long time. The same was the case with the Unani Medical School. It was only after OGH was built that a general hospital for the Unani system was constructed. The Unani Medical School, established in 1891, was upgraded to the Unani Medical College, offering a five-year degree, and a grand building was constructed in 1930 near the Charminar to house it. Similarly, Ayurveda, which was practised since the Qutubshahi period, received state patronage only decades after OGH came into being. A privately run Ayurvedic school started offering a four-year diploma course in 1935. The Nizam's government took it over in 1941 and established a separate Department of Ayurveda as well as Majalis-e-Mashvarat-Ayurveda (Board of Ayurveda).[22]

The riverfront would have had many more institutions, if the original plans had not got hampered due to various factors. After the sites for construction of the City School and the High Court were identified, the Nizam wanted the new university, which was to bear his name, also to be on the riverfront. But the large area needed for a residential university could be found only outside the city. Another plan was to construct the Central Secretariat on the river banks for the use of the Executive Council and the Secretariats of the Central Government.

The City College building on the riverfront (photograph: author)

Since the water flow in Musi got reduced to a trickle due to the two reservoirs, Visvesvaraya suggested developing a serpentine lake in the riverbed with flowing water overlooking the proposed secretariat.[23] His dream was to make the riverfront a Civic Centre and Hyderabad a modern city.

The dream remained unfulfilled as the riverfront district gradually lost its glory in the decades following the merger of Hyderabad with the Union of India and the formation of Andhra Pradesh with Hyderabad as its capital. The city expanded further north, marginalising the riverfront to the edges of the walled city. The only addition to the riverfront was the new building of the Salar Jung Museum on the southern bank. Though famous globally as one of the largest 'one-man' collections of artefacts, it is actually a collection of objects acquired by three generations of the Salar Jungs. A bulk of the collection was acquired by Salar Jung III in the first half of the twentieth century. For many decades, the museum remained synonymous with Hyderabad while connecting the immediate past with the modern present.

5

India's First Vernacular University

Do not, I pray you, regard this movement (Osmania University), or movements of this kind, as, in any way, separatist, provincial or sectarian. They are based upon the first principles of national self-respect, reverence and respect for your cultural traditions which are not the insidious enemies but strongest supporters of national evolution.

–Akbar Hydari,
founder of Osmania University, 1925[1]

We look upon Osmania University as a great vehicle for fostering unity in India through the development of the regional languages.

–Prime Minister Jawaharlal Nehru,
Hyderabad, September 1952[2]

MODERN UNIVERSITY EDUCATION IN INDIA IS considered a colonial transplant. In the late eighteenth century, Warren Hastings proposed the teaching of the English language, along with Arabic, Persian and Sanskrit being taught in oriental schools. The teaching of subjects like mathematics and natural sciences was also introduced in existing schools of oriental learning. European-style colleges teaching arts and sciences made their debut in the early nineteenth century. The change was reflected in a string of new institutions in Bengal and Western India: Presidency College (Calcutta), Elphinstone College (Bombay), Deccan College (Poona), and engineering colleges at Serampore and Roorkee. Medical schools came up in Calcutta, Madras, Dacca and Bombay during this period. Thomas Babington Macaulay, as the law member of the Governor-General's Council in 1835, advocated making English as the medium of instruction and putting an end to the state support for oriental learning. He argued that vernacular languages had not developed to a level where they could become vehicles for the transmission of Western knowledge.

After the revolt of 1857, full-fledged universities offering courses in different disciplines were established in the Presidency towns of Calcutta, Madras and Bombay. The European model of university education inspired colleges and universities at Allahabad, Aligarh and Lahore, around 1875. In princely India, the oriental system of education continued and the progress of modern higher education was slow. Schools started imparting modern education but universities like Baroda, Mysore and Osmania were set up only in the early part of the twentieth century, almost seventy-five years after higher education had been introduced in British India.

In Hyderabad, State support for education was initiated by Mir Turab Ali Khan (Salar Jung I) who became the Diwan in 1853. Darul-Uloom, an oriental college, opened in 1856 with Arabic and Persian as the mediums of instruction. It was to be the centre of oriental learning in the Deccan and the means of diffusing the taste of culture through classics, according to Salar Jung. Four modern languages (Urdu, Kannada, Marathi and English) were also taught to those interested. To attract students, the administration offered scholarships and promised jobs to those completing the course. As the European population grew steadily, English-medium schools— St. George's Grammar School (founded in 1834), All Saints' High

School, Methodist Boys School and Wesley Mission Girls School—
were founded by Christian missionaries. For the children of nobility,
Salar Jung started Madrasa-i-Aliya as an alternate to homeschooling.
Higher education in Hyderabad received an impetus with the
import of academics from outside. The first one was Syed Hussain
Bilgrami, a professor of English literature at Lucknow's Canning
College, whom Salar Jung appointed as his private secretary in 1870.[3]
Bilgrami, who was made the director of Public Instruction in 1885,
reorganised school education across the state. Apart from being the
personal secretary to the sixth Nizam, he was also the tutor of the
heir apparent, Osman Ali Khan. Another scientist–educationist who
came to Hyderabad at the invitation of Salar Jung was Dr Aghorenath
Chattopadhyaya who founded the Gloria High School (also known
as Chaderghat High School) in 1881. It was merged with the City
English School (which was established as a branch of Darul-Uloom)
and upgraded into a second-grade college, Hyderabad College. In
1887, Hyderabad College was further upgraded to form Nizam
College. Nizam College was affiliated to Madras University and
Chattopadhyaya was appointed its first principal. To commemorate
the investiture of Mir Mahbub Ali Khan in 1884, two existing schools
in Secunderabad were merged to form the Mahbub College.[4]

The educational institutions in Hyderabad in the late nineteenth
century were dependent on the university system in British India
for affiliation and examination. The first Matriculation Examination
of Madras University in Hyderabad was held in 1875. Darul-Uloom
became affiliated with Panjab University for its Oriental Titles
Examination in Arabic and Persian.

At this time, new ideas for starting a university were floating
around in Hyderabad. Wilfrid Scawen Blunt, an English evangelist of
education among Muslims, advocated a Mohammedan University as
'the centre of religious thought for all India' in 1884, just after a young
Mahbub Ali Khan was invested full powers of the Nizam. Blunt wanted
the proposed university to provide 'all useful sciences and all branches
of solid learning' like the Azhar University in Cairo. He even coined
a name for it—Deccan University—and sent a note to the Nizam
requesting him to grant a building for it.[5] An old mosque in Kalbarga

and another building in Aurangabad were identified as potential sites to locate the university. Bilgrami, however, struck a note of caution saying 'the Government of India will never consent to such a plan'.[6] Another idea came from Sheikh Jamaluddin Afghani, a pan-Islamist campaigner who favoured 'cultivation and teaching of modern science in the local language of the people'.[7] Syed Ahmed Khan, founder of Mohammedan Anglo-Oriental College in Aligarh, suggested an English-medium university though he was not against giving Urdu a trial.[8]

Though an Islamic institution of higher learning as lobbied by different people did not materialise, the need for an indigenous university in Hyderabad kept cropping up in some form or the other for the next two decades.

The British influence over the administration of Hyderabad increased at the beginning of the twentieth century, particularly as the state faced a financial crisis. Lord Curzon pressurised Mahbub Ali Khan to sign the Treaty of 1902 providing permanent cession of the province of Berar.[9]

Among British civil servants deputed to top positions in Hyderabad was George Casson Walker in the Finance department. In October 1905, Walker invited Akbar Hydari, who was working as an examiner of Government Press Accounts in the Indian Finance department, to assist him. Hydari, the son of a Sulemani Bohra businessman of Bombay, had extensive experience in British India and at one point was invited by Gopal Krishna Gokhale to join the Servants of India Society. His mother was the sister of Badruddin Tyabji, president of the Indian National Congress.

Two years after coming to Hyderabad, Hydari became the finance secretary and took steps to bring the precarious financial situation under control. Among other steps, he appointed Arthur Mayhew, an Indian Educational Service (IES) officer working as deputy director of Public Instruction in Madras, to review the state of public instruction in Hyderabad. Mayhew subsequently became famous as the author of *The Education of India* report in 1926. For Hyderabad, he suggested the expansion of primary and secondary education, along with changes in the functioning of the Education department. For higher education, his suggestion was to develop a composite residential university with Darul-Uloom as its theological section and the Nizam College offering European-style education.[10] This would have ended the dependence of the Nizam College on Madras University for examinations and degrees. In any case, it was felt that the contribution of the Nizam College in enhancing higher education in Hyderabad was marginal. In 1907, just 4 per cent of candidates passed the BA examination conducted by Madras University. The number rose to 12 per cent in 1908.[11] The number of students in Darul Uloom too came down to twenty-two in 1914 from 141 in 1906.

The demand for setting up a new university (the suggested name was Nizam University) was articulated during the diamond jubilee celebrations of the Darul-Uloom in 1911. In 1915, the Hyderabad Education Conference chaired by Akbar Hydari supported the idea of a university where all subjects, including science, were taught in Urdu. By this time, Hydari was secretary to the government in Judicial, Police and General departments that also administered educational matters. Hydari's proposal for a new university made at a public forum received enthusiastic support from the Education department, which he headed, and the Department of Public Instruction, the director for which was Syed Ross Masood. An IES officer, the Oxford-educated Masood was a grandson of Sir Syed.

Armed with Mayhew's report and recommendations of the Hyderabad Educational Conference, Hydari crystallised the idea of a new university. He was joined in this effort by Syed Ross Masood and R.I.R. Glancy, who succeeded Walker in the Finance department. The group decided to make Urdu, not English, the medium of instruction in the proposed university. Glancy informally consulted Michael O'Dwyer, governor of Punjab, who had previously served in Hyderabad. O'Dwyer too supported the idea of the local language as the medium of instruction, but also enclosed the opinions of the director of Public Instruction of Punjab and the principal of the Oriental College, Lahore, both of whom pointed to practical difficulties of doing so through 'a language of which vocabulary is not wide enough to express all modern ideas and which is not equipped with the necessary textbooks etc'.[12]

At the end of these deliberations, the group decided to prepare an arzdasht (petition) on higher education and present it to the Nizam, who could then approve it, instead of going through the Legislative Council.[13] Accordingly, on 24 April 1917, Hydari submitted a thirty-page comprehensive survey of education in India beginning in 1835 and developments in education in Hyderabad to the Nizam. The memorandum argued that making English the sole vehicle of higher education in India was a mistake as 'most of the time which should be spent on the acquisition of the sciences and arts is spent on the acquisition of the foreign medium.'[14] As a result, 'mere memorizing of books is given priority by the students and most of what they develop is other people's opinion with little tax on their own intelligence'. Hydari cited the example of the English-medium Nizam College which admitted 253 students from 1907 to 1914 and only thirteen of them could graduate from Madras University in eight years.

The original drawing of the Osmania University logo, 1918
(courtesy: Chowmahalla Palace Archives)

In the backdrop of such experience, Hydari gave the following reasons for proposing Urdu as the medium of instruction in the new university:[15]

1. Urdu was the language of the widest currency in India.
2. It was the official language of the State in Hyderabad.
3. It was an Aryan language and thus had direct kinship with other languages of the country.
4. It was a language which was understood by a vast majority of the population of the state.

Cognizant of the ground realities of Hyderabad being a multilingual and multicultural state, the memorandum noted: 'It would have been far preferable if four Universities could be established in the state, representing its four languages—Urdu, Telugu, Marathi and Kannada—but the finances of the State would not allow it.'[16]

As decided in advance, the Nizam Mir Osman Ali Khan signed a Firman-e-Mubarak (Royal Charter) sanctioning the new university. The popular versions of history credit the Nizam for deciding on the arzdasht within two days of its submission, but in reality the arzdasht was just a well-thought-out bureaucratic tool to formalise the decision which was a result of long deliberations.

A special day was chosen for the issuance of the firman—the 1st of Rajab, which was the birthday of the Nizam. The firman declared, 'The fundamental principle in the working of the University should be that Urdu should form the medium of higher education but the knowledge of English as a language should at the same time be deemed compulsory for all students.' With this in view, the Nizam said he had ordered that all steps be taken for the inauguration of the University 'to be called the Osmania University of Hyderabad in commemoration of my accession to the throne'.[17] In addition to its primary objective of diffusing knowledge, the university also aimed at the moral training of students as well as providing an impetus to research in all scientific subjects.

An eleven-member panel with Hydari as chairman developed the curricula for Matriculation Examination, Intermediate and BA degrees. Among the members of the panel were Syed Ross Masood (director of Public Instruction), N.G. Welinkar (chief inspector of Schools) and Maulvi Abdul Haq (inspector of Schools). The draft curricula were circulated among 'educational circles' in England and India. Among those who sent detailed comments were Dr M.E. Sadler (chairman, Calcutta University Commission), Rabindranath Tagore (Visva-Bharati), Justice T.V. Seshagiri Aiyer, Professor J.W. Gregory (Calcutta University Commission), H.V. Nanjundayya (vice chancellor, Mysore University), M. Visvesvaraya (Diwan, Mysore State), J.H. Towle (principal, Aligarh College), C.P. Ramaswamy Iyer (fellow, Madras University), Rai Bahadur G.N. Chakravarti (fellow, Allahabad University), Fazal Hussain (fellow, Punjab University) and A. Mayhew (director, Public Instruction, Central Provinces). From within the state, several high officials, judges, professors and poets, including Sarojini Naidu, were consulted.

The syllabus for the two-year Intermediate course included three papers in English modelled after the Bombay University Intermediate Exam. The subjects in Group A were Greek and Roman history, English history, Indian history and administration, European history, Islamic history, economics, one modern language (Urdu, Telugu, Tamil, Kanarese, Marathi, French, German, Persian), one classical language (Arabic, Sanskrit, Latin, Greek, Persian), logic (deductive and inductive) and psychology. The subjects offered in Group B were physics, chemistry, biology, pure mathematics and applied mathematics.[18] In BA, candidates could choose any one stream from languages, history, science, philosophy and law.

The next task was the preparation of textbooks in Urdu for all the courses. For this purpose, Darul Tarjuma (Bureau of Translation and Compilation) was established in August 1917. Help was sought from linguists, subject experts and educationists as well as members of different faculties to select standard texts for translation. A curator, a team of translators and literary experts were employed in the bureau. Experts were consulted from different universities and Committees of Technical Terms were formed for translating technical terms in engineering, medicine and sciences.

Maulvi Abdul Haq, a linguist and lexicographer, led this massive effort. Haq was a protégé of Sir Syed and a product of the Muhammadan Anglo-Oriental (MAO) College in Aligarh. In 1895, he began working for the Hyderabad State Education department as the headmaster of Madrassa Asafia. He advanced through the ranks, and in 1912 he was appointed inspector of Schools in Aurangabad. In the new university, Haq was made the head of the Department of Urdu as well as the translation bureau. Haq migrated to Pakistan in 1949. For all his contributions to the language, he earned the sobriquet of Baba-e-Urdu (grand old man of Urdu).

In May 1920, the University Council approved the use of 'international nomenclature' for medicine and engineering 'in view of the immense difficulties with which the evolution of a complete system of indigenous nomenclature is beset, and the facilities accruing from the use of international nomenclature'.[19] Scientific nomenclature included the binomial system used in botany and zoology, English names of elements and compounds, their symbols and formulae. Chemical equations adopted by scientists were retained in their original form as they were internationally recognised. Transliteration—instead of translation attempted earlier—of such nomenclature, along with the terms of European languages, was rendered into Urdu. Terminology and notations were translated and compiled in Urdu with the help of classical and Indian languages like Arabic, Persian, Sanskrit, Urdu, Hindi and others 'to the extent to which Urdu is capable of assimilation, absorbing and expressing the exact sense of the term'.

Abdul Haq described the translation methodology, saying, 'The translator before starting on his work picks out all technical and scientific terms occurring in the book and submits his list to the Curator who places it before the Terms Committee dealing with the subject. When the terms to be used are finally settled, the translator starts with his work which is examined in detail by the Literary and Religious Censors and by the Curator before being sent to the press. This process although lengthy is necessary to ensure accuracy.'[20] The reference to the presence of a 'religious censor' in the bureau gave rise to allegations of an Islamic bias in textbooks by those who later opposed Urdu as the medium of instruction.[21]

Philosophy, history, law, economics, mathematics, physics, chemistry, biology, medicine and engineering were among the many subjects covered for translation. By 1946, the bureau had published a total of 356 textbooks. Another 150 translated books were under publication. In three decades, nearly 1,00,000 technical terms in different subjects were compiled and incorporated in translated books.[22] The textbooks published by the bureau were widely distributed in British India and outside. Complimentary copies were sent regularly to several British, Indian and foreign universities, colleges, institutions and libraries. The list of recipients included the British Museum, the India office in London, Cambridge University, Paris University, the University of Cairo and so on.

The translation exercise was massive, but certainly not the first as claimed by its proponents. The earliest effort to develop scientific terminology and textbooks in Urdu was made at Delhi College in the 1830s. Dr Springer and Mr Batrons formed a translation society to translate scientific textbooks and laid down principles for translating technical terms into Hindustani. Some 200 books dealing with mathematics, astronomy, chemistry, physics, medicine, natural history, jurisprudence, economics, logic, philosophy, and political and constitutional history were translated.[23] In Hyderabad, Fakhruddin Khan Shamsul Umra II founded a translation bureau in 1826 for preparing Urdu books in modern science for pupils in Madrasa-i-Fakhriya which he had established.[24]

Inspiration from Japan

Language was a tool to assert cultural nationalism as well as to demonstrate a non-British model of education. For both, Hyderabadi officials looked to Japan. Indian provinces under direct British rule introduced Western education and established universities, while education in princely states, particularly with Muslim rulers, was mostly based on traditional systems. Hindu-ruled princely states like Ajmer, Gwalior, Indore and Rajkot opted for the British public school system modelled after Harrow and Eton.[25] Hyderabad and Rampur resented English-style education, which they felt could alienate students from their country and culture. The Nizams ignored nudges from successive British Residents to send Hyderabad princes to Mayo College in Ajmer. Instead, they preferred homeschooling by British and Indian tutors.

In early twentieth century, Japan emerged as a courageous, civilised, developed country and a role model for people in colonies of South Asia. It was seen as an example of achieving industrial progress and modernisation through an indigenous education system. Japan's stature increased particularly after its victory over Russia in 1905. Indian magazines regularly published articles on Japan's successes in various fields. Maharaja Ranjit Singh of Kapurthala and Nawab Hamid Ali Khan of Rampur decided to focus on education after their visits to Japan. The free and compulsory education in Baroda is said to have been inspired by the Japanese educational system.[26] Another eminent Indian impressed with the Japanese industrial development was M. Visvesvaraya, who visited Japan thrice in two decades and exchanged notes with Masood.

Impressed with the Japanese education system during his visit, Rabindranath Tagore included judo and ikebana in the course taught at Visva-Bharati. Punjab governor O'Dwyer felt that 'the precedent of Japan is apposite enough for Hyderabad conditions'. He added, 'I never by the way met a Jap who could approach a well-educated Indian in the knowledge of good idiomatic English or in facility of speaking it. But for all that, and perhaps because of that inferiority, the Jap is probably nine out of ten better equipped intellectually, mentally, and more capable of independent reasoning than even the flower of our universities.'[27]

In a 400-page report on his visit to Japan to study the education system, Masood attributed the secret of Japan's rapid intellectual progress to the country making Japanese the language of instruction at all levels.[28] Japan could do this because of the homogeneity in the Japanese society and Japanese being their sole language, unlike

Hyderabad. For achieving homogeneity, Masood wanted the Education department to inculcate among people 'loyalty to His Exalted Highness the Nizam, love of the country, and knowledge of the official language (Urdu)'. Masood said that just like Japan's Education department, which supplied a copy of the royal edict on education along with a signed picture of the emperor to all schools, all schools in Hyderabad should be provided with a photograph of the Nizam and 'a nicely printed copy' of a message from him. Masood wanted all textbooks to emphasise the 'beneficence of the Royal House of Hyderabad'.[29]

Masood dreamt of developing Hyderabad as India's intellectual capital with Osmania University at its centre. Besides royal patronage and Urdu as a medium of instruction, he needed learned men for this project. And for this, he looked to north India, particularly to Aligarh, which had a strong tradition of higher learning. One of Masood's early recruits was Haroon Khan Sherwani, an academic who had degrees from both Oxford and Cambridge. The two had a common friend in E.M. Forster who was Masood's tutor in Oxford. Masood had inspired Forster to visit India, which resulted in his landmark work *A Passage to India*. Masood and Sherwani remained in touch over the years, exchanging notes while Masood was serving at Bankipore in IES.

Osmania University offered new opportunities for academics, and Masood thought of getting his friend Sherwani a suitable post. In January 1918, he wrote to Sherwani asking him to send a formal application to Akbar Hydari for an appointment in the university. Hydari was the executive home secretary incharge of the Education portfolio.[30] Masood regularly corresponded with Sherwani, sharing his dreams as well as frustrations while trying to develop a modern education system in Hyderabad. In one of his letters to Sherwani, he wrote, 'it is my desire to make Hyderabad the real intellectual capital of India and that can only happen if we have capable men cooperating with each other ... but there are many people in Hyderabad with a strong prejudice'.[31] Sherwani joined in 1919 as an assistant professor in the Department of History at Osmania University. His association with the university was long, spanning almost half a century, including a stint as the principal of Nizam College.

Another Grand Edifice

Teaching at Osmania University started in 1920 but it took another fifteen years for it to get a permanent home—a magnificent building which became a symbol of development under the rule of the last Nizam.

In the beginning, the University College was housed in the bungalow of Agha Syed Hasan, while the Registrar's office functioned from the bungalow of Zal Rustomji, both situated on Gun Foundry Road. Karam Ali and Co. of Bombay was given the contract for supplying the furniture. Two professors and fourteen assistant professors were appointed in the first year, while the appointment of a full-time principal was pending. 'Suitable buildings for the new college and university offices are badly needed' along with a boarding house attached to the college, an official report noted in 1921.[32]

The search for a suitable place to locate the new university began soon after teaching started in 1921-22. At first, it was proposed that a suitable place be found on the riverfront for the construction of university buildings. Another idea was to explore if some royal palaces or the old building of Madrassa-i-Aaliya could be utilised for the university. But the authorities representing the university said they would need a large area to develop a campus, and this could be available only outside the city.

The proposal to construct an independent campus was criticised by some. 'Let us, by all means, copy and adapt the educational methods of Cambridge and Oxford, but by no means follow their system of educational segregation. Let us not make our Osmania University the symbol of royal generosity and affection, inaccessible and costly like Cambridge and Oxford,' wrote Zoolcader Jung, a member of the construction committee, in a dissent note.[33] The majority, however, was in favour of building a separate campus at a spacious location.

Patrick Geddes, a Scottish biologist, sociologist and town planner, was involved in the site selection process. In 1918, Akbar Hydari invited him to visit Hyderabad and share the report on the town planning of Indore with the City Improvement Board.[34] Geddes had prepared nearly fifty town plans for cities in India and emphasised respect for nature as well as tradition. The three shortlisted locations that Geddes inspected for Osmania University in 1923 were Begumpet, Khairatabad and Adigmet. In Khairatabad, he was shown the mansion of Fakhr-ul Mulk as it had a large ground. Among the factors that favoured this site were 'unfinished gardens, its rock ridges, its valleys and its streams' besides its proximity to the rail and road networks as well as to the Nizamiah Observatory.[35]

After a survey and review of several sites, a large area in the old Adigmet (derived from Adhika Metta, which in Telugu means high grounds) village was found suitable. Experts were attracted by 'its elevation, the panoramic view it commands of the City and surroundings, its salubrious climate and its natural ridges and hillocks, affording unique opportunity for an aesthetic layout'.[36] Adigmet was situated about 4 miles from the city centre, the nearest railway station was half a mile away, and the distance from the Secunderabad junction was 2 miles.

A bulk of the 1,240 acres identified for the university project were Sirf-e-Khas Mubarak (Crown lands), so they had to be converted into Diwani Ilakha (government lands). The Building Committee requested the Nizam to let the area surrounding Sirf-e-Khas land be undisturbed as it was without any built-up structures. Since the site was away from the city's municipal limits, the committee wanted 'the university area be kept independent and outside the Municipal jurisdiction' in line with 'the practice observed in other residential universities in the Empire'.[37] Because of increasing expenditure towards rented buildings, it was decided to construct temporary structures in Adigmet for colleges, hostels and other facilities till permanent structures were built.

To give the new university building a look of a monument like the buildings on the riverfront, Hydari wished for an innovative design. Zain Yar Jung, head of PWD (later to be the chief architect), and Syed Ali Raza, superintending engineer of the project, were sent on a world tour to study university buildings. The two visited Great Britain, Europe, Japan, America, Egypt, Syria and Turkey, and submitted a voluminous report. They identified Ernest Jasper, a Belgian architect who had designed 'many fine Saracenic buildings' in Cairo, to work as a consultant architect for the building project.

Akbar Hydari, who was in London to participate in the Second Round Table Conference in October 1931, negotiated the terms with Jasper and cabled Hyderabad that the consulting fee of Jasper would be '1.25 per cent of works cost irrespective of the amount of work entrusted'.[38] Jasper would visit Hyderabad every year to inspect the work, for which he was to be paid first-class return airfare, all expenses for a stay in Hyderabad and a daily allowance of 12 Pound Sterling from the date of leaving Brussels. Hydari mentioned that the terms of engaging Jasper had been approved by Sir Richard Trench, a member of the Nizam's Executive Council who was also a part of the Hyderabad delegation in London.

In 1933, Jasper submitted his design for the main building of the university, which was to house the College of Arts. What he came up with was a blend of the Indo-Saracenic and Mamluk styles of architecture, drawing heavily from the design of the iconic Heliopolis Palace Hotel he had built in Cairo two decades earlier.[39] Jasper also planned other buildings—senate hall, main library, law and training colleges, museum and hostels—on surrounding hillocks, ridges and valleys. Colleges of agriculture and forests, medical and women's colleges were also planned but eventually they were not developed on the main campus, for various reasons. The foundation stone of the main building was laid by the Nizam on 5 July 1934. Zain Yar Jung, the chief architect of Hyderabad, implemented Jasper's designs. While doing so, he made some significant changes such as doing away with a tapering dome (which resembled a Hindu temple from Cambodia) and a crescent on the top.

A hagiography of Zain Yar Jung crediting him for the architecture of the Arts College described the style as, 'Evolution of the new style of architecture of the university buildings which was christened as the Deccani style was a fusion of the Bahmani and Kutubshahi architectures on one side and the Buddhistic-cum-Brahmanic style on the other, which later had blossomed in the Ajanta and Ellora caves and the Hemandpanti style of temple construction in the Deccan and South India.'[40] Jung spoke about the architectural design of the university buildings at the Indian Institute of Architects in 1944 but made no mention of Jasper's design. He said he had studied Hindu and Muslim cultural elements of all the periods in the states and come up with 'a composite whole signifying the evolution of a new style which should distinguish the reign of His Exalted Highness from all other rulers in the history of Asaf Jahi dynasty.'[41]

The Whirlpool of Language Politics

The formation of the Osmania University necessitated the transfer of existing colleges of medicine and engineering to it. The medium of instruction in Hyderabad Medical School was changed from Urdu to English in 1884 and it was regulated first by the Madras Examination Board and then by the Bombay Board. The medium of instruction in Osmania was Urdu, and the medical school (renamed Osmania Medical College by then) reverted to Urdu after nearly four decades. The first Urdu-medium MBBS class was held in October 1926. Medical textbooks, mostly imported from England, were translated into Urdu and all lectures were delivered in Urdu.

The change in the medium of instruction caused student unrest. Some sixty protesting students were dismissed. The British Resident thought, 'The system is hardly likely to be a success in view of the fact that it would be impossible to translate (even) one-tenth of the ordinary medical literature into Urdu except at a prohibitive cost.'[42] The focus on teaching in Urdu from secondary school onward evoked criticism from non-Urdu speakers who represented the linguistic majority of the state. In his arzdasht, Akbar Hydari had forewarned about such opposition but had emphasised, 'While it is true that those whose mother tongue is Urdu are in a minority, yet Urdu is the cultural and official language of the State and polite society, and is generally spoken by those classes from which students proceeding to a College course are drawn.'[43]

In 1928, Peoples' Educational Conference of Hyderabad (PECH), a newly formed group, argued that Telugu, Marathi and Kannada were equipped for higher education as demonstrated in other universities like Andhra University and Mysore University. Moreover, Urdu used at Osmania University was 'highly Arabicised and Persianised'. Forcing all educational institutions to get affiliated with Osmania would lead to 'Urduisation of the vast majority of the subjects' and deny them the benefit of government jobs, according to Laxman Rao Ganu, conference secretary. The conference also alleged that a special officer was appointed in the translation bureau to 'examine its works from a religious and Islamic point of view', which went against the principles of liberal thought.[44]

Another organisation, the Standing Committee of the Hindu Subjects, led by Kashinath Rao Vaidya, a member of the Legislative Council, talked of the adverse effects of Urdu education on the educational status of the Hindus.[45] The committee felt that employment chances of the Hindus were hit as preference was being given to knowledge of English and Urdu in government jobs, particularly in the recruitment to the Hyderabad Civil Service.

At the national level, the language debate focused on developing consensus on a national language, with the Congress leadership, Mahatma Gandhi and Jawaharlal Nehru, expressing themselves in favour of Hindustani—a composite mix of Hindi and Urdu.

Mindful of such criticism and debate about Hindustani in India, leaders of Osmania University tried to project the adoption of a vernacular as a symbol of national unity and 'all-India synthesis', and began referring to the medium of instruction not as Urdu but as Hindustani. For instance, Akbar Hydari told the 24th Session of the Indian Science Congress, hosted by Osmania University, that the use of 'simple Hindustani' as the medium of instruction had given 'our University an All-India character (rather) than a narrow provincial one'.[46] The reference to Hindustani (which then was being projected as India's future national language) and not Urdu by Hyderabad officials was a reflection of their stand vis-à-vis proponents of

Hindi–Hindustani and the campaign to make Devanagiri the script for Hindustani.

The discourse surrounding the need for a national language for India intensified in the 1940s. With newly formed Pakistan adopting Urdu as its national language in 1947, supporters of Hindi wanted it declared the national language of India. After 1948, the language policy of Osmania University was modified. Urdu was not to be the exclusive medium of instruction. Lectures were delivered in Hindustani while students could take the examination in Urdu, Hindi or English.

Keen to bring Hyderabad into the mainstream, the Central government reviewed several matters connected with the future of Hyderabad's institutions including the Osmania University. On 29 October 1951, the Union Cabinet approved a proposal to take over the university and convert it into a central institution, to be run on the same lines as Banaras Hindu University (BHU), Aligarh Muslim University and the University of Delhi, which had been made central universities. It also decided to make Hindi the principal medium of instruction.[47]

Prime Minister Nehru felt that the university 'will deteriorate gravely if it is left to the state when the state is run entirely on a popular basis'. As regards the medium of instruction, he wished Osmania to perform 'a special function both from the linguistic and the communal points of view'.[48] Since Hindi or Hindustani was developing as a national language, in his view, south India should have 'a great educational institution which has this language as its principal medium of instruction'. The university, if properly run, 'could become the centre for bringing about communal harmony' and 'bring the south and the north of India nearer to each other'. The effort seemed to be to convert what started as an experiment in cultural nationalism into a symbol of communal and linguistic unity of the newly independent nation.

Hyderabad chief minister M.K. Vellodi informed the Centre that 'while the changeover of the medium of instruction from Hindustani to Hindi will not be unwelcome', the popular feeling was not in favour of a Central takeover. Vice Chancellor Ali Yavar

Jung proposed a division of the university's assets between the Government of India and the Government of Hyderabad, with the Centre taking over the University College of Arts and Science, Department of Translation and Publications, University Press and Nizamiah Observatory, leaving control of the other colleges with the Government of Hyderabad.[49]

The former Nizam, Osman Ali Khan, proposed a Trust Fund using as a corpus Rs 3.15 crore, which he had advanced to the Hyderabad government in 1949.[50] He suggested that the interest from the fund could be used to run the University College of Arts and Sciences, College of Engineering and the translation bureau, while the Central government could take over Law College, Nizam College, Women's College and Nizamiah Observatory. He proposed that the Trust Fund could support Chairs in Arabic, Persian, Sanskrit, Hindi and Urdu; Chairs in astronomy and geology; Readerships in Deccan history, archaeology and Islamic religion and culture; and Bureau of Arabic Publications (Dairat-ul-Maarif). The trustees could have the power to nominate three members of the University Council. This appeared like a last-ditch attempt by the former ruler to retain some stake in the running of the greatest achievement of his rule.

After the state assembly elections in Hyderabad, Burugula Ramakrishna Rao of the Indian National Congress became the chief minister. The Centre asked Rao to give his opinion on the proposal to make Osmania a Central university, while, at the same time, forming an expert panel to examine the financial and administrative matters of the university. The panel included Central and state officials such as Union Education secretary Humayun Kabir and his Hyderabad counterpart Laxmi Narayan Gupta.

Ramakrishna Rao agreed to the Central takeover but with conditions such as providing 'facilities for local students, rights and privileges of staff and financial viability'.[51] He was severely criticised for his stand. The Hindu editorial that appeared on 1 June 1952 read: 'The fact that Urdu was the media of instruction there till the other day is no point in favour of the proposed change since the original experiment itself was a failure.'[52] Daily News wrote on 7 May 1952, 'It is passing strange that Mr Ramakrishna Rao who had advocated the mother tongue medium in the past should have consented to the proposal of the Central Government.' The Hyderabad government sought to defend the decision by saying that a university with Hindi medium would help 'South Indians in attaining high proficiency in Hindi which would no doubt be required for the Services in future' as Hindi would be the official language. A Hindi Central university in Hyderabad would also foster 'greater cultural unity between the North and the South.'[53]

As the opposition to the proposal grew, Ramakrishna Rao appealed to Nehru in May 1952 to reconsider the matter 'in a clearer perspective'. Nehru, in his detailed reply, feared that 'if the university remained with the Hyderabad government, it will become the plaything of political forces and pulls and intrigues will flourish'. On the language issue, Nehru said, 'When we talk about this being a Hindi university, we simply mean that special attention will be paid to the national languages which should be simple Hindustani and not any Sanskritized type language. Of course, other languages would also have pride of place.'[54] Moreover, he said, much of the university instruction would have to be in English, particularly 'scientific, medical and technical instruction', till an adequate number of textbooks were developed in Hindi.

The Osmania University Bill to make it a Central university, introduced in the state assembly in July 1952, was shelved, and the Centre was requested to form an expert panel to examine the question. Accordingly, a committee under the chairmanship of Acharya Narendra Dev, vice chancellor of BHU, was constituted in September 1952. Rao suggested the inclusion of experts from Hyderabad on this panel. Kashinath Rao Vaidya (speaker, Hyderabad Assembly), Madpati Hanumantha Rao (mayor, Hyderabad Municipal Corporation) and Krishnachari Joshi (member of Parliament) were included in the panel. Dr Suri Bhagwantam, vice chancellor of Osmania University, was made its convener.

The committee turned out to be an exercise in buying time. It did not meet for one year, for various reasons. Meanwhile, Narendra Dev resigned in October 1953 owing to ill health, following which Dr Zakir Husain was made the chairman. The first meeting of the committee finally took place in Hyderabad on 3 and 4 July 1954. Subsequently, Husain too resigned saying it was 'a question of high political policy and not of educational detail'. The Ministry of Home Affairs decided to keep the whole exercise in abeyance. The university was allowed to continue functioning under its original charter.[55] The idea of a Central takeover was finally dropped altogether as the Centre became preoccupied with the larger problem of the reorganisation of states. While Osmania University did not become a Central university, Hyderabad got a Central university two decades later—the University of Hyderabad. It was housed in the Golden Threshold, the family home of Dr M.G. Naidu and Sarojini Naidu which was bequeathed to the university by their daughter Padmaja Naidu.

The Importance of Being Osmania

Though the stated objective of setting up Osmania University was the need to end the monopoly of Madras University over education in Hyderabad, in effect it was a larger cultural, political and nationalist project. The idea of imparting modern, European-style education in a vernacular language was diametrically opposite to theological and Islamic education proposed by the proponents of a Mohammedan university. The language chosen for Osmania University was Urdu, which was widely spoken in the state, besides being the official language. It had a pan-Indian appeal as Urdu was spoken not only by Muslims in north India, Bengal and elsewhere but also by a large number of non-Muslims. This gave the university and its patron, the Nizam, a national profile and the idea a wider reception.

The plan to build a new university appealed to the young Nizam though he had never been to a university himself. He was mostly home-tutored by Hyderabadi and English tutors. He had grown up in the old Mughal-style court traditions and had kinship links with the Paigah nobles. Yet, he showed an urge to break from the past and be looked upon as a modern ruler. Intellectuals like Ross Masood further reinforced such thoughts. For them, Osmania University symbolised an awakening of the Islamic world and a great advance for Osman Ali Khan who they believed 'had the great foresight to be the first to place education in India on a rational and truly national basis'. Masood wrote, 'The day is near when, under his benign rule, Hyderabad will see as great an intellectual awakening as was witnessed by the Islamic world in the days of the great Caliphs of Baghdad.'[56]

The translation project was not merely an exercise to produce Urdu textbooks. It was meant to reinvent Urdu as the language of science and knowledge, breaking its popular image of being a language of sher-o-shayari and royal durbars. The promoters of the bureau wanted to extend the exercise to enrich and modernise Urdu, which went beyond university textbooks. Since 1912, when he became the secretary general of Anjuman-i-Taraqqui-Urdu (founded by Sir Syed in 1886), Abdul Haq was deeply engaged in the promotion of Urdu. He shifted the Anjuman's office from Aligarh to Aurangabad where he served in the Nizam's Education department. His transfer to Hyderabad to head the translation bureau did not dilute his commitment to the Anjuman. New terms coined at the translation bureau were regularly publicised in Urdu, the journal published by the Anjuman.[57] The Anjuman also published a quarterly, Science, to popularise science among Urdu-speaking people, besides subject-wise glossaries of terminology and dictionaries.

The translation work spurred technological advances in Urdu printing. If good quality books had to be printed in large numbers, the challenge was to render the calligraphic style of writing Urdu, known as nastaliq, into moveable type letters. Type letters were necessary if the laborious lithographic printing technique had to be replaced with mechanised printing. The government-funded Osmania Type Foundry produced calligraphic-style type letters in lead, for commercial use.[58] It was supposed to make publishing in Urdu profitable and efficient while keeping intact the essential elements of handcrafted lettering. A full set of fonts was developed. Named 'Osmania style', it included 457 single letters, 102 compound letters and thirty-five extra letters. However, there were no takers for the lead fonts as the cost of a single set was Rs 36,000 in 1933.[59]

The formative years of Osmania University coincided with the period in which the feudal and hitherto politically inert princely state was witnessing the birth of new political and social formations like Andhra Mahasabha, Arya Samaj, Hindu Mahasabha and Majlis-e-Ittihadul Musalmeen (MIM). As the first and only university in the state, Osmania became a nursery of political ideas and gave rise to an educated and politically aware class within a short time. In the 1930s, Osmania University graduates emerged as the new elites who got into government jobs and participated in economic activity.

The growing contacts between the educated elites of Hyderabad and British India influenced the formation of political ideas of linguistic identity and nationalism. The large presence of intellectuals from north India for the translation project and their growing influence in Hyderabad made the local intelligentsia in Osmania University form the Mulki Council (also known as Nizam's Subjects League) to assert Deccan nationalism. The sentiment against ghair-mulki (non-locals) Urdu-speaking administrators and academics from north India was strong since the shift from Persian to Urdu helped to consolidate political power in the hands of such 'outsiders'.[60]

The choice of Urdu as the sole medium of instruction brought to the fore some uncomfortable questions about the position of the Hindu majority in the administration and government jobs. This issue provided an opportunity to express dissent against the Nizam for the first time in his tenure. Newly founded organisations like the Standing Committee of the Hindu Subjects and People's Educational Conference of Hyderabad challenged the promotion of Urdu and the neglect of Hindus in the Hyderabad Civil Service. The choice of language was directly linked to government jobs and preference was given to the knowledge of Urdu for recruitment to the Hyderabad Civil Service. The new associations disputed that Urdu was the only official language, citing the use of Marathi and Kannada in subordinate courts, land records and surveys since the 1880s, in addition to Persian, which was the official language at the time.

The university effectively became a site for aspiration for freedom and development, like other universities in British India and other princely states. As historian Karen Leonard noted, 'Western education had come to Hyderabad, through many channels including Osmania, and it produced in Hyderabad the same kinds of voluntary associations, caste and linguistic mobilizations, Masonic orders, and sporting clubs as in British India.'[61] In later years, the nationalist Vande Mataram movement and the Comrades Association, which inspired the communist-led peasant uprising, had their beginnings at Osmania University.[62] This vein of political activism persisted at Osmania University after 1948 as well, as evidenced by the active role that students and faculty played in the movements for separate Telangana in 1969 and 2010, which eventually resulted in the creation of the Telangana state.

The Osmania Graduates Association (OGA) formed in 1932 was a key element of the social and economic ferment of Hyderabad. Among its founders were Mahmood Ali, Shankerji, Akbar Ali Khan, Premji Lalji and Raja Guru Das. In 1938, the Economic Committee of OGA organised an exhibition of handicrafts and industrial products of Hyderabad to coincide with the silver jubilee of the Nizam's coronation. The exposition called Numaish Masnuaat-i-Mulki became a regular annual feature after that and the Nizam allotted a piece of land in the heart of the city for organising it. Initially, the objective was to showcase the work of state enterprises and Mulki businesses, but over the next few years, the trade show acquired a national profile. The Association formed a separate entity, the All India Industrial Exhibition Society, and opened up the Numaish to small and medium-scale entrepreneurs as well as craftspeople from all over the country. The revenue collected through stall rental and entry charges was used to sponsor educational institutions, particularly those for women. In 2023, the Exhibition Society was running eighteen educational and vocational training institutions with a total intake of 30,000 students annually.[63]

The university remained a state university despite Nehru's desire to make it a Central university after Hyderabad's integration with

India, with Hindi as the medium of instruction. However, Osmania University contributed to the development of Central institutions in Hyderabad. It incubated two national research laboratories—Central Laboratories for Scientific and Industrial Research (CLSIR), which became Regional Research Laboratory (RRL) and moved to its campus, and the National Geophysical Research Institute (NGRI). The location of the university in an area away from the city attracted several research and academic institutions, including the Nutrition Research Laboratories from Coonoor. A Central Institute of English to train teachers in English was established on the university campus in 1958. It expanded its ambit to French, German and Russian subsequently, to become Central Institute of English and Foreign Languages in 1972, eventually taking the shape of the English and Foreign Languages University (EFLU). All this made this part of the city the first knowledge corridor in Hyderabad.

SECTION II

A Knowledge Cluster on the Horizon (1948–1991)

6

An Industrial Laboratory and
a Culture of Science

∽

IN THE LATE 1940S, A NEWLY INDEPENDENT INDIA WAS GOING through the process of establishing a unified democratic republic with the integration of princely states. It was not only a political integration but also economic and administrative. The administrative systems in many princely states were at variance with those in the provinces ruled directly by the British. In Hyderabad, the Central government initiated this process soon after the Police Action of September 1948. Prime Minister Nehru was keen to see Hyderabad join the national mainstream and benefit from the planning and economic development his government had initiated. He wanted key educational and scientific institutions in Hyderabad to be brought under the Central government so they could be assisted and developed, while being free from local political interference. However, his plan to make Osmania University a Central university failed. The second most important knowledge institution, the Central Laboratories for Scientific & Industrial Research (CLSIR) did become a Central institution, but it took a long time.

Nehru's interest in scientific and educational institutions in Hyderabad should be seen in the context of his larger vision of science and technology-led industrialisation, addressing poverty and disease through human development and application of knowledge. He advocated a 'mixed economy' approach based on the confluence of the Soviet socialistic planning and the Western industrial capitalism.[1] The vision was implemented through Five Year Plans, development of river valley projects and dams, heavy industries, building science and technology infrastructure and State support to critical research in nuclear energy. To make science a key player in development, an integrated Ministry of Natural Resources and Scientific Research (NRSR) was created in 1951, with Nehru taking its charge himself.

While CLSIR of Hyderabad, with its primary objective of industrial research, fitted well in this developing scenario, it could not qualify to be a national laboratory as its research orientation was regional. Nor could it be a fundamental research centre like the Tata Institute of Fundamental Research (TIFR) shaping up in Bombay under Homi Jehangir Bhabha or the Saha Institute of Nuclear Physics founded by Meghnad Saha in Kolkata. All this made the process of the integration of CLSIR with India's mainstream scientific community rather painful. Moreover, in 1948 CLSIR was short of funds and headless as its incumbent director Muzaffaruddin Qureshi, who had proceeded to Lahore on home leave in June 1947, did not return.

In November 1948, the government picked Dr Syed Husain Zaheer as director of CLSIR. Zaheer was already in the Nizam government's service. He had been the principal of Government City College for the preceding two years and prior to that, he had had a long teaching and research career at Lucknow University (1930–46). He had personal connections with Hyderabad as he was married to the sister of Ali Yavar Jung, the minister for Constitutional Affairs in the Nizam's government.

A chemist trained in Lucknow, Oxford and Heidelberg, Zaheer had an active political stint during which he was a member of the United Province Legislature, representing the combined universities constituency of Allahabad, Agra and Lucknow. For some time, he served as the parliamentary secretary to the Education minister. Before joining City College, he was selected to serve as an assistant director at National Chemical Laboratory (NCL) by a selection panel chaired by the CSIR president C. Rajagopalachari, but he did not take the offer.[2] By 1948, he had a dozen research papers published in international and Indian journals, including two co-authored with his mentor at Heidelberg University, Karl Freudenberg, who was a celebrated German chemist and an expert in stereochemistry, tannins, carbohydrates, lignin and insulin.

Along with academic work at Lucknow University, Zaheer was a consultant to several industries in north India. For Ram Laxman Sugar Mills in Meerut, he prepared schemes for the manufacture of golden syrup from molasses, cotton wool from raw cotton and caffeine from tea leaf dust and scrapings from tea kilns. He designed a process for the preparation of crystalline glucose for the Government Cooperative Department in the United Province during the glucose scarcity in 1944–46. The technical advice provided by him helped New Delhi-based H.K. Chemical Industries to start the manufacture of potassium permanganate from pyrolusite and yeast from molasses. In Hyderabad, he was associated with the Board of Scientific & Industrial Research (BSIR) as the chairman of its research committee on drugs and pharmaceuticals.

At that time, national laboratories of CSIR focused on specific sectors like chemicals, buildings, ceramics and glass, fuel and so on. On the other hand, TIFR's focus was basic research in physics. Bhabha made it clear that TIFR 'would not directly play a service role in Indian industry' but would 'indirectly influence the industry by setting the standards that were now missing.'[3] In contrast to these trends, CLSIR's focus was on the utilisation of raw materials like coal, forest produce and oilseeds, to develop or adapt processes and techniques for direct industrial application. This helped spur industrialisation in Hyderabad.

CLSIR was in bad shape when Zaheer became its director. Though it was formed in 1944, research work could not begin for several reasons. Zaheer's predecessor Qureshi was away in the UK and USA for a long period as a member of the Fertiliser Mission of the Government of India. New research staff was not recruited, a sufficient budget was not allocated and the accommodation given at Osmania University was inadequate. The Government of Hyderabad allocated a recurring grant of Rs 3 lakh for the financial year (October 1948 to September 1949), of which more than half went towards salaries and allowances, leaving little for the purchase of equipment, apparatus and chemicals.[4]

In December 1950, Zaheer presented to the CLSIR Governing Body an exhaustive list of equipment and staff required to expand the lab and for the construction of pilot plants to demonstrate processes developed for industry. Given the resource crunch, the Governing Body suggested that some work be taken up on priority, and constituted a panel to fix the priorities. The Governing Body included Dr J.C. Ghosh (director, Indian Institute of Technology, Kharagpur), Professor M.S. Thacker (director, IISc, Bangalore), Shanti Swarup Bhatnagar (director, CSIR), J.W. McBain (director, NCL) and K.N. Mathur (deputy director, National Physical Laboratory—NPL).

Among the pilot plants that were identified to be built on priority were those for low-temperature carbonisation (LTC) of coal, briquetting of coal and coke, solvent extraction of oilseed cakes, processing of cotton seeds and custard apple seeds, newsprint production from forest wood, utilisation of molasses for biochemical processes and of cotton dust for making cellulose paints and varnishes.[5] Orders were placed to import an LTC pilot plant from Lurgi in Germany.

Construction work to build a new campus began on a large piece of land in Uppal village on the periphery of Osmania University. The construction work was taken up in phases, to economise on available funds. In the first stage, the basement, ground floor, first floor, two pilot plant areas, gas house, electricity substation and workshop were built. But there was no compromise on essential facilities. For instance, the Priority Committee suggested the acquisition of additional 300 acres for building cottages for staff. These 'cottages', with a floor area of 500 square feet each, for housing technical and scientific staff were built using the design provided by Messrs Heatly and Gresham.

Zaheer was a stickler for details and aesthetics, personally monitoring the building project and actively seeking help from different sources and personal contacts. For instance, he was in touch with a Bombay businessman M.H. Hasham Premji for procuring teak and timber for the laboratory buildings. The two had first met in connection with the transfer of technology for making castor oil at Premji's vanaspati plant at Amalner. In early 1953, Premji enquired about the government tender for the supply of teak and offered his help. Zaheer informed that a quotation from Malai Timber Mart had been received and asked if Premji could suggest other suppliers from Bombay. Premji replied, 'It is no use giving the names of merchants as they are bound to cheat in prices. I shall, therefore, collect quotations and write to you. If you then wish to purchase the items, please arrange to have the money remitted and I shall have the items purchased departmentally and forward them to you.'[6]

For insurance of the new building which was to house costly equipment, Zaheer contacted S.R. Kidwai, an acquaintance working as an agent in the Bombay-based Eastern Federal Union Insurance Company Limited. Kidwai suggested approaching an English insurance firm but felt that 'in the present setup the Central Government' would not prefer an English company'. Then an estimate from New India Insurance was obtained. To address the problem of rats and mice in certain sections of the laboratory, help came from an unexpected quarter—America. During the visit of an executive from the New York–based engineering firm Foster Wheeler Corporation, Zaheer mentioned the pest menace in the laboratory. Upon his return, the executive shipped a can of Warfarin, which had been introduced in the US for pest control.

The Tussle over Control and Role

While the new building was coming up and interim funds were released for running the laboratory, the Hyderabad cabinet expressed its inability to find financial resources for the completion of the CLSIR building and purchase of equipment for some time and requested the Central government to take it over.[7] It argued that shortage of funds would lead 'to the postponement of the utilization of even that portion of the new buildings part of which is now almost ready'.[8] The Ministry of States declined the proposal in October 1951 and asked Hyderabad to approach Planning Commission and NRSR Ministry for funding.[9]

Prime Minister Nehru did not want the laboratory to suffer due to uncertainties connected with the future of Hyderabad. He said, 'There is a possibility of the state being split up. Even if the state continues as an integral unit, there is a likelihood of internal troubles and political conflicts between rival groups. This will bring down the quality of the administration and probably little interest might be taken in the research laboratory.'[10] But he left the question of providing recurring expenses of Rs 5 lakh annually to the finance minister. The finance question was critical as almost one dozen new laboratories all over the country were coming up under CSIR and each of them needed huge resources.

Dr Syed Husain Zaheer belonged to a prominent political family from Uttar Pradesh. His father, Syed Wazir Hasan, was the chief justice of the Awadh High Court and a contemporary of Motilal Nehru, while his elder brother, Syed Ali Zaheer, was the law minister in the interim cabinet formed in 1946. His mother, Lady Wazir Hasan, participated in the Non-cooperation Movement. Dr Syed Husain Zaheer himself worked with Nehru in the Indian National Congress during the freedom struggle and was in prison for one year. As a member of the United Provinces legislative assembly, Zaheer worked with Govind Ballabh Pant, Keshav Dev Malviya and Sri Prakasa, all of whom, after Independence, held important posts in Nehru's cabinet or the Uttar Pradesh government. This gave Zaheer easy access to the corridors of power in New Delhi, yet winning support from the Finance ministry for CLSIR was tough for him.

Nehru, who visited CLSIR along with Maulana Abul Kalam Azad (minister for Scientific Research), allayed the fears that the work of CLSIR was regional. He felt that the research centre was of 'national importance deserving encouragement and support'.[11] Boosted by such support, Zaheer cajoled the Hyderabad government to send a more ambitious proposal to the Centre in September 1953 seeking the following: a non-recurring grant of Rs 19.50 lakh for completion of the building, a recurring annual 'block grant' of Rs 3.10 lakh and a non-recurring grant of Rs 24.72 lakh for purchase of equipment.

Officials in the NRSR ministry were willing to rescue CLSIR to the extent of Rs 2 lakh for non-recurring expenses and Rs 1.5 lakh for recurring expenses, but the ministry's secretary and the director of CSIR Shanti Swarup Bhatnagar rejected the demand altogether, saying 'CSIR gives ad hoc grants and not recurring grants' and that too only to all-India institutions and not those owned by states. NRSR minister Keshav Dev Malviya overruled Bhatnagar, saying research work of CLSIR such as refining of oil, preparing disinfectant from custard fruit seeds and coal washing was of all-India significance. The minister suggested that NCL director Dr G.I. Finch should be sent to ascertain if the research work was 'useful and purposeful' for financial assistance.

The delay in decision-making irked Nehru. He told the NRSR ministry that if Finch, who was sent to inspect the laboratories, had not written his report, he could write directly to him on 'what he thought about the general work of those laboratories'.[12] Nehru told Malviya that the Hyderabad lab should be 'encouraged and given the opportunity to do good work'. He noted, 'It is desirable to have some kind of general laboratories of this type in South India, apart from the specialised laboratories we have. But it is essential to have proper coordination with the other laboratories to prevent overlapping and waste of efforts.[13] Upon his return from a foreign tour, Bhatnagar sought to clarify that he was not personally opposed to the grant of financial assistance to CLSIR.[14]

Two days later, the NRSR ministry wrote to the Finance ministry for a grant-in-aid of Rs 3.5 lakh and asked the state government not to reduce its normal contribution to the running of the laboratory. At the same time, the ministry was suspect of Hyderabad's argument regarding the shortage of funds to run the laboratory as a 'recent examination of the State Government reserves (cash and investment) has revealed that the state has sizeable reserves'.[15] Finally, at a meeting held on 11 October 1954 in Bhatnagar's office, Hyderabad agreed to continue to provide a recurring grant of Rs 5.25 lakh while the additional requirement of Rs 3 lakh recurring and Rs 52 lakh non-recurring expenditure (for building and equipment, etc.) was to be met by the Centre.

To a large extent, it was because of Nehru's interest in CLSIR that the financial grant was agreed, though not to the extent Zaheer would have liked. For Zaheer, it was still a battle half-won. Nehru came to Hyderabad to inaugurate the new building of CLSIR on 2 February 1954.

Prime Minister Nehru, CLSIR director Syed Husain Zaheer, Hyderabad chief minister B. Ramakrishna Rao, Princess Durru Shehvar and CSIR director Shanti Swarup Bhatnagar at the inauguration of CLSIR, 1954 (courtesy: Nehru Memorial Museum and Library)

The decision to support CLSIR was taken at a time when the building of scientific institutions under CSIR was at its zenith.

Eleven new national laboratories and five coal survey stations were under development, and more laboratories were in the pipeline with development grants totalling Rs 5.84 crore in the first Five Year Plan.[16] In an atmosphere of intense competition among different labs for resources, Zaheer had to work hard to retain a distinct identity for CLSIR. To his benefit, he, like Bhatnagar, enjoyed direct access to Nehru as well as to minister Malviya and the bureaucracy in New Delhi.

Bhatnagar passed away on 1 January 1955. Maneklal Sankalchand Thacker (director, IISc) was appointed director general of Scientific and Industrial Research (Bhatnagar was the director). Thacker took charge of CSIR on 3 August 1955, while still in Bangalore. Before this, he submitted the report of another panel that CSIR had formed to examine the modalities of CLSIR's merger with CSIR. Based on this report, on 29 September 1955 BSIR recommended the takeover, saying it should be 'administered the same way as other national laboratories of CSIR.'

After years of uncertainty, CLSIR finally became a part of CSIR. The 'central' in its name was dropped and it was renamed Regional Research Laboratory (RRL). Subsequently, CSIR established more RRLs to handle 'scientific and technological problems of special importance' in their respective regions.[17]

Research Agenda and Institutional Identity

Along with securing much-needed funding from the Central government for the completion of the building project and purchase of equipment, Zaheer needed to build a research programme and teams of scientists and technicians to implement the programme. In the year of its transfer to CSIR, the laboratory had thirty-five research scientists and twenty-eight technical staff. In November 1956, applications were called for the posts of deputy director, assistant directors, senior scientific officers and junior scientific officers. Given that it was an industrial research laboratory, it needed people with both research and industrial experience. Those shortlisted were from industry, defence establishments and CSIR labs.

The first lot of people selected were mostly those who had been working in CLSIR. Dr D.S. Datar, selected as assistant director (heavy chemicals), joined CLSIR in 1946. Dr Gurbachan Singh Sidhu was appointed assistant director (organic, pharmaceuticals and drugs). An organic chemist, Sidhu had research stints in Germany, Austria, Switzerland and the UK in micro-organic chemistry, isotopic compounds and fine chemicals. For the post of assistant director (fuels), Dr M.G. Krishna, a PhD from Leeds, was chosen. Dr K.T. Acharya, a PhD from the University of Liverpool, was appointed as assistant director (oilseeds). Among the senior scientific officers appointed was Dr Pushpa Mitra Bhargava who, after his doctorate, had spent three years at the University of Wisconsin for training in general biochemistry and research in the biochemistry of cancer, besides publishing many research papers. Sidhu and Bhargava were students of Zaheer at Lucknow University in the 1940s.

Dr S.A. Saletore was made the deputy director. He joined CLSIR in 1950 after working in Alembic Chemical Works, Howrah Oil Mills and Snowhite Food Products Company for two decades. He had also been the director of Laxminarayana Institute of Technology, Nagpur. The selection panel found Saletore suitable for appointment on a starting salary of Rs 1,600 per month but wished that he be informed that he should not consider his appointment as 'qualifying in any way as a leading step in the Directorship of the laboratory'. The selection committee report was sent to the prime minister who was also the president of CSIR. Nehru wrote 'I agree' on 22 February 1958.

During his visits to universities and research institutes in India and abroad, Zaheer would identify young, promising researchers. If he spotted such people in scientific symposia or sessions of the Indian Science Congress, he interviewed them informally and invited them to Hyderabad. Formal appointments were, however, made through the Public Service Commission or a research fellowship. 'One day he came to the chemistry department (of Osmania University) to deliver a lecture and I was supposed to introduce him to the audience. After the lecture, he asked me to see him in RRL the next day. He said I could pursue my PhD while working at RRL,' recalled G. Thyagarajan, who joined RRL in 1957 and rose to become its director in 1981.[18] 'Zaheer brought bright people from all over, nurtured them and let them flourish and go out to other places. That's how RRL produced several leaders,' according to Thyagarajan.

Along with these appointments, Zaheer sought higher salaries for some scientific officers who were appointed in CLSIR and then became a part of RRL. This included Bharat Bhushan, Baldev Singh, M.A. Wahab, N. Sambasiva Rao, R.J. Sujir, B.S. Narayan Rao, R. Vaidyeswaran, A. Rahman and I.K. Kacker. Wahab was an MS in ceramic technology from Ohio State University, while Sujir had worked in Canada under a fellowship granted by the National Research Council of Canada. Rahman had a doctorate in biochemistry from Sheffield University and was mentored by J.D. Bernal who pioneered the concept of 'social functions of science'. Kacker was trained in Germany as a recipient of the Alexander von Humboldt scholarship.

The selection committees that went through the elaborate exercise of picking the right candidates for RRL would have hardly realised that they were selecting future leaders of Indian science. Many of those selected were to become directors and founders of labs and even become director general of CSIR in the decades to follow.

The primary objective of the laboratory was to conduct research to facilitate the industrial-scale use of raw materials like minerals, coal, sugarcane, cotton, oilseeds and forest produce available in Hyderabad. The research programme was organised under different sections, such as vegetable oils, fibres, biochemistry, pharmaceuticals and drugs, fuel, heavy chemicals, ceramics and chemical engineering. Once processes were developed, pilot plants were set up to demonstrate their efficacy to the industry.

In the formative years, studies in the vegetable oils section focused on custard apple seed oil (removal of toxicity, isolation of insecticidal principle, industrial utilisation, etc.), preparation of fatty acids, dehydration of castor oil, activation of Hyderabad earths for bleaching purposes, analysis of fatty acids in cottonseed of different Hyderabad varieties, halogenations of vegetable oils and fatty acids, and so on. The laboratory ordered a 7 gallon pilot plant 'to demonstrate practically how castor oil can be processed to give high-quality drying oil for the manufacture of surface coatings'.

The work in the Fibre Research Section involved studying cotton linters and casuarina pulp for making cellulose acetate rayon, developing handmade paper from rags, cotton and hosiery waste, developing processes for making lignin, Masonite board using locally available resins and making paper for lamp shades.

The Biotechnical Section worked on pilot plants for the production of food yeast, preparation of lactic acid by fermentation of molasses (in collaboration with the Nizam Sugar Factory), preparation of calcium levulinate, citric acid fermentation and itaconic acid fermentation.

In the Pharmaceuticals and Drugs Section, work involved the synthesis of analgesics, preparation of sesamin, synthesis of compounds of turpentine oil and conversion of brucine to strychnine. The section received an order from England for the supply of 10 tons of fructose based on the process it had developed for making fructose from cane sugar.

The Entomology Section studied the insecticidal and fungicidal properties of indigenous plants as well DDT (Dichloro diphenyl trichloroethane) resistance in houseflies.[19] Some twenty different kinds of non-edible oilseeds, such as bitter almond and thornapple, were collected from local environments, and their oils were extracted and tested on insects in different concentrations.

Zaheer had worked in an industry-oriented laboratory in Germany and handled industrial consultancy in UP and Hyderabad. He was uniquely positioned to orient the laboratory as an industry-linked research centre. He noted, 'There is a growing realisation amongst all thinking people that while a fair amount of research is being done in various laboratories of India, hardly any of it is adapted on an industrial scale and most of it continued to remain unutilised.'[20] Therefore, RRL not just developed processes but conducted trials on a pilot plant scale to demonstrate the technical and economic feasibility of the new processes and techniques.

Along with pilot plants, Zaheer advocated liaison with industries—'meeting industrialists, coming to know their problems and difficulties by trying to solve them, by allowing our staff to go to factories for the erection of plants and starting of new processes'.[21] In its early years, the laboratory worked on projects for the Tatas in coal and hexachlorobenzene, conducted coal surveys for local collieries, provided technical advice on reorganisation and expansion of Hyderabad Chemicals and Pharmaceuticals, and conducted an investigation on engobes for Taj Clay Works.

A pilot plant at CLSIR, 1954 (courtesy: Nehru Memorial Museum and Library)

Being a major natural resource available in Hyderabad State as well as in the newly formed Andhra Pradesh, coal was a key area of research. The region had one of the oldest coal mines at Kothagudem, initially operating as Hyderabad (Deccan) Company Limited and then as Singareni Collieries Company Limited (SCCL). The state-owned company devolved to the Government of Andhra Pradesh in 1956. RRL developed processes for the utilisation of low-grade coals of Kothagudem by developing technologies for LTC, coal-tar distillation, briquetting of coal-char into domestic coking fuel, moving-bed pressure gasification of coal for power generation and so on. Several processes were transferred to the industry after pilot plant studies at RRL.[22]

Of Smokeless Coal and Town Gas

The first pilot plant for LTC with a capacity of 25 tons per day was imported from Lurgi, a German company, for conducting experiments with the Hyderabad coals. Besides the coal-based fuel coke, the plant yielded tar from which products like petrol, lubricating oils and ammonia fertilisers could be produced.[23] The processes were developed for making smokeless domestic fuel, recovering crude motor spirit from gases released during carbonisation, recovery and fractionation of tar acids from tar oils and liquor, hydrogenation of LTC tars and oils, cracking of LTC tar and briquetting of non-coking coal fines.

In addition to developing processes for industrial use, RRL used the pilot plant to make commercial products. One such product was smokeless coke which could be used as domestic fuel. In a bold move, the laboratory decided to market it under its own brand name, Kolsite, after conducting a market survey during 1958-59 on domestic fuels in Hyderabad and Secunderabad. The survey found that firewood and cow dung cakes were the predominant fuels used for cooking in households as well as restaurants. Just 13 per cent of households used coal and charcoal. Firewood was a preferred fuel because of its low price—Rs 46 to Rs 55 per metric ton. 'If the price of Kolsite can be brought down sufficiently to Rs 60 to Rs 80 per ton (from Rs 124 per ton), with proper propaganda, Kolsite can easily replace firewood,' the survey concluded.[24]

The RRL plant produced about 4,000 tons of Kolsite a year as against the market potential of 7,000 tons in Hyderabad city. The technology for Kolsite production was later commercialised by SCCL which established a plant of 900 tons per day capacity. Zaheer proposed that LTC plants based on local coals available could be established near coalfields in India's four regions for 'convenient production and distribution of smokeless domestic fuels'.[25]

Another idea for the utilisation of coal that Zaheer put forth to the government was the supply of town gas in Hyderabad and Secunderabad using fuel gas produced through the gasification of coal. He proposed a pressure gasification plant near the coal mines at Kothagudem and transportation of the gas to Hyderabad through pipelines at high pressure. On the way, the gas could be supplied to towns such as Warangal, Jangaon and Bhongir. Based on market surveys and projected demands, he proposed a pressure gasification plant with a capacity of 7.5 million cubic feet per day. A long-distance pipeline was proposed along railway tracks, while in the city it was to be along main roads.

Zaheer envisaged a network of gas pipelines from major coal mines to serve domestic as well as industrial consumers across India. At that time, only parts of Bombay and Calcutta were provided with piped gas supply for domestic use. He was keen to pursue the idea, but it was scuttled despite RRL getting equipment to develop a pilot facility in 1966. Zaheer recalled later that Prime Minister Nehru had approved his plan in 1954 but it did not take off because 'it could not be fully comprehended by our technicians and administrators in view of its novelty' and due to the prevailing optimism about 'finding large deposit-reserves of oil in India'.[26]

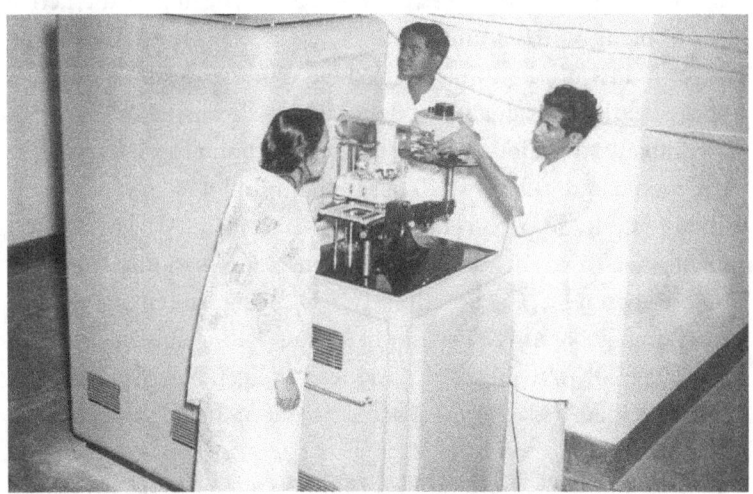

Scientists in a lab of CLSIR (courtesy: Nehru Memorial Museum and Library)

Another technology RRL industrially commercialised was activated or active carbon. Although charcoal was known as a purifying agent for centuries, its purification properties in military operations were demonstrated only during the First World War. Active carbon later found applications in processes for separation and purification in food, pharmaceuticals, chemicals and so on. In India, in the 1950s, active carbon was used for decolorising vegetable oils and glucose as well as for water treatment and in the pharmaceutical industry. RRL developed the know-how for the production of gas adsorption or vapour removal grade of active carbon (used for gas masks for protection against toxic gases) from coconut shells using zinc chloride as an activating agent.[27] The technology was based on a fluidised bed reactor in which raw materials were processed, along with fluidising gases, at elevated temperatures.

Zaheer got in touch with Industrial and Agricultural Engineering Company (IAEC), a trading firm based in Bombay which was importing active carbon from West Germany and supplying to the chemical industry for bleaching vegetable oils, glycerine, sugar and starch solutions; adsorption of solvents and purification of water.[28] Zaheer requested IAEC to explore becoming agents of the active carbon made by RRL under the brand name Hykol. After trials in user industries, he informed IAEC, 'Our carbon is as good in respects as the best quality carbon obtained from ICI.'[29] In 1957, the company sold about 50 tons of active carbon produced at RRL. IAEC purchased it for Rs 840 per ton and sold it at the maximum price of Rs 1,250 a ton after paying for freight, packaging and allowing for discounts and commissions. The National Research and Development Corporation (NRDC) signed an agreement with Bombay-based Voltas Limited after RRL's agreement with IAEC expired. Active carbon produced indigenously and used in the Indian industry was a great achievement of the young industrial laboratory.

Though India had several paper mills making a variety of paper and newsprint, special quality papers like imitation art paper, real art paper, tissue paper, butter paper, airmail paper and parchment paper were still being imported at a high cost. RRL worked on special papers and handmade paper using locally available raw materials. A pilot plant was established for drawing and bond paper as well as filter paper using first-cut cotton linters. Trials were conducted in 1957 for making 'document paper' for the National Archives and high-bursting strength paper for the Ministry of Defence. Sheets of bond paper bearing a monogram as a watermark were prepared for some universities and insurance companies.[30] Handmade paper made at the laboratory was sold commercially to printing presses and other buyers in Hyderabad. RRL's annual report was printed on handmade paper produced at the laboratory.

Several investigations were initiated in the 1950s to study heavy chemicals, fertilisers, catalysts and inorganic chemicals. Pilot plant studies were conducted on the processes developed for the manufacture of white cement from feldspar. A twin-chambered jacketed cement clinker of stainless steel was designed and fabricated for the plant, while marble-limestone, limestone, gypsum and feldspar were procured from Rajasthan. The cement produced at 1,400 degree centigrade was tested for compressive strength by making cylindrical briquettes of cement mortar under stress. The results were compared with the white cement available in the market. 'The cement produced in the Laboratory was whiter than any other Indian brands of white cement and compared favourably with imported brands,' the laboratory stated.[31]

The industry-oriented research projects and pilot plant production at RRL attracted international attention. The new methods for making white cement from feldspar and activated carbon were among the top inventions that were reported in international technical press such as the *Chemical and Engineering News* published by the American Chemical Society.[32]

While keeping its focus on useful industrial research, RRL scientists did not ignore basic research. They regularly published technical papers in leading Indian and international research journals and filed patent applications. Between 1949 and 1963, Zaheer's name figured as a co-inventor in seventy-eight Indian patents in organic chemistry, coal technology, oils and fats, surface coatings, heavy chemicals and fertilisers and other fields.[33] The list of co-inventors included K.N. Moorthy, Baldev Singh, Bharat Bhushan, Sardar Mahboob, C.R. Reddy, G. Thyagarajan, G.S. Sidhu, M.B. Naidu, S. Iqbal Ahmed, N.K.

Sogani, P.B. Sattur, Y.S. Sadanandam, K. Bhanumati, Pramila Rao, Shanta Bai Moray, M.G. Krishna, D.P. Agrawal, B.S. Narayan Rao, D.S. Datar, H.A. Khan, S.A. Satetore, K.T. Acharya, V.P. Harigopal, C.C. Ninan, S. Raghavendar Rao, M.C. Menon, M.A. Sivasamban, E.R. Saxena, Razia Osmani and M.K. Chary.

Fostering Research Culture

The emphasis on pilot plants to demonstrate the know-how developed at the laboratory and proactive engagement with industry formed a part of the 'innovation chain' that sought to link research with industry and society. A crucial part of this chain was operational research in which CLSIR was an early pioneer. While Zaheer was a great proponent of applied and industrial research, the idea of operational research as a tool for the management of scientific and industrial research came from Abdur Rahman who was influenced by the 'social functions of science' theory of J.D. Bernal. Operational research methods were applied to the research activities of the lab as well as to selected industries in the state. The objective was to 'introduce planned work in both, realize the handicaps and bottlenecks, thereby have more of efficiency which we feel is necessary if India is to advance in applied research and industrial production'.[34]

Scientific research, according to Zaheer, had three stages of development. The first stage was of seeking knowledge. The second stage involved exploring possibilities of benefiting humankind and examining the stage of its utilisation in society. The third stage, which Zaheer called operational research, was to examine questions like: Has the discovery been properly employed? Can it be improved? Or should it be discarded in favour of something more efficient? These questions imply ethical, economic, psychological, social and technical examinations of the problem, and statistical data becomes necessary for the correct decision.[35] The involvement of scientists in studying air defence in Britain during the Second World War was an example of operations research. The operational research, Zaheer elaborated, was 'that level of research where different uses of a discovery or invention, its efficiency and degree of utilisation are qualitatively evaluated and conclusions made to serve as a working basis for socio-technical decisions'.

An outcome of this thinking was the Operational Research Unit (ORU) at RRL, which came up in 1949. It consisted of research workers, chemical engineers, operational research teams and the director. It helped in formulating research projects keeping in view their background, perspective of utilisation and multi-sectoral coordination. The unit conducted an economic assessment of a research scheme using available information on prices and availability of raw materials, consumption and requirement of the main product and the extent of the potential market. If needed, fresh market and industrial surveys were conducted to gather relevant information.

After the economic feasibility of a project was established through laboratory and pilot plant studies, a non-technical note was prepared and circulated to the industry and others interested. The note contained information on technical personnel and equipment needed for commercialisation. An example of this practice was the note on high acetyl value castor oil which Zaheer sent in July 1952 to M.H. Hasham Premji, the Bombay-based 'rice, cotton general merchant' who owned a vanaspati factory in Amalner. The manufacturing cost of castor oil of high acetyl value, according to the note, 'will mainly depend upon the choice of the solvent, the efficiency of the plant and the efficient solvent recovery unit'.[36] Premji's company, Western India Vegetable Products Limited, was later rechristened as Wipro Products Limited and finally, Wipro Limited. His son, Azim Premji, took over the business after Hasham Premji's death in 1966 and diversified into information technology in 1979.

The interface of RRL with industry occurred through various means like direct technical assistance to public and private industries and regular visits of scientists to industries to understand technical problems and the functioning of equipment and practices. All research programmes were given a 'project orientation' with clearly defined objectives and targets (short, medium and long term).

Projects were executed by interdisciplinary teams working under a project leader appointed based on competence and not hierarchical seniority. The laboratory staff maintained only two types of relationships—a 'scientific relationship' based on cooperation among members of a research team, and the relationship between an individual scientist and the director to deal with personal problems.[37] Scientists had direct access to the director without 'an intervening hierarchical ladder.'[38]

Zaheer would take a round of the laboratory every day and talk to people about the progress of projects. This helped in addressing minor problems and also helped him develop a rapport with the scientific staff. He would have lunch in the office canteen and instruct the staff not to keep a separate table for him. Scientists wrote to Zaheer about their work and personal issues even while he was travelling abroad. All important decisions were taken in a collective, informal atmosphere and authority was delegated to scientists though the responsibility remained with the director, as per rules. Saturday colloquiums on research topics and general scientific issues in the laboratory, and informal 'Wednesday Group' meetings at the director's residence, promoted an open atmosphere for scientific enquiry and intellectual discourse on broader issues concerning science and society.

In its tumultuous journey that began in 1917 in the princely Hyderabad, the industrial laboratory traversed a long distance to become, in 1955, a part of the emerging scientific infrastructure of an independent nation. From being a small analytical laboratory housed in a government distillery, it transformed into a robust, multidisciplinary research outfit catering to the needs of industrialisation and import substitution. It carved a niche for itself in Nehru's efforts of nation-building through the application of science and technology. In Hyderabad, as the only scientific institution of its kind and size in the city, it became a nucleus of scientific development, giving birth to new ideas and new institutions. It also became the nursery of future leaders of Indian science. One of the most notable contributions of the laboratory was in the development of drugs, as elaborated in Chapter 12.

7

The Early Movers

∽

O N 31 MARCH 1953, A MOMENTOUS EVENT TOOK PLACE IN
Hyderabad. Union Health minister Rajkumari Amrit Kaur laid
the foundation stone for the new campus of Nutritional Research
Laboratories (NRL) in the city. This was the first Central government
scientific institution to be located in Hyderabad. The two existing
academic and research institutions—Osmania University and
CLSIR—were a legacy of the Nizam era and functioned under the
Hyderabad State government. The plan to make Osmania University
a Centrally run institution had run into a political controversy and
CLSIR was yet to be transferred to the Central government. A
colonial-era laboratory, NRL operated at Coonoor in the Nilgiri
Hills for three decades before being shifted to Hyderabad.

The decision to shift NRL from Coonoor to Hyderabad was
mostly for logistic reasons, and it proved lucky for Hyderabad. Maj.
Gen. S.L. Bhatia, formerly an officer of the Indian Medical Service
(IMS) who served in the two World Wars, was posted in Hyderabad
as the inspector general of Medical and Health Services. At the
foundation laying ceremony for NRL, he observed that 'Hyderabad

was not fortunate enough to attract' any of the many national laboratories established in different parts of India. But he expected that 'the establishment of NRL will be the beginning from which we may hope that other similar research institutes may be established here to enable this city and the State to contribute to the general scientific activities of the country'.[1] Bhatia's words proved prophetic. In 2023, Hyderabad was home to an estimated 200 knowledge institutions—universities, academic bodies, research laboratories and commercial R&D units.

The Osmania University and CLSIR, located in what used to be the eastern periphery of the city, became the nucleus for the development of Hyderabad's first knowledge cluster. Before discovering how it happened, let's explore how an unsung organisation, the Hyderabad Science Society (HSS), the first privately run scientific society, contributed to Hyderabad's journey to stardom in the twenty-first century.

In the mid-twentieth century, visiting scientists from other parts of India and abroad were a source of new ideas and inspiration for Hyderabad students interested in science. The visit of Harvard astronomer Harlow Shapely helped M.K. Vainu Bappu, a student at Nizam College, pursue higher studies in astronomy in America as detailed in Chapter 1. One of his juniors, Sanjar Ali Khan, was interested in tinkering with instruments and helped Bappu assemble an astrograph that Bappu installed at his house. Khan, along with his friend Zia Hashmi, decided to pursue this hobby of making scientific instruments. The two pooled their savings and formed the Hyderabad Science Society (HSS) in October 1948. They enrolled like-minded youngsters as members. One of them, S.M. Asghar, offered the garage in his residence at Red Hills to the Society for its activities.

Khan's interest in instrument-making was kindled by his science teacher, an Australian missionary, at St. George's Grammar School. 'He was a gifted person. He built a gas plant in the school to supply gas for the science lab, assembled his car from scrap material, was an expert in carpentry, he fabricated handloom to teach us weaving,' recalled Khan.[2] He found the atmosphere in Nizam College vastly different, consisting of mostly classroom lectures and some basic lab work meant to prepare students for civil and mechanical engineering. The young students wanted to work in new areas of science and so they thought of building their lab. They persuaded their physics professor, J.C. Kameswara Rav, to be the president of HSS. Rav's PhD supervisor was Nobel laureate C.V. Raman.

The first task was to get a proper working space for the Society, which till this point was functioning from the garage of one of its founders. The principal of Nizam College, P.K. Ghosh, wanted to encourage the group but he was unable to give any space in the college buildings as HSS would not qualify as an 'approved academic activity'. The college was housed in what was earlier the palace of Paigah noble Asad Ali Khan. It had several outhouses and stables. The boys enthusiastically welcomed Ghosh's offer to let them use one of the stables because it would be enough for a modest lab and workshop. 'We chose two emerging subjects—nuclear physics and electronics—which were hot favourites after the War,' Khan said. Subsequently, HSS managed to get a two-storeyed building of PWD allocated to it, besides a small grant from the government's Industrial Trust Fund (ITF).

The building of Hyderabad Science Society (photograph: author)

The group's first project was to fabricate a cloud chamber to detect ionising particles. It involved the machining of precision valves, pistons, vacuum-tight seals and so on. Khan and his colleagues then fabricated a Van de Graff high-voltage particle accelerator. The dome-shaped contraption that generates static electricity is no big deal now, but in the 1940s it was a challenge. The Hyderabad boys first built a prototype of 250 kV, and then a dome-shaped accelerator which could go up to 750 kV. 'The different configurations of the dome were hand-hammered over a concrete mandrill, insulating columns were fashioned out of hollow earthen-ware pipes, and we also solved the problem of ever crumbling rubber endless-belt. Building up 500 kV of static electricity in the accelerator was a significant achievement,' remembers Khan.[3]

Encouraged by its success, HSS wrote to the Atomic Energy Commission (AEC) for a grant for further work on the generator. Khan followed this up by meeting AEC chairman Dr Homi Jehangir Bhabha in Bombay. During a visit to Hyderabad in January 1954, Bhabha and NPL director Dr K.S. Krishnan visited HSS to see the accelerator. Another high-profile visitor in the same month was Dr G. Randers, director of Norway's Joint Establishment of Nuclear Energy. Impressed by the effort, Randers arranged to send from Norway a small quantity of heavy water for the production of neutrons.

The indigenous production of electronic measuring instruments and controls was yet to begin. Imports were difficult due to high prices and the foreign exchange crunch. Therefore, scientific and academic institutions looked for alternate sources. Hyderabad Science Society addressed their needs and fabricated a range of basic electronic testing and measuring equipment for institutions in Hyderabad and elsewhere. For Nizamiah Observatory, HSS made many kinds of equipment: a 50-feet antenna, special receiver for atmospheric and solar flares, electron counting photometer, constant frequency drive for its spectrohelioscope and Grubb telescope. Hyderabad Science Society made a nuclear detection instrument for the Radium Institute and Cancer Hospital (later renamed Mehdi Nawaz Jung Cancer Hospital and Radium Institute). Research institutes like RRL, Engineering Research Laboratories and local industries sought its help in electronics and instrumentation. Subsequently, HSS diversified into the development of industrial robots and training aids.

For nuclear research, HSS approached AEC with a proposal to establish a full-fledged Institute of Nuclear Physics jointly with Osmania University. The vice chancellor of Osmania University, Suri Bhagwantam offered a piece of land on the university campus for the building. Atomic Energy Commission was willing to help if 'the university agreed to undertake the responsibility of running the institute'.[4] Meanwhile, Hyderabad was merged with the newly carved Andhra Pradesh in November 1956. The new government wanted the institute to be developed at Andhra University, not Osmania. This was not acceptable to AEC, which said its approval was subject to Osmania University participating in the project. Hyderabad lost the opportunity. Atomic Energy Commission, however, continued to fund projects and, in 1968, Bhabha Atomic Research Centre (BARC) established a radioisotope centre at HSS, the first outside BARC.

At a time when scientific and industrial institutions in Hyderabad were shaping up and expanding their activities, HSS fulfilled the critical need for electronic instrumentation. Through a range of services, it met the requirements of the industry, academic institutions and research laboratories in Hyderabad and the rest of the country. In addition, it helped promote scientific awareness in the general public through outreach programmes. Hyderabad Science Society stands out as a unique example of non-governmental R&D in India.

From Coonoor to Hyderabad

The site identified for the proposed nuclear research centre of HSS was located right opposite the main gate of RRL. The plan for a nuclear centre was shelved but the co-location of Osmania University and RRL attracted other research councils to consider Hyderabad for establishing new research laboratories. The Indian Council of Medical Research (ICMR) was the first one to do so. It shifted its oldest lab, NRL, from Coonoor to Hyderabad. Osmania University allocated 20 acres of land to ICMR to build a campus for NRL.

Set up in 1918, NRL functioned from a few rooms in the Pasteur Institute of South India, which had been functioning in Coonoor since 1907. The Pasteur Institute of South India was a part of the network of such research centres established in many parts of the world in the late nineteenth century as a legacy of the pioneering research in vaccination and bacteriology by the French scientist Louis Pasteur. These institutes produced vaccines for rabies, cholera, plague and other infectious diseases. Two Pasteur Institutes in India were situated in Mukteshwar and Shillong. For South India, Coonoor was chosen because of its salubrious climate. As medical research expanded, Indian Research Fund Association (IRFA) was established for better coordination.

IRFA initiated several 'enquiries' to investigate specific diseases. One such enquiry was on beriberi, a nutritional disease caused due to deficiency of vitamin B. The objective was to explore the role of sanitation, vector control and the relationship between diets and diseases. The project headed by Lt Col. Robert McCarrison was housed in a few rooms in the Pasteur Institute. It was later shifted to the premises of a discontinued jam factory owned by the Government of Madras.[5]

With experiments on pigeons, McCarrison concluded that polished rice was 'the principal dietary factor in the causation of Beriberi'.[6] More nutrition-related studies in animals and observations in humans showed that one of the major causes of goitre was 'deficiencies of vitamin A, C, iodine etc' and 'goitrogenic substances present in foodstuff such as cabbage, groundnuts, maize etc'.[7] Based on its work, the unit was given a wider mandate and renamed as Deficiency Diseases Enquiry in 1925. At the recommendation of the Royal Agricultural Commission which found malnutrition as a cause of physical inefficiency and ill health among masses in India, the lab was converted into a full-fledged nutrition research unit. It was named NRL with McCarrison as its first director.

Dr W.R. Aykroyd, who succeeded McCarrison in 1935, was an expert in applied nutrition. He initiated a systematic analysis of the nutrient composition of commonly consumed Indian foods for assessing the adequacy of Indian diets. Nutritional Research Laboratories conducted diet and nutrition surveys in different parts of the country and also trained workers of public health departments in provinces and princely states to conduct similar surveys on their own.[8]

In 1940, the Hyderabad Department of Public Health created a nutrition unit with an officer trained at NRL as its incharge to conduct a nutrition survey in eight districts. People from different strata, like farmers, agricultural labourers, traders and so on, were surveyed. Along with this, magic lantern lectures were arranged on 'food and nutrition' to educate people about the 'good and ill effects of different types of diets'.[9] The survey found high consumption of milled rice, low intake of leafy vegetables and the presence of fluorosis in some villages. As a remedial measure, the Agriculture department was told to popularise the cultivation of jowar and ragi in place of maize and help the development of kitchen gardens.

Though NRL had an expanded footprint of nutrition research in India, it was not equipped for clinical research and had to depend on hospitals in Madras for clinical studies. A post-War review of the health sector, under the chairmanship of Joseph B. Bhore, found that the government was 'unable to make the fullest use of the Coonoor laboratories on account of their great distance from the Capital'. The panel recommended the creation of 'a strong central nutrition organization with staff and laboratories adequate to form a permanent centre for research, reference advisory and advanced training work'.[10] The recommendations of the Bhore panel led to the reorganisation of IRFA as ICMR after Independence.

The work of NRL also figured in the Constituent Assembly debates. The Assembly recommended that NRL should start a diploma course in nutrition 'to create a larger number of trained medical and non-medical personnel required by states to implement their nutritional policies satisfactorily'. For this, NRL needed better infrastructure and relocation to a central place with full facilities for running the course.[11]

Initially, the Madras government was asked if it could spare some land for the institute. 'The land was not available, except at a very high price, forcing the Governing Body to decide in favour of Hyderabad.[12] The state government in Hyderabad promised a large piece of land in the vicinity of the Osmania University. In addition, it offered NRL access to a certain number of patients at Osmania General Hospital and Niloufer Hospital for Women and Children for clinical studies. The Niloufer Hospital had just been set up with an endowment from Niloufer Khanum Sultan, the Ottoman princess who was married to Moazzam Jah (the second son of Mir Osman Ali Khan).

Nutritional Research Laboratories could also benefit from collaboration with Osmania University's science departments such as biochemistry, physiology and animal husbandry. Other advantages of Hyderabad were its central location with 'easy access to most parts of India' and the prevalence of a variety of dietary practices.[13] The foundation for a new building for NRL was laid on 31 March 1953, and the lab was fully shifted from Coonoor to Hyderabad in January 1959.

For guidance and material support, NRL looked to CLSIR, which by now had become a Central institute called RRL. V.N. Patwardhan, the first Indian to become the director of NRL in 1947, was in touch with RRL director Zaheer in early 1957. He visited RRL with a view to 'profit from its experience' and consulted Zaheer on 'some matters pertaining to the equipment'. After the building got ready, he wrote to Zaheer saying 'members of my staff may, on occasions, need to refer and consult books and journals in the library of your institute'. Zaheer readily agreed and arranged a meeting between Dr P.G. Tulpule of NRL and Baldev Singh of RRL.

After it shifted to Hyderabad, NRL's research agenda expanded rapidly. Its research covered a wide spectrum: the nutritive value of Indian foods, childhood malnutrition, protein-rich foods, Lathyrism, energy metabolism, fortification, pellagra, Kwashiorkor, fluorosis, drug toxicology, protein energy malnutrition, vitamin A deficiency, pregnancy and lactation. During the golden jubilee of NRL in 1968, NRL was renamed as the National Institute of Nutrition (NIN) in recognition of the wide scope and impact of its work. It was given the task of conducting 'operational research connected with planning and implementation of national nutrition programmes' such as the Integrated Child Development Scheme (ICDS) and the Mid-day Meal Scheme. The lab added new facilities like the National Nutrition Monitoring Bureau and the animal house (which later became a national facility, National Animal Resource Facility for Biomedical Research, located in Genome Valley). The development of nutrient requirements for Indians and recommended dietary allowances (RDA) was a landmark work.

Exploring the Earth and the Atmosphere

Long before India became independent, the planning for economic development and industrialisation was set in motion under the aegis of the National Planning Committee (NPC) formed by Subhas Chandra Bose, the president of the Indian National Congress. Natural resource planning was one of the key areas of this process. The National Planning Committee stressed the economic value of systematic exploration of natural resources and their use for economic development. Soon after Independence, reorganisation of existing scientific institutions was initiated to align them with national needs like utilisation of natural resources, demand for energy and power generation.

In addition to prospecting for mineral resources by the Geological Survey of India (GSI), small scientific groups were engaged in airborne geophysical surveys to collect magnetic and gravity data using different sensors mounted on aircraft. The Oil and Natural Gas Commission (ONGC) was engaged in prospecting for petroleum, while the Survey of India conducted geodesic and triangulation studies. Seismological observations were conducted by the India Meteorological Department (IMD). Geophysical studies were thus underway in different organisations. But the country was dependent on the services of foreign companies like Fairchild Aero Corporation for conducting aeromagnetic surveys. The newly established Department of Atomic Energy (DAE) formed the Atomic Minerals Division (AMD) to explore mineral resources needed for atomic energy and develop indigenous equipment and survey capabilities. In 1974, AMD was shifted from Delhi to Hyderabad. There was no single organisation that took care of all aspects of geophysical research.

In 1947, Meghnad Saha, who headed the Planning Committee for Geophysics, foresaw the need for a national centre devoted to geophysical research. For better coordination of the geophysical work of different agencies and universities, the panel recommended the formation of a Standing Committee and a Central Geophysical Institute. As a follow-up, the Central Board of Geophysics (CBG) was constituted in GSI in January 1949. For almost a decade, it acted as a clearing house for geophysics-related projects of IMD, GSI and so on and promoted postgraduate education in applied geophysics.[14] Two units were developed for research—the Geophysical Research Wing at GSI in Calcutta and an Oceanographic Research Wing at the Indian Naval Physical Laboratory at Cochin.

The control of CBG and the two research units was passed on to CSIR in April 1961. In October 1961, CSIR transferred the geophysical research unit and CBG from Calcutta to Hyderabad, renaming them as National Geophysical Research Institute (NGRI) and Geophysics Research Board, respectively. The National Geophysical Research Institute was India's first research laboratory meant for both applied and basic research in geophysics and earth sciences—subjects vital for the exploration of minerals, hydrocarbons and groundwater. It had to draw up its R&D programmes in a manner that supplemented ongoing work in different organisations while exploring new areas of research.[15]

Osmania University became the first home of the new laboratory, just as it was for CLSIR two decades earlier. The National Geophysical Research Institute operated from a few rooms in the basement of the Department of Chemistry, while its administration and finance departments were housed in a rented building near

RRL. Dr Hari Narain, who was the director of ONGC's Research and Training Institute in Dehradun, was invited by CSIR director general Syed Husain Zaheer to take over as NGRI director after Dr M.S. Krishnan's retirement. As the space in Osmania University was too small for NGRI, Narain convinced RRL to accommodate NGRI in its newly constructed staff quarters. The open space around the quarters was used to erect sheds for workshop and maintenance services.

Eventually, NGRI was allotted 150 acres in the Uppal area not far from RRL, to construct its campus. It could move to this new campus only in 1970 as the construction got delayed due to restrictions imposed during the 1965 war. The main building of NGRI was designed by CSIR architects. The building used Y-shaped concrete columns typical of the brutal modernist style of architecture that was preferred for institutional buildings in the 1960s. Pakistani painter Sadequain, who was visiting India in 1982, came to Hyderabad to paint murals. Sadequain was born in Amroha in Uttar Pradesh and was related to a senior scientist of NGRI, Dr Mohammed N. Qureshy. At Qureshy's request, Sadequain visited the laboratory and found the ambience so inspiring that he decided to paint a large mural reflecting the functions of the laboratory. The mural that adorns the wall in front of the main hall became one of the significant works of the artist in India.[16]

In the initial years, NGRI took up detailed surveys for mineral exploration using integrated airborne, magnetic, ground gravity, electrical and electromagnetic surveys. Over the years, NGRI conducted extensive studies of the lithosphere and the earth's interiors; exploration, assessment and management of groundwater; exploration of hydrocarbons and energy resources, including gas hydrates and geothermal energy; earthquake monitoring and hazard assessment; and shallow surface geophysics and geo-environment.

A seismological observatory, the first one in the Indian peninsular shield, was established on the campus and its instruments were calibrated to conform to the Worldwide Standard Seismograph Network (WWSSN) 1966. It so happened that the United States

Geological Services (USGS) established a global network in which
five stations of IMD were included. 'NGRI was not one of them but
Dr Hari Narain was keen to have such a facility in NGRI. I worked
with the USGS scientists at Central Seismological Laboratory in
Shillong, which was an IMD station in the network. A year later
when I joined NGRI, I was asked to set up a station similar to those
in the USGS network but without formal help from the US agency,'
recalled Dr Harsh Gupta, who joined the institute in its formative
years.[17]

*The mural was made by Pakistani artist Sadequain at the National
Geophysical Research Centre in 1982 (photograph: author)*

The observatory recorded a major earthquake that occurred
at Koyna in western Maharashtra on 10 December 1967, which
set Gupta on the trail of his landmark work on reservoir-triggered
seismicity (RTS). He showed that large reservoirs can induce
earthquakes as water permeates to depths, modifying pore pressures
either by reducing the normal pressure on faults or by altering the
chemical composition of the fault material. In the Latur region, a
borehole was drilled to find the nature of faults and the role of fluids

in the generation of earthquakes. Gupta's first book, *Dams and Earthquakes*, published in 1976 when he was just thirty-four, shot him into global fame. Gupta had opted to pursue applied geophysics at the instance of his brother, a mechanical engineer who was working in ONGC. He rose to become the director of NGRI and a key policymaker as the secretary of the Ministry of Earth Sciences. In 1983, Gupta led a pioneering scientific mission to Antarctica, during which India constructed its first wintering station, Dakshin Gangotri, there.

Given the foreign exchange crunch and import restrictions in the 1960s, NGRI took up the fabrication of geophysical instrumentation in India. For instance, a range of precise magnetometers and sensors were developed for airborne magnetic surveys. Electrical resistivity meters, seismic timers and rubidium vapour magnetometer were other instruments developed. The know-how for such instruments was also transferred to the industry in Hyderabad, including to units floated by former NGRI scientists.

The laboratory made serious efforts to develop capability in airborne geophysical surveys in its early years. Hari Narain, who had spent eight years in ONGC before joining NGRI, was acutely aware of the need for such a capability for the exploration of natural resources. The scientists at NGRI modified an ELSEC Proton Precession Magnetometer imported from the UK to make it suitable for airborne work and borrowed from AMD other equipment like an altimeter and a recording camera. The equipment was mounted on a Dakota DC-3 aircraft to conduct an experimental survey over the iron-ore belt of Kudremukh in Karnataka in April 1967.

Aeromagnetic surveys were conducted in Karnataka, Madhya Pradesh and UP. In the same year, two multi-sensor airborne surveys were conducted with foreign assistance—Operation Hard Rock sponsored by the US Agency for International Aid (USAID) and Compagnie Generale De Geophysique sponsored by the French agency BRGM.[18] To independently conduct such surveys, a new organisation, Airborne Mineral Surveys and Exploration (AMSE), was constituted. Yet another collaborative project—this one with the International Institute for Aerial Survey and Earth Sciences,

Netherlands—in 1966 led to the formation of the Indian Photo-Interpretation Institute (IPI) in Dehradun to deal with the analysis of aerial survey data.

Simultaneously, policymakers started looking at the systematic development of aerial surveys and remote sensing. In September 1971, Planning Commission constituted a task force to examine all aspects related to aerial surveys. It had representatives of all organisations concerned—GSI, IMD, AMD, NGRI, ONGC, Indian Space Research Organisation (ISRO) and so on—and it consulted potential users of geophysical data. Mohammed N. Qureshy, an NGRI scientist, was its convener while his colleague D. Gupta Sarma served as a member. After a detailed analysis of remote-sensing techniques, instrumentation, aircraft, ground facilities and manpower, the panel identified a 'technology gap in the use of remote-sensing methods in natural resources surveys' in India and recommended the creation of a dedicated agency for promoting the use of remote sensing and 'generating capability for integrated remote sensing surveys.'[19]

The task force wanted NGRI to be involved in the 'operational, developmental and interpretational aspects' of the remote-sensing programme. Indian Photo-Interpretation Institute was to train technical manpower, along with the Centre for Survey Training and Map Production, a unit of Survey of India in Hyderabad. Today, satellite images can be accessed on smartphones by anyone, but satellite-based remote sensing was yet to be introduced in India in the early 1970s. The newly formed ISRO had just begun work with NASA to get images from the Earth Resources Technology Satellite (ERTS) A and B, as well as Skylab. The proposed national agency for remote sensing was to handle the acquisition, processing, interpretation and compilation of all data (including that obtained by ISRO), and its dissemination for proper utilisation.[20] The agency, the panel recommended, should have at its disposal several aircraft to be operated and maintained by a civil national authority. Indian remote-sensing satellites were not even on the drawing board.

The National Remote Sensing Agency (NRSA) was registered as an autonomous society under the Department of Science and

Technology (DST) in September 1974 and it started functioning in April 1975 in Hyderabad. A piece of land was acquired from Hindustan Aeronautics Limited (HAL) for the construction of a building for NRSA at Balanagar on the outskirts of Hyderabad. A Research Flight Facility was established in Bangalore with a fleet of survey aircraft—Canberra, HS 748, Beaver and Dakota. The unit suffered a major setback in April 1977 when a Dakota on an aero-magnetic survey crashed near Kanigiri in unified Andhra Pradesh after taking off from Madras airport. Five scientists belonging to AMD and five IAF crew members on deputation to NRSA perished in the crash that occurred when the plane 'hit a hillock and came down in flames.'[21]

Meanwhile, IPI, working in Dehradun, was made a part of NRSA in 1976 and four years later, NRSA itself was shifted from DST to ISRO. This change reflected in data acquisition—from aerial photography to satellite imagery. NRSA had to develop the capacity to receive data directly from the satellite and interpret it. NRSA director Wing Commander K.R. Rao was earlier involved in the construction of satellite earth stations at Ahmedabad and Arvi. He used this experience to establish an earth station to receive data directly from NASA's Landsat-2 and Landsat-3 satellites. The state government provided 316 acres of land at Shadnagar for the earth station. The earth station was soon modified to receive data from French SPOT and Franco-German TIROS-N satellites as well. Scientists and technical staff were trained in the operation and maintenance of the earth station with financial assistance from the United Nations Development Programme (UNDP). The data reception facilities at Hyderabad were expanded further when India launched its remote-sensing satellites in 1988.

The potential of remote-sensing data in non-civilian use helped NRSA to convince policymakers to give the go-ahead for rapid expansion of NRSA. For instance, when the Expenditure Finance Committee was deliberating upon the question of funding an upgrade of the earth station for the Landsat-D satellite, K.R. Rao pointed to the 'defence angle'. He explained that the Hyderabad earth station covered 'areas in the North up to southern China and Indo-

Tibetan border, in the East beyond Burma and Bangladesh, and the West including Pakistan and Afghanistan and also parts of Russia and Iran.[22] The pictures obtained from Landsat-C gave 'sufficient details including man-made features like dams, roads, airfields, so forth while Landsat-D can produce even clearers pictures, as the resolution will be up to 30 meters as against 70 meters in Landsat-C'. DST secretary M.G.K. Menon quoted newspaper reports to add that 'the US government is providing China with a sophisticated satellite ground station which could have military applications'.[23]

In addition to the capacity for data acquisition from satellites, NRSA developed facilities for processing data received from remote-sensing satellites with different instruments like optical, microwave and hyper-spectral sensors. In this area, B.L. Deekshatulu, who joined NRSA as head of its Technical division in 1976 and became its director in 1982, played a pivotal role. Before joining NRSA, he was engaged in research in control systems at IISc after completing PhD in electrical engineering there. In 1971, he went on a sabbatical to work at IBM's TJ Watson Research Centre where he developed an interest in digital signal processing and remote sensing. He continued to work in this area, encouraged by IISc Director Satish Dhawan, who was soon to become the chairman of ISRO.

'My team and I built a drum scanner using an old discarded lathe machine in the workshop premises. Darkroom conditions were met using a large tarpaulin cloth draped over the machine and (by) operating the scanner during the night only. One had to bend and get under the tarpaulin cover to work on the scanner,' recalled Deekshatulu in 2020.[24] The team then built a colour drum scanner under a project sponsored by ISRO. Dhawan encouraged Deekshatulu to collect remote-sensing data using the Pushpak aircraft of IISc, after retrofitting it with multispectral cameras. 'We could perform numerous aerial surveys over the nearby places like the citrus plantations in Gonikoppal and the sandalwood plantation at Bannerghatta. We engaged in many interactions with scientists at the University of Agricultural Sciences, the State Horticulture Department, so forth. This being the first time, all of us were excited at the results of photo interpretation,' recounted Deekshatulu.[25]

At NRSA, he established facilities for processing of remote-sensing data, image processing, photo processing and for archiving data. A range of remote-sensing equipment was developed in collaboration with the industries located in Hyderabad—additive colour viewer, image analyser, dual densitometer, microfiche camera, path recovery scanner, data digitiser, optical reflection projector and satellite images processing systems. For data application, NRSA worked with users in sectors like agriculture, land use, disaster management, natural resources management, urban development, forestry and so on. A seminal contribution of NRSA was using remote-sensing data for the preparation of a forest map of India. The map based on satellite data showed large-scale deforestation. This finding was at variance with the maps produced by the Forest Survey of India (FSI). After initial resistance, FSI incorporated a remote-sensing–based technique in its mapping process. This episode demonstrated the operational use of remote-sensing data and it was subsequently introduced in areas like agriculture, hydrology fisheries, land use studies, town planning, disease surveillance and so on.

Over the decades, NRSA, which was renamed as National Remote Sensing Centre in 2008, became the nucleus for further institutional development. In 2010, its Dehradun unit was reorganised as a separate centre of ISRO—Indian Institute of Remote Sensing. Scientific programmes of National Remote Sensing Centre (NRSC) catalysed the formation of new institutions in Hyderabad—Indian National Centre for Ocean Information Services (INCOIS) and Advanced Data Processing Research Institute (ADRIN). INCOIS provides daily ocean forecasts and advisories for fisherfolk. It is recognised as a regional tsunami service provider and shares tsunami warnings with countries in the Indian Ocean Rim.

8

The Chemistry of Life

∽

THOUGH THE USE OF FERMENTATION FOR MAKING alcohol has been known in many cultures for ages, the understanding that fermentation is a chemical process brought about by using microorganisms is relatively new. It was only in the nineteenth century that French chemist Louis Pasteur demonstrated through experiments the action of living yeast in transforming glucose into ethanol.[1] In 1897, German chemist Eduard Buchner showed that living organisms or cells were not necessary for fermentation and that it could take place even with enzymes extracted from dead cells. This knowledge gave birth to a new field of science called biochemistry.

Gilbert John Fowler, a chemist from the University of Manchester, pioneered biochemistry research in India at the Indian Institute of Science in 1915. He trained scientists from Hyderabad in industrial fermentation, which remained a key research area at the Industrial Laboratory, which was merged with CLSIR in 1944. As a part of the reorganisation of research in 1950, a Biochemistry division was formed in CLSIR. Syed Husain Zaheer, the director of CLSIR, recruited a small group of researchers to work under Pushpa Mitra Bhargava who returned from the US in 1958 after completing postdoctoral research. Bhargava initiated new studies in cellular and molecular biology, including those on the mechanism of the formation of itaconic acid, the effect of cell concentration on biological properties of individual cells in cell suspension, metabolism of tissue cells in suspension, protein metabolism of liver cells and metabolism of nucleic acid in bovine sperm.[2]

It was an exciting period in biochemistry globally but most universities in India were teaching it either as a part of chemistry or physiology, or were ignoring it altogether. Given this, the University Grants Commission formed a Biochemistry Review Committee in 1959 to examine the state of biochemistry education and research. The panel chaired by Bires Chandra Guha, an eminent biochemist, included Zaheer among its members. Robert H. Burris, chairman of the Department of Biochemistry at Wisconsin University, who was in India under the Wheat Loan Programme, participated in some of the deliberations. The panel recommended that while university departments should engage in fundamental work in biochemistry, national laboratories could take up 'certain specialized aspects of fundamental work in drug research (rational approach to chemotherapy, enzymes, toxicology, cytology, etc.)'.[3]

Zaheer participated in planning biochemistry research and education, with Bhargava providing critical inputs. But the biochemistry unit in Zaheer's laboratory faced an existential crisis. A review panel formed by CSIR questioned the relevance of biochemistry and organic chemistry research in a regional laboratory. Some members felt the subject was in the domain of National Chemicals Laboratory (NCL) and the work at RRL amounted to duplication of research efforts. CSIR then appointed a Specialists Committee to suggest ways of avoiding duplication among national laboratories. Predictably, the panel which had NCL director as a member voted against an independent Biochemistry division at RRL. As a result of this exercise which smacked of turf war, three divisions of RRL—biochemistry, organic chemistry and drugs and pharmaceuticals—were clubbed under a new division, the Division of Technical Services.[4] This was a blow to the young scientists as the biochemistry group lost autonomy and identity in the lab at a time when the field of biochemistry was witnessing exciting developments globally. The situation somewhat changed in 1962 when Zaheer was elevated to the post of director general of CSIR and G.S. Sidhu, a protégé of Zaheer, was made the director of RRL in 1964.

Meanwhile, Bhargava pursued his idea of developing an informal group of biochemistry researchers in India. As a postdoctoral research scientist in Wisconsin in the 1950s, Bhargava had been fascinated with the concept of the Gordon Research Conference (GRC) that encouraged free-wheeling scientific discourse among peers. He discussed the idea with some like-minded scientists on the sidelines of annual sessions of the Indian Science Congress held in Madras and New Delhi in 1958 and 1959. Bhargava had G.P. Talwar, D.P. Burma and B.K. Bachawat with him. The group decided to meet every year to discuss developments in modern biology in an atmosphere of 'free, frank and objective criticism of scientific work' unlike formal scientific meetings.[5]

The first meeting of the group took place at Khandala on 6 and 7 January 1960. The hill station became an unlikely venue of this meeting due to Zaheer and his social network. His close friend author Mulk Raj Anand had purchased an estate in Khandala for use as his writing retreat.

The property had a Hyderabad connection. It originally belonged to Himayat Nawaz Jung of Hyderabad. Anand purchased it in 1951, with help from Zaheer.

The Khandala meeting was a great success, with nineteen biochemists attending it. It became an annual feature and took the shape of a scientific society. Subsequently, it was named Guha Research Conference, in memory of B.C. Guha who passed away in 1962.

Bhargava also networked with the rising stars of new biology globally. He was the only Indian scientist at the landmark GRC on Nucleic Acids in 1964 where the who's who of modern biology was present. Har Gobind Khorana was the vice-chairman of the meeting.

Bhargava organised India's first major international symposium on molecular biology in January 1964 where a major discovery in molecular biology, 5S RNA, was announced by Roger Monier. Among the participants in the meeting were stalwarts like Francis Crick and Schramm.[6] By the mid-1960s, Bhargava was emerging as a star of new biology in India.

Biochemistry research and education got a boost as a result of the groundwork done by the UGC panel and the parallel efforts of scientists like Bhargava and Talwar. As the director general of CSIR, Zaheer wanted to attract young researchers to this field from institutions in India as well as Indians working in America and Europe. He would often forward to Bhargava letters received from Indian scientists willing to return and work in India. To one such request from Soma Kumar, Zaheer—based on the draft reply prepared by Bhargava—asked if he (Soma Kumar) was interested in taking up planning and organisation of fine biochemical production under the auspices of CSIR. G.P. Talwar from All India Institute of Medical Sciences (AIIMS) referred to Zaheer a request from Har Gobind Khorana from the University of Wisconsin about an Indian faculty member Saran Adhar Narang—specialising in nucleotide chemistry—willing to return to India in 1966.

Zaheer was pursuing the idea of setting up a National Biological Laboratory (NBL) under CSIR. Expert panels had earlier supported the idea, noting that revolutionary discoveries like the three-dimensional structure of the DNA had opened new vistas into studying human and plant health, and biology was no more a mere descriptive science.[7] The governing body of CSIR approved the plan in 1964 and a site in the Kangra Valley (then in Punjab) was identified for setting up the new institute. Chemistry and biology puritans within and outside CSIR consistently opposed the proposal on the grounds that biological research was best done in universities, frustrating Zaheer, who was already under criticism for his unconventional ways of running CSIR. Bhabha was among those opposed to the idea of NBL. He wrote in 1964 that he was not in favour of setting up the NBL and 'if at all such a national laboratory had to be set up, it should be set up near a university and arrangements made for close cooperation between the institute and the university.'[8]

When Zaheer's tenure as the director general ended in 1966 amidst allegations of flouting rules while appointing scientists to senior posts, Dr Atma Ram, the founder of the Central Glass and Ceramics Research Institute in Calcutta, succeeded him. Atma Ram went on a witch hunt, targeting Zaheer's appointees. RRL was severely impacted. Several projects came to a grinding halt. Siddhu offered to resign, along with other directors appointed by Zaheer— Hari Narain of the National Geophysical Research Institute (NGRI) and S.R. Valluri of the National Aerospace Laboratory (NAL).

Bhargava had helped Zaheer in preparing the NBL plan, which had proved to be a non-starter. In addition, the controversy created by the new director general vitiated the research atmosphere in RRL. But Bhargava kept nursing the idea of developing an independent institute devoted to modern biology. In 1975, RRL proposed to CSIR to expand the scope of the Biochemistry division by converting it in a separate centre for cellular and molecular biology. The lab justified its proposal giving the same arguments that were advanced for an NBL. The main objective of the centre was to 'research in frontier and multi-disciplinary of modern biology and to seek potential applications of this work.'[9] Y. Nayudamma, the director general of CSIR, referred the proposal to a panel of scientists and industry experts: G.P. Talwar, Obaid Siddiqui, S. Ramachandran and T.V. Subbiah. The panel gave the go-ahead to form a semi-autonomous entity within RRL. On 1 April 1977, the Biochemistry division of RRL became the Centre for Cellular and Molecular Biology (CCMB), and two years later it was accorded the status of a full-fledged national laboratory of CSIR.

It was the moment that Bhargava had waited for nearly two decades. Nayudamma offered him a large piece of land in the nearby NGRI but Bhargava opted for a smaller area within the RRL premises so that common facilities like the library, workshops and so on could be shared until a new building came up. The creation of CCMB settled a long-drawn question about the relevance of cellular and molecular biology in a chemical technology laboratory. It paved the way for more such centres devoted to modern biology like the National Institute of Immunology (NII) led by G.P. Talwar in Delhi in 1981 and the National Centre for Biological Sciences (NCBS) under Obaid Siddiqui in Bangalore in 1991.

Having been an active participant in the building of RRL under the leadership of Zaheer in the 1950s, Bhargava had imbibed certain core values of pursuing scientific research from his mentor. Both believed in the social function of science, developing an intellectual and creative environment for research, attracting and nurturing young scientists, actively encouraging multidisciplinary interactions and fusion of science with art. Bhargava believed that 'science and art are related, inter-dependent and are two sides of the same coin— creativity.' He pursued this by providing opportunities at CCMB for scientists and creative people (artists, musicians, social scientists and writers) to share their thoughts and creative pursuits, and explore common ground. This went beyond mere acts of patronage like hosting an occasional painting show or music concert.

Bhargava introduced several novel elements in the functioning of CCMB while it operated from a few rooms in RRL. Room 240 represented the new culture—tea and coffee were available in this room which scientists were free to visit any time. They could interact with a colleague and discuss research problems by making use of blackboards kept there. Bhargava believed that research was not a '9 to 5' job. Researchers were not supposed to sign attendance registers; their performance was judged by their research output. Unlike the strict division of work and hierarchies in RRL, CCMB did not have watertight compartments. People were encouraged to address each other by their first names. All this may sound normal in the present times, but it was quite unconventional for a government laboratory in the 1970s.

As the new building for CCMB was coming up, Bhargava wanted to incorporate all these elements into its basic design. His thinking was somewhat influenced by Frank Lloyd Wright who propagated the 'form follows function' approach. Bhargava had been exposed to several Wright buildings in Wisconsin as a young post-doc there. The house of his research mentor Charles Heidelberger, where he stayed for some time, was also designed by Wright. Taking cue from that, in CCMB, Bhargava emphasised aesthetics and cost-effectiveness, along with functionality. Three wings of the new buildings had identical designs and at the end of each floor, a common instrumentation facility was built with deep storage, centrifuges, shakers and so on, needed for molecular biology research. Anyone from any research group could use these facilities that were open around the clock.

The plot of land given to CCMB had a tennis practice wall that Bhargava decided not to pull down. When M.F. Husain, a frequent visitor to RRL and a friend of Bhargava, saw the wall, he offered to paint a mural on it. Once the building was ready, Husain was like an 'artist-in-residence'. Room number 9 in the guest house was reserved for him. He could stay there whenever he wished, for any length of time. Husain made some of his early paintings of the Mother Teresa series during his extended stays in CCMB.

M.F. Husain made the mural at the Centre for Cellular and Molecular Biology in 1987 (courtesy: CCMB)

The main building had a sunken court which served as an art gallery and a public place for holding music concerts. Hyderabad artist Surya Prakash was later appointed as 'artist-in-residence' and the lab regularly hosted art camps. Li Yan, called the Picasso of China, too spent a month at CCMB as the 'artist-in-residence'. The tradition of art displays in the ground floor foyer has been kept alive all these years.

'The laboratory complex resembles a queen's abode with rock gardens, flower pots, paintings and colour-matched curtains, and coffee machines on each floor as well as a "gardened terrace" that can hold parties for 1,000 and a guesthouse with 32 air-conditioned rooms,' reported the news agency Press Trust of India (PTI).[10] Scientists from other labs sarcastically referred to the new building as 'Pushpa Sheraton' after the well-known international hotel chain. In scientific circles, CCMB was often called a 'five-star' laboratory.

'Bhargava saw science as a creative pursuit because you are taking a path where nobody had gone before; you are pushing the boundaries. Art is also an expression of the struggle and thoughts taking place in the minds of artists. The sunken court (in CCMB) was like Room 240 in the RRL building—a place for informal conversations and creative thinking across disciplines,' recalled Chandana Chakrabarti, Bhargava's long-time associate.[11] The idea behind creating an aesthetic workplace was also to inculcate a sense of belonging among researchers. The lab was built as a place that inspired and motivated its occupants.

CCMB attracted bright minds from all over. Dr Lalji Singh joined CCMB after long research stints at Banaras Hindu University, Calcutta University and the University of Edinburgh. His work focused on understanding the mechanism of sex determination in snakes. In Edinburgh, he succeeded in isolating sex-specific 'minor satellite DNA' from Indian Branded Krait (Bkm). Singh, along with his mentor Ken Jones of Edinburgh, visited CCMB to participate in a scientific symposium. After the meeting, Bhargava offered Singh a position in CCMB and followed up with a formal letter. But Singh was reluctant to return to India given his experience of working in Indian universities that lacked research facilities. He put certain pre-conditions to join. Bhargava got all of them accepted, including equipping the lab with instruments he had suggested. Singh joined CCMB in 1987.

Meanwhile, British scientist Alec Jeffrey developed a 'DNA fingerprinting probe' from human DNA and patented it in 1985. 'Dr Bhargava was aware of my work with Bkm. When I returned to India, he asked me to develop our own DNA probe as Jeffrey's probe was patented. It took me about a year to develop this probe from snake satellite DNA by cloning,' Singh recalled in 2014.[12] The DNA fingerprinting probe was the breakthrough from CCMB that caught national and international attention. Only America and UK possessed this technology then.

As the development was reported in newspapers highlighting its potential applications in forensics and settling disputes of paternity, Singh was flooded with requests to provide necessary evidence through DNA fingerprinting in legal disputes. DNA evidence helped investigation agencies solve many famous cases of this period: the Naina Sahni murder case, the Beant Singh assassination, the Swami Premanand case and so on. The most important case was establishing the identity of the 'human bomb' that assassinated former prime minister Rajiv Gandhi. By analysing the DNA of different body parts collected from the blast site and flesh stuck to a denim belt, Singh helped the investigating team identify the assassin. Very soon DNA identification received legal approval, and most forensic labs now use the technique routinely for solving cases. The same technology was deployed to certify the purity of economically important export commodities like basmati rice. Another application of the technology was developed for wildlife forensics. A separate unit, Laboratory for Conservation of Endangered Species (LaCones) was constituted in 2007 for this.

Because of the wide scope of research and services around DNA fingerprinting, Centre for DNA Fingerprinting and Diagnostics (CDFD) was established within CCMB in 1990 with Lalji Singh as the officer on special duty. CDFD became a full-fledged research institute under the Department of Biotechnology in 1999.

The Centre for DNA Fingerprinting and Diagnostics, an offshoot of CCMB (photograph: author)

'I came from Madras University and found the culture in CCMB very different. The lab was never locked; you could work in any lab; there were no restrictions. I used to spend almost 18 to 20 hours in CCMB,' recounted Dr K. Thangaraj who joined CCMB in 1993 and became the director of CDFD two decades later.[13] 'My group leader, Lalji Singh, gave me full freedom to work, so I made optimum use of it to excel in the field. That's how I could publish my research on human genetic diversity in top journals and collaborate with leading groups in India and abroad including Harvard, Oxford and Cambridge.'

Besides the DNA probe, Lalji Singh worked on population genetics, establishing that Andaman and Nicobar tribes were the earliest Indians to have migrated from Africa 60,000 to 70,000 years ago. In 2009, Singh and Thangaraj published their landmark study that reconstructed the history of the Indian population through gene screening.

As an offshoot of its research work on genetic disorders, CCMB established a laboratory for the diagnosis of rare genetic diseases occurring due to chromosomal disorders, and to offer counselling to families with such genetic defects. 'We have diagnosed genetic disorders related to children born with mental retardation, birth defects and delayed development; women not attaining menarche or delayed puberty and miscarriages; couples with infertility issues,' said Dr Lakshmi Rao Kandukuri, chief scientist, who joined CCMB in 1995.[14] She has counselled several families on the need to avoid consanguineous marriages, a practice prevalent in South India.

Like its parent lab, CCMB has matured like a tree, with multiple offshoots.

9

Electronics, Nuclear Fuel and Missiles

∽

O N 20 OCTOBER 1962, CHINESE TROOPS LAUNCHED AN
unprovoked action on the borders of Ladakh and the North-
East Frontier Agency (NEFA, later Arunachal Pradesh). The
sudden and synchronised attack caught the Indians unprepared.
The People's Liberation Army (PLA) far outnumbered Indian
troops on both fronts. As the war continued and Indian casualties
mounted, army commanders reported to the Ministry of Defence
in Delhi that some crucial equipment were failing. They were not
rugged enough to work at high altitudes and sub-zero temperatures.
Army commanders were worried as importing the spares at short
notice was impossible.

Cabinet secretary Sucha Singh Khera sent an SOS to the
Department of Atomic Energy (DAE) secretary Homi J. Bhabha.
Being an ex-officio member of the Atomic Energy Commission (AEC)
that Bhabha chaired, Khera was aware of the ongoing electronics-
related work in DAE units. As soon as he received the message from
Delhi, Bhabha summoned R.V.S. Sitharam who was working in
the microwave engineering and electronics group.[1] The immediate

requirement of the army was a set of transit-receive switches for an imported radar system. Sitharam quickly developed the radar switch, providing the much-needed support to the Indian Army.

Even before the war, Bhabha and his team of young scientists and technologists were acutely aware of the strategic nature of specialised electronics and data processing machines, and the problems associated with imports. Among the early recruits of Bhabha were engineers and scientists conversant with electronics and computing. Ayyagari Sambasiva Rao (A.S. Rao), who returned to India in January 1948 armed with an electrical engineering degree from Stanford University, was one such engineer. Bhabha tasked Rao with building Geiger–Müller Counters, which he needed for cosmic ray experiments.

At the Atomic Energy Establishment at Trombay (AEET), Rao assembled a group of technicians and organised a workshop for designing and building control systems for Apsara, the first nuclear reactor under development, and later for the Zero Energy Reactor for Lattice Investigations and New Assemblies (ZERLINA). Rao's electronics group worked under difficult circumstances in the initial years. Scientists would often go to Chor Bazaar in the Mohammed Ali Road area in Bombay to buy war surplus materials like electronic units used in signalling and communication and salvage useful components like vacuum valves, oscilloscope parts and so on from the junk. The first analogue computer fabricated by the team used such material.[2]

Developing capability in nuclear electronics was critical for building nuclear reactors. These instruments could not be bought off-the-shelf and were considered strategic. So A.S. Rao organised a full-fledged electronics production unit at AEET in 1958. 'At that time, I proposed that this should be made into a much bigger unit so that it would become an independent commercial organization to prove not only the technical but commercial viability of our instruments,' he recalled in an interview.[3] The young engineer had foreseen the situation which unfolded during the 1962 war.

The war experience made the Central government realise the importance of and the need for self-reliance in electronics. Cabinet secretary Khera suggested the constitution of a committee to examine the country's requirements of electronics in different sectors, not just defence. Thus was born the Electronics Committee in August 1963, with Bhabha as chairman and A.S. Rao, Suri Bhagavantam and Vikram Sarabhai as members. Bhagavantam, a physicist trained under C.V. Raman, had served as the director of Indian Institute of Science (IISc) before being appointed the head of the Defence Research and Development Organisation (DRDO) and scientific advisor to the defence minister. Sarabhai was the director of Physical Research Laboratory and chairman of the Indian National Committee for Space Research, which would eventually become ISRO.

After extensive consultations involving scientists, academics and industrialists, the committee prepared a series of reports. But the final report could not be submitted to the government as the Indian scientific community suffered a big jolt—on 24 January 1966, Bhabha perished in an air crash on his way to Vienna. The report was subsequently presented to Prime Minister Indira Gandhi by the three members of the panel. It provided a detailed blueprint for planning an indigenous industry for electronics, computers, communications and components, based on R&D, design, training and limited foreign inputs.[4]

From Trombay to Hyderabad

India's first nuclear reactor, Apsara, went critical on 4 August 1956, marking the country's entry into the nuclear club. It was a landmark scientific achievement for a newly independent nation. The reactor was designed and fabricated by Indian scientists and engineers but the enriched uranium fuel elements used in the reactor came from the UK. For further work on nuclear energy, India needed to be self-reliant in fuel. In the early 1950s, DAE started exploring the possibility of mining and extracting uranium minerals from Jaduguda in Bihar. Simultaneously, development work started for fabricating a plant for producing enriched uranium from the low-grade ore obtained from Jaduguda. More efforts were required to be able to generate nuclear power at a commercial scale, which was the ultimate goal of DAE.

S. Fareeduddin and H.N. Sethna were tasked with the responsibility of setting up a uranium metal plant at Trombay. Fareeduddin, a graduate of Osmania University and a postgraduate from the University of Michigan, had returned to India in 1951. He worked for some time in the Department of Applied Chemistry at Osmania before joining DAE in March 1953. Bhabha deputed him to visit uranium mining and extraction facilities in the UK, France, Canada and the US. Upon his return, he led a team that worked out the process and equipment design to convert uranium concentrate into nuclear-grade ammonium diuranate.[5] The first uranium ingot from the plant came out on 30 January 1959. Fareeduddin then designed a large uranium mill that was erected at Jaduguda.

The next task was to convert the milled metal into fuel rods that could go into a nuclear power plant. For this, a project code-named 'Project Faggots' with Brahm Prakash as its leader, was initiated. The group developed a fuel fabrication facility at Trombay for making uranium oxide fuel rods encased in aluminium alloy tubing. Very soon, aluminium was replaced with zirconium. Keeping in view the plan to construct a series of pressurised heavy water nuclear reactors, DAE wished to establish a large facility to produce nuclear fuel at a central location, away from Trombay. Meanwhile, Bhabha also agreed to A.S. Rao's long-standing demand for a commercial production unit for electronics to serve the needs of research as well as the upcoming nuclear reactors. The Department of Atomic Energy then looked for suitable sites for the two proposed units— electronics and nuclear fuel.

A site selection team consisting of N. Kondal Rao, P.R. Dastidar and C.V. Sundaram visited several places in South India and held talks with state government officials. The team zeroed in on Hyderabad as the preferred location for setting up the Nuclear Fuel Complex (NFC) as well as a nuclear electronics production facility named the Electronics Corporation of India Limited (ECIL). The Andhra Pradesh government allocated a large area of 1,200 acres overlooking the Moula Ali Hill which housed a Sufi shrine dating back to the Qutub Shahi era. Besides the assurance from the state government to provide this large area for the projects, the reasons for selecting Hyderabad were 'low humidity and favourable environmental conditions'.[6] Homi Bhabha, along with H.N. Sethna, Brahm Prakash, A.S. Rao and Kondal Rao, visited the proposed site in December 1965. Bhabha passed away a month later and the two projects were pursued by his successor, Vikram Sarabhai.

The Department of Atomic Energy also decided to co-locate the Balloon Flights Facility of Tata Institute of Fundamental Research (TIFR) in this cluster. Hyderabad was particularly suitable for balloon flights as it was away from the coastline and was well connected by road. In 1961, the city was chosen for conducting a large scientific project—the Joint Indo-US Balloon Flight Programme—with TIFR playing a lead role. High-altitude balloons were launched from the cricket ground of Osmania University to study stratospheric particulate material and the distribution of natural aerosols, as well as primary cosmic rays, using photographic emulsion and electronic counters, and also to gather data on various meteorological parameters.

Until the new campus of ECIL got ready, it operated from sheds rented in Sanathnagar Industrial Area which had several engineering and manufacturing industries. A.S. Rao was appointed the first managing director of his dream project in 1967.

If the 1962 Indo-China war propelled policymakers and scientists to plan an indigenous electronics industry, the Indo-Pakistan war of 1965 speeded up the process of implementation. The shortage of critical communications equipment and spares cropped up again during the war as America restricted the supplies on political grounds. The only defence electronics production unit in operation at that time was Bharat Electronics Limited (BEL), which worked with know-how acquired from foreign companies. Just a handful of electronics units were operating in the private sector. Hyderabad had three units engaged in professional electronics—ELICO founded by D.V.S. Raju made pH meters, ITL set up by former BARC scientist S.S.R.L. Swamy made regulated power supplies and Kadevi Industries headed by M.B.S. Purushotham made antenna systems for defence applications.[7]

In the field of data processing and computing, scientists felt the need to develop indigenous capability because of the growing influence of multinational companies, IBM and ICL, which had a near monopoly of the commercial data processing market of India. The two companies brought discarded equipment and mainframe computers from Western countries, refurbished them in India and leased them out to users at high rentals. The DAE leadership wanted to break the foreign monopoly. The mandate of ECIL, therefore, was to go beyond the stated objective of commercialising indigenous know-how developed at AEET, which was renamed as Bhabha Atomic Research Centre (BARC) after Bhabha's demise in 1966.

In one of the largest exercises of its time, the entire electronics production unit at BARC, consisting of about 300 scientists, engineers and technicians, was shifted from Trombay to Hyderabad, along with equipment and ongoing projects. Senior scientists who moved to Hyderabad with A.S. Rao included E.V.R. Rao, Vadali Rama Rao, S.V. Kasargod and U. Venkateshwarlu. While core scientific and technical staff came from Bombay, ECIL recruited a large number of engineers and technicians through the Employment Exchange and directly from campuses. A batch of twenty glass blowers was recruited from Gudur, which had an Industrial Training Institute with courses in glass and ceramics techniques. They came in handy in fulfilling an export order of Geiger–Muller counters.[8]

At its peak in the 1970s, ECIL had a workforce of about 8,000. 'One half of my class proceeded to America, as was normal then, and the other half was hired by ECIL,' said Badri Vishal Bajaj, who joined ECIL after completing BE in electronics and communication engineering from Osmania University Engineering College in 1975.[9] 'There was mass recruitment in 1971. I was selected to work as a trainee technician and placed in the R&D division which worked mainly in the indigenization of imported instruments. There I learnt the intricacies of making a PCB (printed circuit board),' recalled Yadaiah, who joined ECIL soon after he passed the Intermediate course.[10]

ECIL became a highly diversified company manufacturing a range of products spread over eleven divisions: nuclear instruments, measuring instruments, resistors and capacitors, semiconductors, television, power reactor instrumentation, servo controls, microwave, antenna, computers and special products (defence). It manufactured about 250 products in 1976. Most were meant for government projects in atomic energy, defence, space and broadcasting, and for use in universities and national laboratories. Television sets and computers were sold commercially to the public.

The working style of ECIL was more like an R&D-based production house rather than a mass manufacturer. Projects came from DAE, ISRO, armed forces and other government agencies; ECIL provided them custom-made equipment, installed and commissioned the equipment and trained the people to operate them. For instance, BARC developed a radiation monitoring system for naval ships and gave it to ECIL for commercialisation. 'I was sent to Trombay for training, and subsequently I worked on three generations of the same device and commissioned it on 60 Indian and foreign frigates and submarines,' recalled Yadaiah, who retired as a deputy general manager in 2012.

In the same manner, engineers worked with user organisations to develop new systems for them. 'I handled several development projects—seismic studies in Krishna–Godavari Basin, computerization of voter data for preparing identity cards, an anti-collision system for Calcutta Metro, and field-training simulators for the army's tankodrome. The idea was to take care of everything—from concept and design to training and maintenance—and we would work with users in the field for months at a stretch,' recounted Badri Vishal Bajaj.

Though ECIL manufactured a range of professional equipment and instruments, it was a consumer product—the television set—that made it a household name in the 1970s. Research work on high-voltage supply module, display tubes and transistor circuits was taken up at BARC by U.V. Warlu, M.A. Gaffar and R.S. Prakasam as a part of the project to develop oscilloscopes. The research was redirected towards developing a television receiver to meet the

need for TV sets under a large project that Sarabhai had initiated—
Satellite Instructional Television Experiment (SITE).[11] The project
envisaged direct television broadcast to thousands of villages across
the country. As a part of the planning for SITE, Warlu was deputed
to America to study TV receiver processes at Fairchild and General
Electric.[12] He favoured developing an Indian design suitable for the
varied environmental conditions in remote villages.

Unlike other available brands, which were valve-based, ECTV
was India's first fully solid-state television set. It consumed much
less power and could be repaired easily as it was built of modules.
It was the first consumer product that ECIL sold in retail markets.
For this, the company developed a sales and service network. It
had its showrooms and pioneered a 'service franchise' model with
service engineers provided with a motorcycle for quick service.[13]
All these factors made the TV much sought after. ECTV had a
waiting period of six months to one year while TV sets of private
sector companies could be bought off the shelf. The company
shared the manufacturing know-how with several state electronics
development corporations who launched their own TV sets under
brands names like Uptron, Keltron, Konark and so on. However,
when colour transmission was introduced during the Asian Games
of 1982 and the import of colour picture tubes liberalised, ECIL
could not cope with competition from the private sector.

Electronics to Computer Development

The computer development activity at AEET had started along
with nuclear electronics development for the Apsara reactor. A.S.
Rao convinced DAE to move the computer group from Trombay to
ECIL in 1971, arguing that ECIL could commercialise the systems
developed in Trombay.

A contemporary of Rao was Sivasubramanian Srikanatan who
joined AEET in 1957. He was in the reactor control division where
he worked on an Electronic Analogue Computer (EAC-62). For
his PhD, Srikanatan proceeded to the University of Pennsylvania
in 1960. Upon his return, he proposed that AEET should work on

digital computers instead of analogue ones. It was a tricky decision because TIFR was also working on digital computers. A.S. Rao requested R. Narasimhan of TIFR to oversee the computer work at AEET. Another TIFR scientist, P.V.S. Rao, was also associated with this work. The result of this effort was India's first indigenously designed digital computer—Trombay Digital Computer (TDC-12). It was modelled on the lines of PDP-8 of the American firm Digital Equipment Corporation (DEC). TDC-12 was a large mainframe, second-generation computer based on transistors, with a ferrite core memory of 4 kilobyte.

Though TDC-12 was designed for nuclear reactor controls, ECIL decided to offer it to other users as well. The first TDC-12 built in Hyderabad was installed at Seismic Array Station at Guaribidanur in Karnataka, in March 1972. It made 'detection of seismic events and preparation of event files simpler and less time-consuming'. Another system was installed at the Fast Breeder Test Reactor at Kalpakkam for the acquisition of reactor parameter data. For the space station at Sriharikota, ECIL made a TDC-12 machine for the acquisition and analysis of telemetry data.[14] TDC-12 was an 'on-line' system meant for specific functions like nuclear reactor control, industrial process control, engine performance studies and so on.

The Trombay Digital Computer (TDC-12) was launched by the Electronics Corporation of India Limited (ECIL) in 1972 (courtesy: E.V.R. Rao)

By the time, ECIL rolled out TDC-12, the technology had become obsolete with commercial manufacturers shifting to the next generation, integrated circuit (IC) based systems. ECIL took another three years to introduce TDC-312 based on ICs. However, since TDC-312 was mostly a scientific computer and had no application software for commercial use, ECIL couldn't find any commercial users for it. Then came TDC-316, which was similar to PDP-11 of DEC and could be used for commercial applications. To develop, operate and write application software, ECIL recruited postgraduates and doctorates in physics and mathematics and trained them. A training centre was set up. The software group at ECIL developed a general-purpose operating system as well as compilers for standard programming languages, FORTRAN and COBOL.[15]

The next logical step for ECIL should have been to develop a microprocessor-based computer (fourth-generation), which by then was the rage in the Western world. ECIL did launch Micro-78 with an Intel 8008A processor, but this happened by accident, not by design. 'As a student in the US in the early 1970s, I used to keenly follow the development of microprocessors. But in ECIL I found that technical managers were not interested in it. They thought that microprocessors are toys and could never replace minicomputers,' explained Sridhar Mitta, who joined ECIL in 1973 as a technical manager.[16]

Mitta's father wanted him to become a doctor as the family owned a pharmacy in Chittoor in unified Andhra Pradesh, but his school teacher thought he was good in mathematics and put him in the engineering stream. After obtaining a degree in electronics and communications engineering from Jawaharlal Nehru Technological University (JNTU), Hyderabad, in 1967, Mitta pursued a Master's at IIT Kharagpur. It was at IIT that he was introduced to first-generation computers and programming. He followed it up with a doctorate in control systems from Oklahoma University.

An enterprising group of engineers like Mitta somehow acquired an Intel processor and informally started developing a system in their free time. Every year, ECIL announced new products at the time of declaring annual results. For 1978, it did not have anything new to announce. 'Someone informed the top management that a microprocessor system was working in our lab; they came and saw it. It was promptly named Micro-78 and announced as India's first microprocessor-based computer,' added Mitta.

By the late 1970s, ECIL's computer division was facing a crisis. The reasons were obvious—focus on building custom-made computers for scientific purposes and inadequate attention to developing commercial applications. Following the stringent self-reliance dictum set by A.S. Rao, ECIL built computers from scratch, including all its components. It developed even the core memory systems for its computers. Then policy changes led to the entry of several new minicomputer companies with better technology suitable for commercial users.

'Their (ECIL's) limited and inefficient production facility meant that their computers cost several times more than their equivalents in other countries. Their computers were "mini" in capability but not in size and cost,' points out Mathai Joseph, a computer scientist at TIFR from 1968 to 1985.[17] For instance, the cost of TDC-316 was equivalent to 1,60,000 dollars (at the prevailing exchange rate in 1978) while a similar computer from DEC was available in international markets for 10,000 dollars. This was because ECIL made everything, from circuits and components to the cabinet, unlike manufacturers like DEC who would buy most of the components and then assemble them.[18]

Several private companies, like DCM, ORG and HCL, introduced faster microcomputers for commercial applications. 'We were seeing ourselves as a development organisation, not as a commercial organisation. Why did we not go into EDP (electronic data processing) earlier? Why did we insist on self-reliance? It was our basic orientation. We saw ourselves as doing development. Commercial considerations were secondary,' explained Srikantan in an interview with Indian Institute of Management–Ahmedabad (IIMA) professor S. Manikutty.[19]

In the early 1970s, the Department of Electronics (DoE) projected ECIL as the 'national champion' in electronics, which ensured necessary protection to the public sector company. This was achieved through controls on import or restricting local production of computers (by IBM and ICL) that were in the range of ECIL's ongoing or planned production programme. By 1980, the situation changed and DoE was under severe criticism for its overt control and regulation.

Another interesting project that ECIL executed in the mid-1970s was designing an electronic voting recording system for both houses of the Parliament. Shyamlal Shakdhar, secretary general of the Lok Sabha, was instrumental in executing this project. He was appointed chief election commissioner in 1977. This was the time when the credibility of the election process was under severe stress due to 'booth capturing' and fraudulent polling using counterfeit paper ballots and other such practices. On a visit to ECIL in February 1977, Shakdhar threw up a challenge, 'You people developed the electronic vote recording system for the Parliament. Why don't you think of electronic voting for electing members of Lok Sabha?'[20] The company accepted the challenge and formed a task force on 'automation of general elections'. It proposed various options like punched cards to record voting data which could then be 'read' by a mainframe computer. These ideas were not workable.

Finally, a team in the Nuclear Instruments division led by T.N. Swamy developed a prototype of an 'electronic voting instrument'. Other members of the team were K.S. Rao, N. Sunder Rajan, T.V.P. Kameswara Rao, Ranga Ramanijam, G.R. Koteswara Rao and V. Keerthi Vasan. The work began in September 1979 and by April 1980, the prototype was ready.

'I decided to use push buttons for my instrument and initially kept the number of candidate buttons to 4. A rotary slide switch could be kept to set the number of candidates. An audio alarm and an indicator lamp were kept to show that a voter has voted. Four non-volatile memory pockets were provided to store the votes of each candidate separately,' recalled Swamy.[21] The software was developed by K. Yashoda, who had a doctorate from IIT Kharagpur.

Swamy then contacted several microprocessor and LED manufacturers like HP, ALTERA Semiconductor Corporation, and decided to use the 8-bit microprocessor of RCA. The company, however, refused to send samples as it was barred to do so under a contract with NASA. The first prototype was built using components from ALTERA and another prototype was built with the microprocessor from RCA when it arrived a few months later. The EVM finally used in elections was technologically much superior than the early versions and underwent major upgrades in 2006 and 2013.

The design and functioning of the electronic voting machine (EVM) being explained to chief election commissioner R.V.S. Peri Sastri at ECIL in 1988 (courtesy: E.V.R. Rao)

There was euphoria in ECIL when Swamy demonstrated the prototype in a mock election on the campus. After several design changes and technical upgrades, the group prepared the final prototype of an electronic voting machine (EVM). It was demonstrated to leaders of political parties as well as Prime Minister Indira Gandhi in August 1980. Gandhi herself operated the machine as a voter and as a presiding officer for over forty minutes and tallied the results with notes she took. 'In my presentations (to the leaders of political parties), I used the words "embedded" and "tamper-proof" because I had tried all tricks including EMI interference on the calculator LSI chip but I was not able to fool it. I had discovered a tamper-proof product and decided to use the same technology in EVMs to make them tamper-proof,' explained Swamy.[22]

Unaware of this work in Hyderabad, BEL developed a voting machine for use in in-house trade union elections. After the news about ECIL's machine got published, BEL demonstrated its machine to the Election Commission of India. E.V.R. Rao, the head of ECIL's instruments group, reached out to BEL for a consensus on further development. It was agreed that both the machines would look similar externally but would be configured independently. After their use on a pilot basis in the Assembly and Lok Sabha elections, EVM finally replaced ballot papers throughout India.

The second unit of DAE in Hyderabad, NFC, became operational in 1971 with several critical facilities: zirconium oxide plant, zirconium sponge plant, zirconium fabrication plant, natural uranium oxide plant, ceramic fuel fabrication plant, enriched uranium oxide plant and enriched fuel fabrication plant. Initially, NFC had Brahm Prakash as project director. Kondal Rao succeeded him in 1972 and was designated as chief executive in 1975.

Over the years, NFC has supplied nearly one million fuel bundles, consisting of uranium oxide encased in zirconium alloy casings, to nuclear power plants in the country. In addition, it supplies thorium oxide pellets and core sub-assemblies for fast breeder test reactors. It also makes seamless alloy steel, titanium tubes and special high-purity materials for a range of nuclear and non-nuclear applications.

Missiles and Defence Units

In the early 1960s, DRDO was a fledgling body trying to organise its research units to reduce dependence on imports. In 1961, defence minister V.K. Krishna Menon picked up physicist Suri Bhagavantam to head DRDO. Menon had worked with Bhagavantam in the Indian High Commission in London where he was the High Commissioner and Bhagavantam worked as the scientific liaison officer. Bhagavantam convinced Menon and his successor, Y.B. Chavan, of the criticality of building a strong R&D base for India to achieve self-reliance through the indigenisation of weapons and equipment.[23]

Bhagavantam directed DRDO labs to diversify into new areas like electronics, radars, missiles and rockets, aeronautics and naval research.[24] Several new laboratories and production facilities were created and colonial-era technical development establishments (TDEs) that functioned in the armed forces were repurposed. Hyderabad benefited from all this. The reason was its central location, away from international borders.

The first defence laboratory opened in Hyderabad was Defence Electronics Research Laboratory (it goes by the short name DLRL) in 1962. It participated in a high-priority project—the Air Defence Ground Environment System (ADGES) plan of the Indian Air Force (IAF). DLRL developed the secondary surveillance radar designed to decode signals from airborne transponders.[25] The radar later went into mass production at Bharat Electronics Limited, Ghaziabad.

TDE (metals), housed in the British-era ordnance factory at Ishapore in West Bengal, was absorbed into DRDO and bifurcated into the Defence Metallurgical Research Laboratory (DMRL) and Chief Inspectorate of Metals. DMRL was moved to Hyderabad in 1962, to be developed into a modern metallurgical laboratory. An eminent metallurgist, R.V. Tamhankar, was appointed its director in 1963. This was a deviation from the practice of appointing only uniformed officers as directors of defence labs. DMRL built competence in strategic materials and alloys needed for aircrafts, tanks, missiles and electronics. Tamhankar proposed that it would not be possible for DMRL to carry on its developmental work without having a sophisticated industrial unit.[26]

The idea was referred to a committee headed by Brahm Prakash, a distinguished metallurgist who had worked with both space and atomic programmes. It resulted in the formation of Mishra Dhatu Nigam (MIDHANI) in 1973. A large number of scientists and engineers of DMRL were deputed to work in the production unit.

The first breakthrough of DMRL and MIDHANI was maraging steel—a critical alloy for rocket casings and centrifuges for uranium isotope separation (for making atomic bombs). The material was under export control and technology embargoes by Western countries.[27] Another early success was the development of aircraft brake pads made of metallic ceramics. There was an acute shortage of brake pads for MIG planes of IAF, as the Soviets controlled the supplies. The Indian Air Force had informed the prime minister that the MIG fleet would have to be grounded if the USSR did not supply the pads.[28] The powder metallurgy group of DMRL developed the pads indigenously within a few weeks and their efficacy was tested at Hindustan Aeronautics Limited (HAL), Nashik. The pads were commercially manufactured at the Hyderabad unit of HAL.

The quality of Indian brake pads was so good that the Soviets sought them when they urgently needed some, recalled V.S. Arunachalam, who was then the director of DMRL. Later, he went on to head DRDO.[29] Over the years, DMRL developed expertise in making a range of strategic materials including friction metals, heavy alloys for armaments, steel projectiles and armour, ultrathin high-strength alloy steel, titanium and titanium-based alloys, superalloys, investment castings for superalloys for aircraft and electro-steel castings for guns. Materials developed in DMRL and MIDHANI found critical applications in nuclear reactors, advanced jet engines, battle tanks, missiles and so on.

Around the same time when DMRL was formed, Hyderabad got another strategic unit. The Defence Research and Development Laboratory (DRDL) has its origins in a small group called the Special Weapons Development Team, which was floated in 1956 to study the science and technology of rockets and missiles. In 1960, the Central government decided to convert it into a full-fledged R&D unit. DRDL was housed in the Defence Science Laboratory in Delhi the following year. Bhagavantam decided to shift DRDL to Hyderabad in 1962, and it started working out of some military barracks and rented buildings.

The first project of DRDL was the development of a wire-guided anti-tank missile which underwent hundreds of flights and user trials by the army. The laboratory also worked on missile components like gyroscopes and accelerometers. Yet another big initiative was codenamed 'Project Devil' and involved the progressive indigenisation of SA-75, a medium-range surface-to-air missile system being imported from the USSR. DRDL worked on liquid propulsion and inertial navigation of this missile system, besides undertaking the design and development of ground electronics. For the K-13 A air-to-air missile system, the laboratory developed a semi-active homing head.

These capabilities in missile technology came in handy when DRDL was given the task of developing a range of missiles under the Integrated Guided Missile Development Programme under A.P.J. Abdul Kalam who took over as the director in 1982. DRDO had acquired a large area near the DRDL for building an anti-tank missile testing facility. When Kalam took over as the director, he requested the Andhra Pradesh government to allocate land for letting him establish a new research facility to support the missile programme. It was named Research Centre Imarat (RCI) and it engaged in the design, development and production of missile avionics.

The Making of a Techno-industrial Cluster

The postcolonial period saw India embark upon a journey of social and economic development through the tool of national planning. The planning envisaged the use of natural raw materials, science and technology, and human capital to overcome the crunch on financial resources. Heavy industry, agriculture, scientific research and higher education were prioritised to address unemployment, hunger, poverty and disease. For all this, India needed technical manpower and institutions dedicated to each area of expertise. This explains the frenzy of institution-building in the decades immediately after the Independence.

Hyderabad's participation in this activity was somewhat delayed due to the uncertainty about its political future after its integration with India in 1948. But once it was a part of the mainstream, Hyderabad witnessed hectic institution-building from the 1960s to 1980s. All this was largely State-led and involved the establishment of national laboratories, public sector undertakings, defence production units, R&D institutes, Central universities, technical education institutes, training centres, agriculture research centres and so on.

These developments had a seminal impact on the private sector through encouragement to ancillary units, small and medium enterprises, entrepreneurial firms and led to manpower development. Together, they contributed to the creation of technical skills and employment and boosted industrial growth, besides helping achieve national goals of self-sufficiency and technological self-reliance in key sectors like electronics, drugs and pharmaceuticals, space, atomic energy and defence.

The institutions whose journeys have been traced in Section II of this book (Chapters 6 to 9) had vastly different growth trajectories, but Hyderabad's central location was a key advantage for all of them. The city was well connected by road to the rest of India and could be reached from anywhere in the country within a couple of hours by air. Yet, it was far away from the coastline and the international borders—a key attribute for the location of the array of strategic units in the city.

The salubrious climate for most of the year was another geographical or natural advantage of Hyderabad. Hyderabad was chosen for ECIL because it had 'low humidity and favourable environmental conditions' needed for electronic production.[30] The typical agro-climatic conditions were directly responsible for the location of agriculture-related national labs and international projects in the 1960s. Hyderabad was chosen for locating the International Crops Research Institute for the Semi-Arid Tropics (ICRISAT) in 1971 as it offered a typical semi-arid climate. A unique feature of Patancheru where the centre is located is that it has tracts of both red and black soils. Hyderabad was chosen from about a dozen sites shortlisted in India and Sub-Saharan Africa. Other Indian cities considered were Varanasi, Indore, Poona and Bangalore. Hyderabad, according to the site selection committee, had advantages like 'communication facilities and opportunities for education of children of expatriate scientists'.[31]

Politically, Andhra Pradesh was an important state ruled by the Congress party. Lok Sabha members elected from the state were critical for the stability of the Central government. This helped to smoothen the process of approvals of projects and institutes. For instance, the Central and state government approvals for ICRISAT, including land transfer and diplomatic immunity (since it was a UN centre), came within three months and the institute was functional within nine months.[32] The shifting of the electronics unit of BARC to Hyderabad to form ECIL was opposed by local politicians in Bombay on the ground of loss of employment to the locals. The issue was sorted out after the then prime minister Indira Gandhi intervened.[33]

Another political factor that benefited Hyderabad in the 1960s was the shift of businesses from West Bengal due to labour problems and the Naxal movement there. 'Most of the investment in the 1960s came from PSUs and the Marwari capital that shifted from Calcutta to Hyderabad. The Birlas were the first to move, followed by large in-migration of Marwari businessmen into Hyderabad,' according to Sanjaya Baru, economist and author.[34] An unrelated fallout of the Birlas' industrial foray in Andhra Pradesh was the construction of the Birla Temple on the Naubat Pahad Hill, in the middle of Hyderabad, followed by the establishment of the Birla Planetarium and Science Museum. In the 1970s, chief minister Jalagam Vengal Rao began the transformation of Hyderabad as a business and industrial centre after the political agitation for separate Telangana and Vishalandhra settled down.

The foundational developments witnessed from the early 1960s onwards made Hyderabad, by the late 1980s, ready for the next leap—globalisation.

SECTION III

A Window to the World (1992–2022)

10

Manna from Heaven

I agreed to join CMC but said that I would like to be based in a non-metro city. Dr Gupta said why don't you go and see Hyderabad. I came here and liked the place. I could put this pre-condition because I had returned from the UK. He agreed and said, 'Ok, we will set up a Research & Development centre in Hyderabad.'

—Ramesh Jhunjhunwala,
founding R&D head, Computer Maintenance Corporation,
1976[1]

I had put a condition that I would not join if the company was located anywhere North of Hyderabad. So, they chose Mysore—an industrially backward area then as the place of manufacture to increase the probability of getting a license. Bangalore was chosen to locate the corporate office. That's how Wipro came to Bangalore.

—Sridhar Mitta,
founding R&D manager, Wipro, 1980[2]

BELLA VISTA, A FRENCH-STYLE VILLA HOUSING THE Administrative Staff College of India (ASCI), is perhaps one of the few surviving links between the bygone princely state and modern-day Hyderabad. It may sound unlikely but this is where the city's journey to becoming a destination for high-technology exports took its roots in the 1970s.

Before 1948, the villa was the official residence of Prince Azam Jah, the eldest son of Mir Osman Ali Khan, the last Nizam, and his wife Durru Shehvar, the daughter of the deposed Ottoman Caliph of Turkey. Azam Jah was the chief commander of the Hyderabad army and the titular prince of Berar. However, he could not succeed his father as Mir Osman Ali Khan chose his grandson (Azam Jah's son) Mukarram Jah as the heir. The ownership of the palace overlooking the Husain Sagar Lake was transferred to the Government of Andhra Pradesh in 1956.

As a part of the exercise of building technical education institutions, in 1953 the Central government wished to develop a centre for management education for top managers on the lines of Britain's Administrative Staff College at Henley. Hyderabad was selected as the location for the college, in line with the policy to spread out national institutions in different parts of the country. At first, the Residency House in Bolarum was considered for housing the new college, but eventually Bella Vista was selected. The Residency House was repurposed as the winter retreat palace for the President of India and renamed Rashtrapati Nilayam. The state government leased Bella Vista to ASCI for a nominal monthly rent of Rs 3,000. Subsequently, ASCI purchased the building with a grant it received from the Ford Foundation. General S.M. Shrinagesh, who had just retired as the chief of the Indian Army, was appointed the first principal in 1957. The pioneering contribution of his father Dr Shrinagesh Mallannah to plague research in Hyderabad has been discussed in Chapter 3.

Research and consulting were integral to the work of ASCI where practising managers from the government and private sector underwent management training. In the 1960s, the college introduced the use of computers in management and administration in its training programmes. ECIL, which began computer production in the early 1970s, wanted to attract commercial users for its mainframe computers. It installed a TDC-12 system at ASCI to help it develop management-oriented software and to undertake data processing for other users. After three years, ECIL replaced the mainframe computer with a new one—TDC-312. ASCI became interested in programming and software and purchased a Soviet system, Reyad-1030, in 1975 for independently developing applications. Several postgraduates from IIMs and IITs were recruited for this work.

With two large computers and a sizeable group of 110 programmers, the computer centre at ASCI developed several software packages like Project Management System and Vehicle Scheduling Programme. It trained hundreds of executives from the public and private sectors and handled consulting assignments for government departments, agencies and research laboratories. For instance, it processed examination results for SSC and Intermediate, developed an electricity consumer billing system for Andhra Pradesh and software for inventory control, scheduling, routing and fleet management for the Andhra Pradesh State Road Transport Corporation. All these were among the earliest known application of computers in government utilities. The ASCI computer centre was perhaps the largest software group in the country in the mid-1970s.

'We did an operations research study on water distribution for Delhi; we developed a financial accounting package; for Khadi Village Industries Board, we designed how they can grow their sales network; we analysed data from household surveys for tribal areas; developed econometric modelling for ICRISAT, a payroll package for Allwyn. The learning from such experience was very rich for all programmers,' recalled Arvind Sharma, an electrical engineering graduate from Osmania University who joined ASCI in March 1974 after a short stint with Indian Telephones Industries (ITI) in Bangalore.[3]

ASCI also pioneered software exports from Hyderabad. Since foreign exchange was scarce, the government permitted imports only under certain conditions. The Russian system that ASCI imported came with an 'export obligation'—a part of the foreign exchange used to import the system had to be earned back through exports. So, ASCI was forced to export. The software packages that were developed for financial accounting, vehicle scheduling, classroom scheduling and so on using the Russian computer were exported to Bulgaria and other countries in the Eastern Bloc. 'We went beyond the mandated export obligation and could generate surplus foreign exchange. We went to work at customer sites in Russia—what came to be known as onsite work. At one point, of our total budget of Rupees 11 million, the computer division accounted for almost Rupees 9.5 million,' according to Sharma.[4]

In July 1979, Joseph Bain D'Souza, former chief secretary of Maharashtra, was appointed principal of ASCI. While reviewing the functioning of the college, he felt that the software activity was a deviation from the college's mandate of training practising professionals. Following this review, the software group dwindled and most of the programmers quit. 'The college decided to move away from software development for computer manufacturers and routine data processing, to more creative areas of application of computers in management and administration, along with augmenting the computer component in all our teaching and training programmes,' explained B.S.S. Gupta, who was incharge of the computer centre in 1980.[5]

The closure of ASCI's software group gave rise to the first set of small software firms in Hyderabad. 'We carried out the work that ASCI's computer division earlier used to do,' recalled C.V.S.N. Murthy, who left ASCI to start his firm, ACS Computers, in 1980.[6] Radig Cybernetics, ERA Computers and Infotech Enterprises were some of the companies floated by former programmers of ASCI.

IBM's Exit and Birth of a Software Firm

The software programming underway at ECIL, ASCI and the nascent private software firms in the 1970s was intrinsically linked with the fortunes of American multinational IBM and its eventual exit from India in 1977. The Foreign Exchange Regulation Act (FERA) that came into effect on 1 January 1974 required multinationals to dilute foreign equity to below 40 per cent or cease operations in India. IBM was already under fire for its 'As Is' programmes under which it leased refurbished computers to Indian customers at exorbitant rentals. A parliamentary investigation found that the company had made 'excessively high profits without making any substantial or significant contribution towards India's attainment of self-reliance in critical areas of computing' and therefore, 'must no longer be tolerated in this country'.[7]

However, the government faced a dilemma—the maintenance of a large number of data processing machines and mainframe installations of IBM and ICL in the country. IBM customers were also worried about this. The Department of Electronics (DoE) proposed that computer maintenance services should be nationalised and it established a public sector company—Computer Maintenance Corporation (CMC)—to handle it. TIFR scientist R. Narasimhan was made the chairman of CMC. For the post of managing director, DoE secretary M.G.K. Menon reached out to Prem Prakash Gupta who was the head of marketing at ICL India. 'He said, "Prem, IBM has informed us that they will leave India in June 1976. Do you think you can maintain their systems?" I said I will try. He said, "No, you don't have to try, you have to do it." Our first task was to provide support to all IBM installations of any age, any type, anywhere in India,' recalled Gupta.[8]

With a doctorate from London University in the application of computers in power engineering, Gupta worked with ICL in the UK before being posted to India. Before that, he was with another British computer firm, Ferranti Limited, in London. He was fairly well known in bureaucratic, social and scientific circles in India as his father, Laxminarayan Gupta, was a senior member of the Hyderabad Civil Service and had held key positions in the Hyderabad State and unified Andhra Pradesh. These connections helped the young Gupta while he worked for multinationals. For instance, in April 1961, RRL director Hussain Zaheer introduced him to NPL director K.S. Krishnan as 'a brilliant young man with advanced training in computer science and applications' who was interested in exploring how his training 'may be beneficially utilized in the country'.[9] Prem Prakash Gupta (fondly called PPG) joined CMC on 6 October 1976.

Around the same time, another young engineer, Ramesh Jhunjhunwala, returned to India from London with a desire to serve the country. 'I always wanted to return and work for India because my parents had nationalistic and patriotic background, having lived in Sevagram in Wardha,' said Jhunjhunwala.[10] In the UK, he worked in IBM's development lab in Manchester as a member of the team that designed the central processing unit (CPU) for IBM 370. IBM offered him a position in India but he was not interested in mere maintenance work. So, he quit and returned home. Jhunjhunwala consulted Professor J.R. Isaac, his mentor at IIT Bombay. At Isaac's suggestion, he met Narasimhan. 'He told me, "Your knowledge of IBM will be useful to the company." But I told him I was more interested in development work. In that case, he said you can work in R&D,' Jhunjhunwala recalled.

Jhunjhunwala and PPG knew each other from their days in London. PPG agreed to situate CMC's R&D centre in Hyderabad and asked Jhunjhunwala to head it. Jhunjhunwala joined CMC on 1 December 1976. The company did not have an office at that time and worked out of the office of the Electronics Commission in the Air India building in Bombay. Jhunjhunwala conceptualised the role of the new company and presented his thoughts at the annual meeting of the Computer Society of India (CSI) in Pune in January 1977. Jhunjhunwala assured the gathering that 'CMC will try and make India self-sufficient in services and will do everything except manufacturing'.[11]

As the first employee of CMC, Jhunjhunwala landed in Hyderabad in January 1977 and started working out of Electronics Testing and Development Laboratory located near ECIL. His first task was to somehow extend the life of existing systems like IBM 1401 because importing new ones was difficult owing to the foreign exchange crunch. The Soviet Union and Eastern Bloc countries were ready to sell on Rupee payment their systems which had architecture similar to IBM and ICL systems. Jhunjhunwala devised a novel strategy through a project codenamed Integra—getting CPUs from the Eastern Bloc, peripherals (disk drives, tape drives, card readers, printers) from non-IBM Western companies, and integrating them. CMC engineers would build a layer of software that would help the two systems work as a single unit. This gave birth to a new line of business—system integration.

'One of the key activities of Integra was to enhance the memory of existing and new machines. For example, we developed add-on memory of 256 KB and 512 KB for RC-1030—the Russian system operating at IIT Bombay—and for EC-1040 imported from East Germany. A Robotron computer system—an East German computer equivalent to IBM 360—was integrated with peripherals from an American firm, Calcomp, with necessary modifications in software drivers. This was done for Engineers India Limited in Delhi,' recalled Surendra Kapoor, who joined CMC in 1977 after a stint as a programmer at the Computer Centre at IIT Kanpur.[12]

Though IBM had installed several computers in the government and corporate sectors, they were mostly engaged in routine work like payroll, accounting and inventory management, sales records and so on, and not for core functions of organisations. The Indian Railways, for instance, was one of the largest users of IBM systems but it was not using them for passenger reservation or freight traffic management. The main hindrance was the lack of application software. CMC saw an opportunity in this and diversified into innovative software projects for Indian public utilities.

CMC engineers worked on prototype software for freight management for the Railways under a UNDP project. This sparked their interest in the passenger reservation system. 'Whenever we used to go to the railway station, we used to find long queues; at one window a lot of people standing and at another none; so, we thought we should do something about it. We developed a small prototype and invited the Railways to see it. They said it won't work, scrap it,' said Arvind Sharma, who was among the earliest to join the R&D department of CMC after quitting ASCI.[13] PPG, who used to divide his time between Hyderabad and Bombay, once had firsthand experience with the reservation system. His sister was supposed to travel to Bombay by Charminar Express, so he went to Nampally (broad gauge station of Hyderabad) to book her ticket. Gupta had to stand in the queue for four hours. The next day, he declared to his team, 'We have to computerize the passenger reservation system.'[14]

As the manager of the reservation project, Sharma had a tough time. The Railways simply handed over its commercial manual saying, 'Develop a reservation system that meets all these rules.' Most of the rules were 150 years old and each had several exceptions. For instance, one of them allowed passengers to take along their mule but with a set of conditions. 'We had to design hardware, and write software; no database was available so we had to write our own recovery routines. Once we started coding, we wrote 1,400 programmes in six weeks. From concept to commercialization, it took 12 months,' said Sharma.[15]

When the passenger reservation system was launched in 1985, it was the first Indian project in which the core functions of a public utility—interface with public and service delivery—were computerised and not just managerial functions like payrolls and accounts. This made it a pioneering e-governance project even though the phrase was not coined by then. It ensured faster delivery of service, eliminated the scope for petty corruption, improved the public image of a large utility and helped the Railways open new reservation centres and expand to stations which previously did not have reservation counters. The Railways project paved the way for branch-level computerisation in banking and other sectors.

Around 1986, CMC started looking at international markets, with an office in London. 'At that time, the London Underground was looking at reducing its costs. We offered them that we could help them. They sent a team of managers to check us out. The day the team visited us, we were celebrating CMC Day at our R&D centre. Employees could bring their spouses and kids to the office on that day. We had nearly one thousand people on our campus. The visiting engineers were impressed seeing all this. This was one of the major factors we got the contract to develop scheduling and signalling of London Underground,' said Gupta.[16]

In the initial period, CMC operated out of a rented premises in Posnett Bhavan, a commercial building developed in the premises of CSI Wesley Church at Ramkot in central Hyderabad. It was named after the German pastor Charles Walker Posnett, and it was constructed with aid from Kindernothilfe, a West German Christian charity. CMC subsequently moved to another commercial building, Chenoy Trade Centre (CTC), in Secunderabad. The company constructed its campus on the outskirts of the city at Gachibowli in 1992. Called the CMC Centre, it had buildings and working spaces that merged with the rock formations and were built using local material. The complex was designed by Satish Gujral, a leading Indian architect and artist, while the interiors were done by the Swedish designer Carl Christiansson. With CMC functioning out of CTC, the building became a hub of computer hardware and software trade and continues to be so till today.

Software Export by Private Firms

IBM's exit not only boosted the business of government firms like CMC but also the growth of several private companies like DCM Data Products, PCS, HCL, ORG and Wipro. They got a share of the emerging market as computer technology shifted from mainframe and minicomputers to PCs and workstations. The software got unbundled from hardware, paving the way for software products and services to become an industry by itself. Still, the economic and industrial policies were restrictive, inward-looking and somewhat hostile to the private sector.

Many engineers who left IBM and ICL joined private companies and others became entrepreneurs. Since formal courses in computer science and software programming were yet to become available, companies looked for trained personnel from the public sector. ECIL became the hunting ground for private firms looking for engineers trained in design, hardware and software.

'Ashok Narasimhan, who was General Manager (finance and planning) at Wipro, convinced me. He said, "We want to start a computer company and you also want to do something on your own. You can get the experience of doing something from scratch with somebody else's money. If it works fine, you can continue. If it does not work out, you will learn how not to do things. Either way, you win." It was a good enough reason for me to join them,' recalled Sridhar Mitta, who had developed Micro-78 at ECIL.[17] He joined Wipro as its first R&D manager in Bangalore on 7 May 1980. He hired others from ECIL including Sadasivam, who was incharge of production, Dr A.L. Rao from the software group, B.V. Venkatesh from marketing and Muthyam from hardware design group. ECIL thus provided Wipro its first set of employees who were experienced in hardware design, software, production and marketing. This group then worked with scientists at IISc to develop Wipro's first minicomputer—Wipro 86.

Hindustan Computers Limited (HCL) was expanding its footprint all over the country. Shiv Nadar had left DCM Data Products along with a group of engineers and floated Microcomp, which then formed HCL as a joint venture with UP Electronics Development Corporation (UPTRON) to manufacture computers. In Hyderabad, HCL hired B.V.R. Mohan Reddy, a mechanical engineer from the engineering college at Kakinada with master's degrees from IIT Kanpur and the University of Michigan. He had worked for some time in the DCM group (not in Data Products) and then joined MICO Bosch as a programmer. He was made senior area manager incharge of the Andhra Pradesh state. HCL sold its systems in Hyderabad to several PSUs as well as to small and medium enterprises who were all first-time users of computers.

Voltas, a Tata group company, in technical collaboration with Dr Raj Reddy, a professor of computer science and robotics at Carnegie Mellon University, applied for a licence to manufacture computer workstations in Hyderabad in 1982. Dabbala Rajagopal Reddy—or Raj Reddy as he is popularly known—had studied engineering at College of Engineering in Madras and completed his doctorate from Stanford University. By the 1980s, he was a familiar name in the Indian academic and business circles. In 1994, Reddy was awarded the Turing Award, which is considered the Nobel Prize of computer science. Reddy is considered a global pioneer in artificial intelligence and robotics.

Unlike PCs, workstations had large local memory and CPU as well as the ability to work in a 'local area network'. Workstations were meant for special applications like computer-aided design (CAD) and computer-aided manufacturing (CAM). The technology was new and only three American companies (Apollo, Sun and PERQ) were making such computers. PERQ was floated by students of Raj Reddy, so the new joint venture, named OMC Computers, had access to PERQ technology. The company applied to Andhra Pradesh Electronics Development Corporation (APEDC) for financial support.

Around the same time, Mohan Reddy was planning to start on his own and had received a manufacturing licence too. He also approached APEDC for assistance. Jayabharat Reddy, the chairman of APEDC, liked Mohan Reddy's proposal but advised him to join hands with an established company like Voltas, which was looking for someone to lead its new venture. Mohan Reddy took the suggestion and joined OMC as its founding CEO. 'I married my thinking on engineering and computers, and for the first time in India, we introduced CAD/CAM computers. It created a new market segment. We showed that computers can do design, engineering, analysis and so on,' recalled Mohan Reddy, who worked with OMC Computers for about a decade.[18] The success of OMC made other Indian companies enter the workstation segment—HCL brought Apollo workstations to India, while Wipro tied up with Sun Microsystems.

Meanwhile, the government policy began to change with the return of Indira Gandhi to power in January 1980. She gave the go-ahead for injecting new technology into telecommunications, ordered the expansion of the television network, eased the import of electronic components and permitted the import of picture tubes of colour televisions in 1982. Her cabinet approved a New Computer Policy (NCP) that liberalised hardware imports and recognised software development as an industry. Rajiv Gandhi, who took over as the prime minister after Indira Gandhi was assassinated on 31 October 1984, announced NCP. It was followed by the 'policy on computer software export, software export and development' in 1986, permitting software exports via 'satellite data links and consultancy delivered at the location of foreign clients abroad'.

The two policies were a landmark development, mainly for two reasons. One, software development was recognised as an industry (till then, software came bundled with large computers) and its export was permitted through data links. Until then, software or data was exported like any other physical item—on magnetic spools and large floppies—via the regular infrastructure of ports and airports, or programmers would travel to a foreign customer and write the software at customer site. Two, data links and satellite communication were just emerging, and their use for software exports was considered a revolutionary idea.

The change opened a new window of opportunities. American companies moved quickly to take advantage of the availability of cheaper technical manpower in India. Citibank opened a software development centre in Bombay to serve its in-house requirements. Texas Instruments (TI), an American semiconductor chipmaker which was facing rough weather at home, opened a design centre in Bangalore in February 1987. In a first, it established a dedicated satellite link for data transfer from Bangalore to its facility in Dallas.

In the same year as TI's entry into Bangalore, another American firm, Intergraph, opened its software development centre in Hyderabad. The Alabama-based Intergraph was engaged in engineering and spatial information management software. This was a growing business as users transitioned from minicomputers to networked workstations in the 1980s. In Hyderabad, a group of five youngsters led by Shakti Sagar, who had previously worked with Microcomp in Bombay and Microsense Computers in Hyderabad, formed a software company which developed a package for the retail industry. 'A friend of our group member was working in Intergraph. Through him, we came to know that Intergraph was looking to set up a software development centre in India. He told us, "Why not set up the centre in Hyderabad since you people are already doing some consultancy work?" We agreed,' recalled Sagar.[19]

Intergraph Consulting Private Limited became functional in 1987 from a nine-bedroom house in the tony Banjara Hills area. It was a fully owned subsidiary of Intergraph and registered as a 100 per cent export oriented unit. 'It was the first full-fledged software export unit in Hyderabad,' said Sagar. The first set of twenty mechanical engineers was recruited from IITs at Kharagpur and Kanpur and sent to America for training. As the business grew, Intergraph decided to move into a larger building close to the Begumpet airport.

'While the building was under construction, some thought it is going to be a hotel because it did not look like a typical office structure. We made sure that when people from inside looked out, they should see greenery instead of the humdrum of the road traffic,' explained Sagar.[20] Very soon, the building with Intergraph boldly written on it became a symbol of the nascent software industry in Hyderabad. It was the first business building visitors saw as they emerged from the airport. Government officials trying to market Hyderabad to potential foreign investors would bring them to the Intergraph office to showcase possibilities of offshore software development.

Another software firm formed in 1987 was Satyam Computer Systems. It was funded by the Raju siblings—Byrraju Ramalinga Raju and Rama Raju—and their cousin D.V.S. Raju. The company engaged in 'software consultancy, design and programming of systems' and operated from a house in P&T Colony in Secunderabad with twenty employees. The Raju brothers belonged to a farming family from West Godavari. A commerce graduate from Loyola College in Vijayawada, Ramalinga Raju went to Ohio University to pursue an MBA. On his return from America, he dabbled in entrepreneurship, starting a spinning mill (Sree Satyam Spinning) with finance from APIDC in 1982, followed by a construction company. These projects were not great successes but Raju continued to dream of making it big in business.[21]

The idea of diversifying into software came from his brother-in-law C. Srinivasa Raju (Srini Raju), who was a software engineer in America. He arranged some consultancy work for Satyam in America.[22] Satyam engineers went to work with American customers in what was referred to as 'body shopping'. Satyam's first client was Illinois-based tractor maker John Deere and Company. As the long-distance data links became feasible, Satyam proposed to its American customers that it could provide services from India using data links and make use of the idle time of their mainframe computers at night. The time difference of about twelve hours between India and America would be ideal for such an arrangement, it argued.

John Deere evinced interest but was not fully convinced. Raju rented a building across the road from John Deere, named it 'Little India' and deployed ten engineers. John Deere and 'Little India' were connected through a 64 kbps data link. '(Our) engineers were prohibited from interacting directly with anyone at John Deere and they worked only during the night to simulate the way offshore engineers would have to do their jobs,' Raju wrote of the experiment in 2007.[23] This was a practical demonstration of Raju's idea of utilising the Deere computer via communication links for programming from India. That's how Satyam 'discovered' its offshore model in 1991. Two decades back, Narendra K. Patni, founder of PCS, did a similar experiment to test if remote work was feasible.

B.V.R. Mohan Reddy resigned from OMC after working for close to a decade and started software exports. He sold his 4.5 per cent stake in OMC for Rs 20 lakh and launched two companies— Infotech Enterprises in Hyderabad and InfoCAD Enterprises (with a partner) in Brussels. Though OMC was a hardware company, it had a software product for drafting and Mohan Reddy handled its export to American customers during his last year at OMC. This gave him an insight into the export potential of the product. He noticed that large engineering firms were transitioning from manual drafting to electronic drafting. The work involved digitising manually made paper drawings. Mohan Reddy sensed an opportunity in this. Infotech Enterprises started with such labour-intensive tasks to gain a foothold in the market and slowly moved into digitising maps for sophisticated applications like Geographic Information System (GIS).

The digitising business helped the firm understand how different industries worked and opened new avenues. 'We had to understand what a circuit diagram is, how a telephone network works, so forth. Once we did the drawings, we would tell customers that you are doing a new network, and can we do it for you. We can design new power lines for you. We had the ability to design the engine that goes in a brand-new aircraft for one of our customers. We also scaled up and had several thousand people working by the end of the 1990s,' recalled Mohan Reddy.[24] This work became a new segment— engineering services. A breakthrough came in 2000 when aerospace giant Pratt & Whitney signed up with the company.

The Gamechanger STP

At the beginning of the 1990s, about a hundred software export firms were registered with DoE with most of them being in Bombay, New Delhi, Bangalore and Pune.[25] Hyderabad had ten firms that exported software worth Rs 1.58 crore in 1989. Most of this business came from only three companies: System Research Group (a division of Ajay Automation of Raj P. Penemetsa), Rs 51 lakh; Satyam Computer Services, Rs 35.34 lakh; and Prajna Computer Services (proprietor V. Chandru), Rs 23.35 lakh. Intergraph did not figure in the list since it was registered with the Ministry of Commerce and not DoE.

Other Hyderabad firms in the business were the Academy of Computer Education (Ashok Kumar Agarwal), Constellation Information Systems (Sikandar S. Chandrani), Era Electronics (K. Ravindra), Era Software Systems (K. Shankar), Frontier Information Technologies (V.K. Premchand), Indotronix Computer (Chandra S. Turaga) and Information Management (K. Venkata Ramana Rao).

In addition to those in the export business, small software firms came up in homes and garages in residential colonies like Banjara Hills and Maredpally in the mid-1980s to serve domestic customers. 'There was a demand for Indian language software because from

computerization of electoral rolls to railway reservation charts—
everything needed Indian language software. I developed software
for Urdu typesetting or desktop production; Vision Labs of Dr Raja
Rao did software for Telugu fonts. Venugopal did finite element
analysis which was used by HAL and BHEL for fault analysis of
turbines; another company developed CAD software which was
also sold to PSUs,' recalled Ashhar Farhan about the early days of
his first startup, Computer Corporation.[26] Farhan helped *Siasat*, the
leading Urdu daily, introduce desktop publishing in Urdu for the
first time in India, in 1989.

In over two decades since ECIL came to Hyderabad in 1967 to
make electronics and computers, the city developed a fairly good base
of electronics, computers and software industry. Large government
schemes were promoting the use of computers. A sizeable number
of people were working in large PSUs like ECIL and CMC as well
as in dozens of small firms selling hardware and software. At least
one major foreign firm, Intergraph, had established a software
export unit in the city and several smaller firms were eager to enter
the export markets. The city, by now, possessed a reasonable pool of
technical manpower.

Still, Hyderabad was way behind other cities. Bangalore
firms were ahead when it came to exports. For instance, Infosys
Consultants exported software worth Rs 2.38 crore, Wipro Rs 69.49
lakh and Texas Instruments Rs 4.61 crore. The national tally was led
by TCS with exports worth Rs 48.14 crore in 1989.[27]

The TI unit in Bangalore was a demonstration of India's potential
in software exports, arousing curiosity in Western technology circles.
It proved the feasibility of virtual exports, that is, data transfer via
satellite links, as opposed to the export of physical goods which
needed infrastructure like roads, ports and airports. However, small
entrepreneurial firms could not replicate the TI model because of
the high cost of data communication service of the government
monopoly, Videsh Sanchar Nigam Limited (VSNL).

There was another hurdle in software exports via satellite links.
The Ministry of Home Affairs and the Intelligence department felt
that such data transmission was a security risk. So a security clause

was included in the licence and the companies were told to share a copy of all data transmitted via satellite for verification, whenever asked. An official of DoE was posted at the TI unit to ensure no secret or sensitive information was transmitted from Bangalore to America. The job was given to a young technocrat from Andhra Pradesh, J.A. Chowdary, who had joined DoE in 1985 after stints in ISRO and BHEL. It was technically an absurd idea but Chowdary had to send periodic reports to Delhi which were shared with the Committee of Secretaries and even the Prime Minister's Office.

'When I took over DoE, it was perceived to be worrying more about the security aspect of data communication than software exports,' recalled Nagarajan Vittal who was appointed DoE secretary in June 1990 during the tenure of the National Front government under Prime Minister V.P. Singh. 'One day Cabinet Secretary Vinod Pande called and told me "Arun Nehru (Commerce Minister) thinks India has a lot of potential in software. Why don't you meet him?" I never met Arun Nehru, but noted the suggestion,' Vittal said.[28]

Learning from the TI experience and bureaucratic hurdles involved in the process, DoE formulated an innovative scheme— Software Technology Parks of India (STPI)—to help small software firms. The scheme offered them office space, access to a mainframe computer and single-window clearance for licensing and duty concessions. It was a unique initiative to address key stumbling blocks—lack of computing infrastructure, high cost of data links, delays in clearances—faced by entrepreneurial software firms. Vittal took up the issue of cost of data links with VSNL but it refused to bring down the price. He then took a bold decision to set up earth stations at software technology parks (STPs) with DoE funds. The first such link became functional at the Bangalore STP with J.A. Chowdary as the director. Vittal approved similar parks for Pune, Bangalore and Bhubaneswar in 1990. In early 1991, four more were added to the list—Gandhinagar, Noida, Thiruvananthapuram and Hyderabad. Chowdary was given the charge of the Hyderabad STP as well.

The Bangalore STP started functioning in a pre-existing industrial zone, Electronics City, but Hyderabad did not have a dedicated area for the electronics or software industry. One suggestion was to locate the software park in the vicinity of ECIL but the idea was dropped because it was far away from the city. While searching for a suitable place, Chowdary noticed that a new office block, Maitrivanam, developed by Hyderabad Urban Development Authority (HUDA) in Ameerpet, was unoccupied. He approached HUDA chairman R.P. Agarwal who agreed to lease five floors in this building at a throwaway price. This allowed the STP to become functional.

A few small firms took office space in this building but export was still not feasible due to the lack of a data link. DoE officials were hesitant to invest in an earth station as the STP was still waiting for more tenants. Chowdary convinced the state government to part-finance the earth station. Industries secretary Hari Narain agreed to give an interest-free loan of Rs 1 crore, while DoE gave a matching grant. The software park was a prestigious project for chief minister N. Janardhan Reddy who was keen to promote export-oriented businesses in the state. So for the earth station, the state government offered 10 acres of land at Madhapur village on the western periphery of the city.

The expansion of the STP network coincided with a series of new policies that came to be referred as economic reforms and liberalisation. As the foreign exchange reserves dropped to precarious levels, the Central government under Prime Minister P.V. Narasimha Rao had to borrow money from the International Monetary Fund (IMF). As a part of the pre-conditions for the bailout loan, the government agreed to 'structural adjustments' in the national economy. The strategy of a planned economy was ended and doors were thrown open for foreign direct investment (FDI) under the industrial and economic policies announced in July and August 1991. The new buzzword was 'export' instead of 'import substitution' followed since the 1960s. Corporate taxes, excise taxes and import duties were slashed. Duty protection for the private sector was withdrawn and public sector monopoly in most areas abolished.

The new policies introduced a sense of competition among states to attract FDI. The chief minister of Andhra Pradesh, N. Janardhan

Reddy encouraged export units in electronics and computers. He laid the foundation stone for the Hyderabad STP at Madhapur on 21 May 1992, coinciding with the first death anniversary of Rajiv Gandhi whose tenure in the 1980s was known as the era of the computer revolution. APEDC announced that fifty-one units were willing to locate their offices to the park. Only eight units were functioning from the premises at Maitrivanam at that time.

APEDC had big plans to develop the area around the earth station as an electronics hub by developing 'at least 200 acres from the total area of 600 acres available at Madhapur for the park'. The managing director of APEDC R. Parthasarathy announced that Motorola, AT&T and Ericsson were among the potential investors.[29] In addition, Japanese companies were keen to invest in an electronics hardware park for which three potential sites were identified at Kesara, Medchal and Madhapur. APEDC planned to develop multi-storeyed buildings with facilities needed for electronics industries.[30]

The satellite earth station at Madhapur was projected to be operational by the end of 1992 but the project faced a technical hitch. Companies in Maitrivanam were supposed to get connected to Madhapur via a microwave tower in the 'line of sight' of the earth station. The Airports Authority of India objected to the erection of the tower saying it would fall in the flight path of planes bound for the Begumpet airport. The STP was forced to search for an alternative location that was in the 'line of sight' of Maitrivanam but not in the flight path of commercial aircraft. The search ended with a piece of land on the premises of Dr Marri Chenna Reddy Human Resources Development Institute at Road Number 25 in Jubilee Hills. The state government obliged once again and allocated the land. The earth station was erected there in 1993, connecting companies at Maitrivanam to the world through a shared 64 kbps data link.

Maitrivanam incubated the first set of eighteen software service firms floated by resident Hyderabadis as well as non-resident Indians (NRIs). Many of them like SoftPro, Smart Soft, DataTree and so on were acquired by large corporations very soon. This automatically brought big names to Hyderabad. The US-based networking software firm Advanced Computer Communications

(ACC) was one of them. In 1996, it deputed an Indian engineer, Srinivas Chilakalapudi, to check the feasibility of offshore product development from India. Srinivas found that office space in the STPI was costly for what was to be a one-person operation. He told the Hyderabad STP director Chowdary that he would prefer Bangalore where affordable shared office spaces were available.

'He immediately took me to the library which was next to his cabin and told me that if it was fine with me, I could use that space to start my work. It was an amazing option. I could start the very next day with the internet connection available in STPI,' remembers Srinivas.[31] ACC grew rapidly and Ericsson acquired it in the US, making the Hyderabad unit a part of its global telecom operations. Chowdary showcased Ericsson's presence in Hyderabad to attract other players in telecom software like Nokia and Motorola. Srinivas's success drove his younger brother, Rajiv, back to Hyderabad. On his return from America, he launched an animation firm called Green Gold Animation, which went on to create the legendary Chhota Bheem character, among several others. Since then, this segment of the industry has grown tremendously. In 2023, Hyderabad had some 150 companies working in the visual effects (VFX) sector employing 30,000 people. Visual effects and animation for some blockbusters like *Life of Pi* and *Baahubali* were done in the city. The animation, visual effects, gaming and comics (AVGC) industry has attracted leading players like Sony, Walt Disney and Electronic Arts to the city.

Spectra Software, a very large scale integration (VLSI) design firm founded in 1993 by Sandhya Khode who returned from America after a long stint with Cyrix, had a similar trajectory.[32] It started as an independent semiconductor design firm and soon found a customer in the US-based CrossCheck founded by Tushar Gheewala. As the work grew, Spectra was renamed CrossCheck Technologies Private Limited and eventually became the R&D centre of CrossCheck. In 1997, CrossCheck in America was acquired by Duet Technologies started by design automation pioneer Prabhu Goel. So, CrossCheck Technologies in Hyderabad became a part of Duet.

The opening of the R&D centre of CrossCheck—one of the first firms at the Software Technology Park—in 1995. It was headed by Sandhya Khode (extreme right) (courtesy: Sandhya Khode)

In the meantime, Khode rose to prominence in Hyderabad's booming software industry and organised a high-profile industry event called VLSI Conference in Hyderabad. Khode was subsequently chosen by Motorola to oversee its development centre when it opted to locate it in Hyderabad.

The policies promoting liberalisation gave rise to what was called the 'new economy', denoting new sectors that were not dependent on manufacturing. Software development and services were at the forefront of the new economy. They involved highly labour-intensive tasks like coding, testing and debugging. As technology platforms changed, a shortage of technical manpower which could perform these tasks developed in the West. Companies located in India used multiple strategies to grab this opportunity, supported by domestic policies that incentivised service exports. The companies followed the practice of sending programmers to work onsite with clients under the clients' supervision (widely known as 'body shopping'), offshore work (using data links at STP), running dedicated development centres for overseas firms and so on.

The presence of a STP in the heart of the city spurred the growth of IT and software-related businesses in the vicinity. Smaller firms which could not afford a full office in the park operated from residential blocks nearby. Independent of the companies in the park, several consultancy firms dedicated to 'body shopping' were established in this area. These consultancies acted as recruiting agents and sent technical workers from Hyderabad to work with clients in America and elsewhere.

Aditya Enclave, a six-storeyed residential block constructed in 1993 near Maitrivanam, became the hub of such consulting firms. In nearby lanes and bylanes came up training centres teaching coding and programming skills needed for clients in the West. 'Several families whose children went to US graduate schools were sending work back to Hyderabad in suitcases. This material came here and was digitized and sent back. To do this kind of data processing work, many coaching centres came up in Ameerpet because of its proximity to colonies like Vengal Rao Nagar and Sanjeev Reddy Nagar where these families were located and had connections to coastal Andhra districts from where young people were coming to Hyderabad for work,' explained Anant Mariganti, founder of Hyderabad Urban Laboratory.[33]

Franchisees of leading IT training companies NIIT and APTECH also opened their offices in the Ameerpet area. In a few years, the locality became the favourite place for youngsters wanting to hone their technical skills quickly and try for an IT job in Hyderabad or America. This earned the area the sobriquet of 'United States of Ameerpet'. 'No university can accomplish what Ameerpet has accomplished,' notes Mariganti.

The Hyderabad STP operating out of Maitrivanam and the ecosystem that developed around it opened a new window for young entrepreneurs to connect to the technology world in America and Europe. This was the beginning of outsourcing business but the turning point in Hyderabad's journey to high-tech stardom, however, was still a few years away.

11

Two Coups and 20/20 Vision

Whenever I used to go to COMDEX and other international shows, I would request companies to come to Hyderabad. They would ask: Hyderabad? Pakistan? Those days Hyderabad Sind was better known than Hyderabad Deccan. They would ask: how far it is from Bangalore? How far it is from Bombay? I would draw a map of India and show them where Hyderabad was located.

—J.A. Chowdary,
director, Software Technology Park,
Hyderabad (1990–98)[1]

Hyderabad is being known now as Cyberabad. ... And he (Chandrababu Naidu) is becoming very well known in the United States and very much admired for all these remarkable achievements.

—President Bill Clinton,
Hyderabad, 24 March 2000[2]

THE EARLY 1990S WAS A PERIOD OF POLITICAL TURMOIL IN Andhra Pradesh. Hyderabad witnessed communal riots. The left-wing extremist formation, People's War Group, indulged in violence in many districts. There was political instability with the Congress party changing its chief minister in Andhra Pradesh frequently. In the state assembly elections in December 1994, the party lost and NTR's Telugu Desam Party (TDP) bounced back to power. It was the third time NTR became the chief minister in one decade.

The new term of NTR as chief minister saw the rise of Narra Chandrababu Naidu, NTR's son-in-law, who had handled the political crisis of 1984 deftly and steered the party in the midterm elections in 1985. Until that time, Naidu only handled the party affairs and had not been a member of NTR's previous two governments. When TDP was voted back to the state assembly in 1994, NTR inducted Naidu into his cabinet and entrusted him with important portfolios of finance, revenue and planning.

The first two terms of NTR were marked by welfare-oriented measures—Rs 2-a-kilo-rice scheme, subsidised housing for the poor, concessional electricity for farmers, and reservation for women in educational institutions and jobs. In the campaign for the 1994 elections, he promised to relaunch the subsidised rice scheme and introduce prohibition. After he was made the finance and revenue minister, Naidu realised that the welfare schemes of NTR were proving to be a drain on the state exchequer. In 1995-96, the rice subsidy alone was about half of the total budgetary allocations for education and health together.[3] As much as 94.5 per cent of tax and non-tax receipts of the government went towards the salary and pension of government employees.[3] Moreover, the state revenue nosedived because of the ban on liquor sales. The industrial growth rate slipped from 5.4 per cent in 1989-90 to 3.8 per cent between 1990 and 1997. The state was lagging behind Karnataka, Maharashtra and Tamil Nadu in attracting foreign investment. Naidu sensed that 'a major (financial) crisis was building up' and that the state was 'heading towards bankruptcy'.[4]

To boost economic growth rapidly, Naidu decided to focus on the emerging areas of IT and biotechnology rather than manufacturing.

At the time of joining politics in 1978, Naidu was pursuing a doctorate in economics and had developed an understanding of business and industry. As a minister, he told the bureaucrats to identify sectors in which Andhra Pradesh could compete with the better-performing states and devise new strategies for growth. A suggestion came up that the chief minister could lead a delegation to the United States, where Telugus make up the largest Indian community and excel in fields like technology. 'The idea was that we could talk to them and figure out the inherent strengths of the Telugus, and try to promote those industries. (We believed) it will be a faster and relatively less risky way of promoting growth,' recalled Sheela Bhide, a civil servant with a doctorate in international trade who was the industries secretary in 1995.[5]

Naidu followed the advice and went to America. There he met several members of the two prominent community organisations—the Telugu Association of North America (TANA) and the American Telugu Association (ATA). These interactions revealed that Telugu professionals and entrepreneurs had an edge in knowledge-based sectors like software, biotechnology, pharmaceuticals, specialty chemicals, medical equipment, healthcare and so on. Data from software industry groups also showed that 23 per cent of Indian software professionals in America were from Andhra Pradesh. Naidu made a pitch to the expatriate Telugus to invest and start new businesses in their home state and promised all help.

The ground reality in Hyderabad, however, was different. The state was not ready for new businesses. Despite STP offering tax incentives, faster clearance and high-speed connectivity, leading software firms were reluctant to shift to Hyderabad. Officials were perplexed by the situation and wanted to know the reasons behind this reluctance. In June 1995, a trip to the Santacruz Electronics Exports Processing Zone (SEEPZ) in Mumbai helped them gain a better understanding. Executives of the businesses in this export zone pointed out that Hyderabad lacked basic infrastructure essential for software export business: an international airport, uninterrupted power supply, reliable telephone service, suitable office buildings and a higher technical institute like an IIT which could assure the supply of high-quality engineers. The social infrastructure was weak and liquor sale was banned.

The officials briefed Naidu about their visit, but at that point the minister had much more than software on his mind. In September 1995, he upstaged NTR in a dramatic political coup and installed himself as the chief minister. In the preceding weeks, he had quietly won over key members of the NTR clan who were unhappy with NTR due to his new wife Lakshmi Parvati's rising interference in government affairs.

NTR's first wife, Basava Rama Tarakam, had passed away in 1985 due to cancer. Parvati, a folk artist and writer, came in contact with the actor–politician when he was out of power in the early 1990s and the two got married in 1993. His marriage with the much younger Parvati alienated him from his sons, daughters and sons-in-law. After he was re-elected, there was a rumour that NTR would make Parvati the deputy chief minister. Naidu channelled the growing disenchantment with the ageing patriarch into support for himself. He revolted, along with a majority of legislators, and installed himself as the chief minister. Just a few months later, a despondent NTR passed away.

As soon as he became the chief minister, Naidu asked a group of officials to prepare a White Paper on the state's financial position. The paper pointed to the need for fiscal prudence, slashing subsidies and downsizing loss-making government companies. Naidu accepted the recommendations and opted for broad-based economic reforms, in a clear break from the past policies of TDP. He also began implementing the suggestions he had gathered in the preceding months. He summoned J.A. Chowdary of STP and bluntly asked him, 'Tell me, how can we beat Bangalore?' He appointed a tech-savvy IAS (Indian Administrative Service) officer Randeep Sudan, to develop an information management system in the chief minister's office. A postgraduate in economics from Jawaharlal Nehru University (JNU), Sudan had just returned from the London School of Economics (LSE) after completing another post-graduation degree. He was a computer enthusiast having introduced the use of computers in district administration in the 1980s. Other highly qualified officers included principal secretary to Naidu, S.V. Prasad, who had a degree in management from IIM Ahmedabad.

A large economic restructuring plan was launched in October 1996 with an assistance of USD 1.58 billion received from the World Bank. It prioritised improvements in basic infrastructure, beginning with power generation to ensure quality electricity supply, especially for proposed technology parks. To shore up the state revenues, Naidu gradually eased the ban on liquor sales and tweaked the rice scheme to slash the subsidy bill. Regulations on construction of buildings were changed to permit high-rise buildings and multi-level parking to help develop modern office space needed by IT companies.[6]

In spite of all these actions, it would have still taken a long time to develop the basic infrastructure in the entire state to be able to attract investors. The Industries department, therefore, suggested a shortcut—the creation of an enclave for the IT industry where necessary infrastructure could be built on priority. Madhapur was the obvious choice for such a park because it had been earlier identified for setting up the STP earth station and had surplus land available. It was a rocky area with scanty habitation and was close to the city.

Industries secretary Bhide hurriedly put together a note and took the file herself to her senior, S.R. Govindarajan, special chief secretary (industry). As she entered the room, she saw Anumolu Ramakrishna, chairman of L&T, having a chat with Govindarajan. Ramakrishna had come to meet Govindarajan to explore new opportunities in his home state for L&T before he retired. When Bhide heard this, it was music to her ears. She told him about the plan to develop an IT park, the file relating to which was in her hands. Ramakrishna instantly got interested and said, 'We are not an IT company, but we can develop the infrastructure.'[7] The officials were happy with the prospects of partnering with a leading infrastructure company as state agencies lacked the necessary capacity to develop the specialised infrastructure for an IT park.

Over the next few days, the Industries department formalised the idea of a 200 acre IT park in Madhapur to be developed in public–private partnership (PPP) mode. Tenders were floated and after the due process L&T was selected.

Public–private partnership was still a new concept. It was a byproduct of economic liberalisation that facilitated infrastructure development jointly by the state and private sector entities. In the case of the IT park, the state government was to provide the land and develop the roads, water and electricity facilities while the rest of the infrastructure was to be developed by the private partner. In addition to L&T, bids were received from Reliance Industries, BPL Engineering Limited, Western India Services and Estates Limited, Chesterton Technology Park, Synergies Limited and Global Techno-Industrial Parks Limited.[8] L&T formed a joint venture with AP Industrial Infrastructure Corporation (APIIC) where it held 89 per cent equity. The venture was named Hyderabad Information Technology Engineering Consultancy City or HITEC City.

The idea of developing an IT 'city' or park had first cropped up when the state government allotted land for the STP at Madhapur in 1992. Since DoE did not have the expertise to develop a technology park from scratch, it decided to get a private player on board. Reliance Industries signed a memorandum of understanding and formed a new company, Reliance Infocity, but the venture did not take off. 'The concept of HITEC City was at the planning stage before I became the Chief Minister. What we have done subsequently is to build on what already existed and draw up a structured framework for making the state a premier IT centre of India,' Naidu wrote in 2000.[9]

The first building developed by L&T was named Cyber Towers. The column-free circular building was built from scratch within fourteen months. The ten-storeyed tower had four quadrants with a fountain in the middle of each of them, with a total floor area of over half a million square feet. Companies operating from the STP at Maitrivanam were the first to shift to Cyber Towers. Prime Minister Atal Bihari Vajpayee inaugurated it on 22 November 1998. Describing the building as 'a symbol of Naidu's vision and commitment', he hoped that 'Andhra Pradesh will soon be known as Cyber Pradesh' considering the pace of its progress.[10] At this event, Naidu formally announced the birth of Cyberabad, as a triplet to the twin cities of Hyderabad and Secunderabad.

Cyber Towers gave Hyderabad a new identity and a new icon, next only to the medieval monuments of Charminar and Golconda. The building was featured among the tourist attractions in publicity brochures.

The Second Coup

Along with measures to develop infrastructure to make Hyderabad a desired destination for technology businesses, Naidu and his team stepped up efforts to attract big names in the industry to Hyderabad. Their logic was that if one leading company selects Hyderabad, then others would follow.

While Cyber Towers was under construction, Naidu's office received information that Microsoft chairman Bill Gates was going to visit India. Microsoft was scouting for locations in China, Israel and India as it looked to expand its business. Among the possible locations shortlisted in India were Delhi, Bombay and Bangalore. Naidu's aides contacted Microsoft India with a request to include Hyderabad in Gates's itinerary. When this did not work, Naidu spoke to US Ambassador Frank Wisner who happened to be in Hyderabad to attend a conference. Wisner said he could not possibly alter Gates's programme to include Hyderabad in it but promised Naidu to get a few minutes exclusively with Gates at the dinner he was hosting in Delhi. On 5 March 1997, Naidu would meet Gates at Roosevelt House in New Delhi.

Naidu's team wanted to make the most of the meeting. 'We worked very hard to prepare a PowerPoint presentation (PPT). We deliberately decided to use a Compaq laptop—it was the same model that had figured in Gates's book *The Road Ahead* published in 1995', recalled an official. 'We had three asks for Gates—a software development centre in Hyderabad, a strategic partnership between Microsoft and AP Technology Services and its participation in the information technology institute which was in the making,' recollected Sudan who was present in the meeting along with Rajiv Nair, president of Microsoft India.[11] Gates was impressed that the chief minister of a state with 80 million people was using a Microsoft product—PowerPoint—to make a presentation to him. He did not commit anything but assured Naidu that he would send a team to Hyderabad to evaluate the options.

By this time Naidu had come to be identified with PPTs. He was the first Indian politician to carry a laptop to public events and make PPT presentations. It was during his engagement with the president of the World Bank James Wolfensohn that Naidu, for the first time, used a laptop to make a presentation on a flight from Hyderabad to New Delhi. In the months and years that followed, Naidu's love for PPT presentations earned him the nickname of 'PowerPoint Prophet' in the Western press. This was at a time when some chief ministers looked at IT with disdain, as reflected in the infamous statement of Bihar chief minister Lalu Prasad Yadav, '*Ye IT-YT kya hai? Kya computer doodh deta hai?*' (What is this IT? Does a computer give milk?)

Within a few weeks of Naidu's meeting with Gates, a Microsoft team led by Sanjay Parthasarathy visited Hyderabad. The CM's team made presentations and showed them around Madhapur where HITEC City was proposed to come up. 'All we had on the ground were rocks and shrubs. Sanjay told me, "Who knows Hyderabad may become Cyberabad one day. But I need a world-class building to locate Microsoft, which you don't have right now." It was a casual remark but I thought it was a smart play on words—Hyderabad and Cyberabad. I mentioned this to CM in the evening. He instantly liked it and said, "Yeah, this sounds smart, let's name it Cyberabad." That's the genesis of the name Cyberabad,' Sudan recollected.[12] After a couple of more visits during which Microsoft officials could see Cyber Towers rising fast, Microsoft decided to locate its first overseas software development centre in India—and that too in Hyderabad.

Naidu's meeting with Gates was nothing short of another coup for the chief minister. 'The demonstration value of that one coup was considerable,' Naidu said later. 'The confidence level of other would-be investors received a big boost. They felt that Microsoft must have done a thorough analysis of the pros and cons before choosing Hyderabad.'[13] Microsoft brought the focus on Hyderabad in the technology world in India and the West, causing a ripple effect.

In June 1998, Oracle signed a deal with the Andhra Pradesh government. Subsequently, it acquired 8 acres of land. The plan was to invest USD 20 million in five years and hire 3,000 professionals to work on e-business applications for its global customers.[14] Motorola launched its new software centre for designing wireless solutions for CDMA handsets, 3G systems and network management solutions for satellite communications. Motorola's Hyderabad centre was one of its ten development centres around the world.[15] It hired design automation expert Sandhya Khode to lead this operation. In November 1999, Ericsson started a similar software centre in Hyderabad for designing software for its internet and data communication networking products. By early 2000, Cyberabad had software design and services wings of IBM, Lumley Technology, Toshiba, Metamor, Baan, DE Shaw, Ericsson and HSBC.

Over the years, many Indians had joined Microsoft in America and climbed up the corporate ladder. Instead of hiring more Indian engineers in the US, Microsoft reasoned that it could have a development centre in India itself. The India Development Centre (IDC) of Microsoft was assigned to work on core technologies such as Windows NT and Microsoft BackOffice. In April 2000, Microsoft launched, for global markets, its Windows Services for UNIX 2.0 which was designed and developed in Hyderabad.[16] During his visit to Hyderabad in September 2000, Gates announced an investment of USD 50 million in IDC. He again came in November 2002 and announced another investment of USD 100 million in the Hyderabad facility. Eventually, IDC grew to become the largest such facility outside Microsoft headquarters in Redmond. Typical projects at IDC were 'a mirror of software development at Microsoft in Redmond' with groups working on end-to-end core technologies and products in networking, storage and mobility, among others.[17]

Backroom operations, popularly called business process outsourcing (BPO), emerged as a new sector of the outsourcing industry in the late 1990s. Driven mainly by the revolutionary changes in telecommunications and internet, corporations in the West sought to take greater advantage of the low-wage labour in countries like India and the Philippines. BPO involved shifting business processes from inside the organisation to external service providers overseas. Typical services like payroll and benefits administration, customer support, call centres and technical support were outsourced. By doing so, companies could reduce transaction costs and free up resources to focus on their core areas of activities.

Large companies either established their service centres or farmed out this work to service providers. Usually, such operations involved employing thousands of workers. In June 1999, APIIC allocated 30 acres of land to GE Capital International Services, which initially employed 4,000 workers. It was among the largest such venture in the BPO space at that time. More such companies chose Hyderabad in the years to come, making it the leading BPO hub in the country, along with Noida, Gurgaon and Bangalore.

Some of the early occupants of Cyber Towers were Microsoft, Patni Computer Systems, Oracle Corporation, GE Capital, 7 Hills Business Solutions, AppLabs, Keane, Prithvi Information Solutions, Orbees and Four Soft. Another large building complex, Cyber Gateway, which was designed for ITES and BPO services with multiple redundancies for connectivity and power, attracted large offshore processing operations. Dell, General Electric, Capitol Records, Lanco Global Systems and Microsoft were among the first companies to start operations in the Cyber Gateway. They were followed by Oracle, Virtusa, Vertex Computer Systems and many others. Several of them very soon grew in size and operations and built their campuses. Then other technology parks such as Cyber Pearl, Ascendas and Mindspace were developed and these housed dozens of companies employing several thousand IT workers. In addition, large Indian companies like Wipro and Tata Consultancy Services (TCS) built their facilities here.

Inspiration from Cyberjaya

The rapid transformation of the area around Cyber Towers and Cyber Gateways was a result of the realisation by Naidu and his advisors that one building (Cyber Towers) and one anchor firm (Microsoft) were not enough to fulfil their dream of developing an IT city. In the first two years, though Madhapur was named HITEC City, all that it had was Cyber Towers. Once a Korean delegation was taken around Madhapur and they could only see rocks, boulders and thorny bushes on the other side of the Cyber Towers. One member of the delegation asked officials, 'Does one building make it a high-tech city?' It was an embarrassing question and set the officials to brood over it.[18]

Here is how one building became the nucleus for a new city.

Just a few weeks after he met Gates in Delhi, Naidu was invited to visit Japan. On the way back, he stopped over in Malaysia to see the Multimedia Super Corridor (MSC), an ambitious project of their prime minister Mahathir Mohamad, launched in 1996 as a part of his Vision 2020 programme. Mahathir Mohammad was an ophthalmologist and had borrowed the concept of 20/20 being the perfect vision.

The visit to Malaysia proved to be a turning point for the fledgling Cyberabad. Naidu decided to expand Madhapur from one building to a city, just like MSC, and develop a Vision 2020 for Andhra Pradesh, like Malaysia. He was told that McKinsey was behind the strategy to develop MSC, and told his team, 'Let's call them (McKinsey) here. Why reinvent the wheel?' As a result, the consulting firm was hired to develop a vision document and propose strategies to attract foreign investors. A McKinsey team consisting of Pramath Sinha, Manish Kejriwal, Sunish Sharma, Nishant Sharma, Noshir Kaka and Deepak Goyal was embedded in Naidu's office from 1997 to 2004.

On 26 January 1999, Naidu released the Vision 2020 document that identified thrust areas in agriculture, industry and services (IT, tourism, knowledge-based industries and logistics). The grand vision was to transform unified Andhra Pradesh into 'a knowledge society by leveraging information technology to attain a position of leadership and excellence in the information age.'[19] Information technology was to be deployed 'to improve the quality of life of its residents and help them achieve higher incomes and employment'. Naidu wanted the state to leapfrog from agriculture to services using IT rather than running 'the course of transformation from agriculture to industry to services'.[20] The vision document was peppered with examples of rapid economic growth attained by Singapore, Malaysia, Thailand, Taiwan and China.

HITEC City was the first step to developing infrastructure essential for the IT industry. But the enclave was spread over a stretch that was barely 1 square kilometre as against Cyberjaya in MSC which was spread over 30 square kilometre and the Silicon Valley in America that extended over an 80 kilometre strip. So a blueprint was prepared to develop an integrated city with offices, residential complexes, hotels, clubhouses, shopping malls, captive power plants, waste water management, etc. Cyberabad was to emulate Cyberjaya and have business areas with 'cutting edge facilities' supplemented by 'outstanding residential facilities and living conditions'.[21] The private sector was involved in the fast-track development of housing blocks, borrowing the strategy adopted by Singapore Housing Development Board. After Cyber Towers, L&T built another office block, Cyber Gateway. Then chunks of land were leased or sold to individual companies as well as to builders like DLF and Raheja to develop more IT parks, hotels and so on.

While the inspiration to develop a full-fledged city around the HITEC building came from MSC, the business model was borrowed from Ireland's International Financial Services Centre (IFSC). Established in 1988, the financial hub housed top banking, financial and insurance companies. The first phase of IFSC was developed by Dublin's Customs House Dock Development Authority. The companies in this hub employed thousands of workers who handled transactions relating to international banking, securitisation, fund administration and so on. IFSC spurred the growth of IT and IT-enabled services (ITES) in Ireland. It was conceived as a special economic zone (SEZ) where financial services firms were given tax concessions and other benefits. These kinds of benefits were given to IT, ITES and software units affiliated with the STP in Hyderabad. In addition, the state government provided concessional power tariffs, relaxation in zoning regulations, and exemption from pollution control regulations and labour laws.

In 2001, an area of 52 square kilometre was carved out from the jurisdiction of Hyderabad Urban Development Authority (HUDA), along with fifteen surrounding villages, and was incorporated as a new municipal area, Cyberabad, on the western periphery of Hyderabad.[22]

'A Coming Asian Tiger in India'

Naidu adopted an aggressive strategy to market Hyderabad. This was necessary because of several reasons. Though the Indian economy was opening as a result of the reforms implemented progressively since 1991, foreign investment was slow to come. One of the key factors was the political instability at the Centre with motley coalitions capturing power after the Congress party lost the elections in 1996. In addition, a negative perception had developed among foreign investors due to the failure of a power project of an American firm, Enron, in Maharashtra. Then, there was competition among states to attract foreign direct investment (FDI).

Styling himself as the CEO of Andhra Pradesh, the chief minister made it a point to attend all major investor fora, domestic and foreign, and make his trademark PowerPoint presentations. He specifically targeted Fortune 500 companies. To be on the radar of potential investors, Naidu believed, face-to-face sessions with CEOs and meeting them in their own countries were crucial. This had to be done continuously to 'put Hyderabad as a possibility' in their minds and to generate the confidence necessary for them to finally invest.[23] This was similar to what Mahathir did to market MSC—he went on a world tour to meet specific IT communities and technology companies.[24]

The World Economic Forum (WEF) annual meeting at Davos provided a perfect setting to market Hyderabad. The chief minister's backroom team, which now included McKinsey consultants, carefully worked out a pitch for his first visit to Davos in January 1998. There was an air of anticipation around this trip, given the positive press Naidu was receiving. The *International Herald Tribune* described Andhra Pradesh as, 'A Coming Asian Tiger in India'. The PowerPoint presentation to be shown to CEOs at Davos by Naidu was brief—running precisely for three minutes and two seconds. This was also the length of *Imagine,* the 1971 song by John Lennon. The chief minister was no pop music buff, but Sunish Sharma of McKinsey suggested that the song should keep playing in the background as Naidu pitched Hyderabad to potential investors. The proposal went something like this—when the slide talked about infrastructure and incentives, it would coincide with 'It's easy if you try'; the slide on faster clearances would have the 'no hell below us'

Andhra Pradesh chief minister N. Chandrababu Naidu on one of his promotional tours in the Silicon Valley (courtesy: J.A. Chowdary)

line in the background; and 'you may say I am dreamer' synced with the slide on Vision 2020.

Naidu met Gates a second time in Davos. Others whom he met were John Chambers of Cisco, Sanjay Kumar of Computer Associates, Carly Fiorina of Hewlett Packard, Michael Dell of Dell, Masayoshi Son of Softbank and Philip Condit of Boeing. Later in the same year, Naidu went to America to hold follow-up meetings with Gates and Chambers, besides meeting Jack Welch of GE and Louis V. Gerstner of IBM. Microsoft was already in Hyderabad, while Cisco invested in a centre in Bangalore. Both GE and Dell, around this time, were exploring expanding their presence in the emerging BPO segment.

Keen to get Dell to Hyderabad, Naidu reiterated his pitch to Michael Dell when he met him again at Davos in 2001. Dell deputed vice president Kip Thompson to visit Hyderabad and Bangalore and commissioned a study on the potential of the two cities. The outcome of this was not in Hyderabad's favour. The study indicated that the telecom infrastructure in Hyderabad was inadequate for large BPO operations. This information trickled down to Hyderabad through the informal channel of Telugu techies working in Dell headquarters. Andhra Pradesh officials took pre-emptive action and convinced leading telecom companies to rapidly extend their services in Hyderabad. They then requested Kip to come to Hyderabad, knowing fully that Dell had made up its mind on Bangalore. As a part of the pitch made to Kip, a meeting was arranged with several telecom companies—Reliance, Tata, Bharti, BSNL and so on—and as agreed in advance, all the companies assured Dell of their commitment to provide the necessary quality of telecom links to the US. A possible hurdle was thus overcome through proactive action.

Not only this, officials arranged a meeting with Naidu in a rather cinematic style. Naidu was travelling and was scheduled to return to Hyderabad just thirty minutes before Kip's flight to Bangalore. 'We took him to the Institute of Administration. The CM landed there in his helicopter, and he met Kip for ten minutes. We then flew Kip in CM's helicopter to the airport. It landed right next to the

*Andhra Pradesh chief minister N. Chandrababu Naidu meeting
CEOs in America to market Cyberabad (courtesy: J.A. Chowdary)*

aircraft, and Kip could catch his flight to Bangalore in time. Kip said,
"It doesn't matter if Dell comes to Hyderabad or not, I will always
remember how responsive this government is." This is how we
targeted companies individually, putting in a lot of effort,' recounted
Sudan.[25] Dell did come to Hyderabad in March 2003.

Producing Techies and Managers

The plan of developing a new metropolis based on technology
and service industries could not be achieved without assuring an
adequate supply of a highly skilled labour force. Low labour cost
was one of the key drivers for large technology firms to operate in
Hyderabad or outsource their services.

For nearly two decades after Hyderabad's integration with
India, Osmania University was the sole, significant institution
of higher learning in the Telangana region which historically
lacked higher education facilities. In the 1970s, the University of
Hyderabad, Jawaharlal Nehru Technological University, Andhra
Pradesh Agriculture University, Kakatiya University and Regional

Engineering College (renamed NIT Warangal in 2002) were developed. Andhra University and Sri Venkateswara University catered to the higher education needs in the coastal Andhra and Rayalaseema regions respectively. Until the late 1980s, these institutions served as a source of manpower for both private businesses and public sector enterprises.

Beginning in the early 1990s, a growing 'industry' of private engineering colleges emerged. In 1995, unified Andhra Pradesh had thirty-two engineering colleges, producing 8,000 graduates annually. Naidu's government relaxed the rules in 1995 to encourage the setting up of private institutions, especially in revenue districts that lacked colleges. In ten years, the number of colleges jumped to 267 with an annual enrolment of 80,000. Setting up an engineering college was a capital-intensive activity and also required a large piece of land. Therefore, wealthy farmers in the coastal Andhra region with surpluses from agricultural income invested in setting up engineering colleges. According to economist and author Sanjaya Baru, 'The Green Revolution in coastal Andhra played a very important role in the emergence of a rural rich class which first invested in education (private engineering and medical colleges) and then came into the business.'[26]

Researchers believe that initially the growth of these colleges was driven primarily by a social demand for engineering education, which was seen as a passport for well-paying employment, and not so much due to the industry demand.[27] Local demand became a factor when the IT industry started to take roots. By the late 1990s, the state possessed a sizeable pool of English-speaking engineers, several of whom were hired by the services sector and trained in specialised skills like the Y2K problem. 'Hyderabad had a large pool of talent in the early 1990s itself. There were many computer training centres and colleges producing engineering graduates. Youngsters from districts came here for training in computer skills. All this got a boost with the Y2K business growing in the late 1990s,' explained Mudraganam Chandrashekhar, an IT consultant who studied computer engineering at Wayne State University and returned to Hyderabad in 1990.[28]

For higher-end work, like software systems development, the industry needed engineers with superior skill sets in computer science, systems development and research. Hyderabad lacked a research university like the Indian Institute of Science, an IIT or an IIM that could cater to this demand. In the 1970s and 1980s, the computer and software industries benefited from technical institutions like IITs. For example, IIT Kanpur's Computer Centre was equipped with a variety of contemporary IBM and CDC machines that were used to train both students and industry executives. Several IIT graduates were employed in companies like ECIL and CMC and also floated entrepreneurial firms in Hyderabad in the 1980s. By the 1990s, IITs were more than just engineering colleges; they had developed into a global brand, and any prospective technology hub had to have one. Hyderabad required a prominent institute to be recognised as a technology centre.

Getting a Centre-sponsored IIT sanctioned for Andhra Pradesh would have taken a long time and required much political manoeuvring. The architects of Cyberabad, therefore, took a decision to build an IIT-like university with assistance from businesses. This gave birth to the Indian Institute of Information Technology (IIIT or Triple–IT), with schools supported by different companies. The first school was established by Microsoft, followed by the IBM School for Enterprise-wide Computing, the Oracle School for Advanced Software Technology and the Metamor School of Software Development Methodologies. These schools formed the core of IIIT with the state government providing the infrastructure. To kick-start the institute without waiting for a new building to be constructed, the government assigned a government building to IIIT that was nearly finished and meant to house the Collector's office and District Courts of the Ranga Reddy district. It was in an institutional area close to HITEC city. Overnight, courtrooms became classrooms and judge's quarters became dorms. IIIT became fully functional within three months of its conception.

To give the institute a global profile, Naidu persuaded Raj Reddy, a well-known computer scientist from Carnegie Mellon, to serve as the chair of its Governing Council. Narendra Ahuja, a leading computer scientist from the University of Illinois, agreed to be the founder director. He developed a truly international faculty, which included Kamlakar Karlapalem (a doctorate from Georgia Institute of Technology), Jayanthi Sivaswamy (PhD from Syracuse University who was teaching at the University of Auckland) and C.V. Jawahar (PhD from IIT Kharagpur), among others. The course combined research with teaching, which was a novel attempt at the undergraduate level in India then. 'The goal was to set up a research-oriented institution that can start new companies, a Silicon Valley in Hyderabad,' recalled Rajeev Sangal, who was the head of the Department of Computer Science and Engineering at IIT Kanpur before joining IIIT.[29]

Since IIIT was not established by the Central government but was an initiative of the state government, the Central Ministry of Human Resources Development objected to it using 'Indian' in its name. IIIT was asked to change its name, dropping 'Indian' from it. In response, its governing body in 2001 decided to replace 'Indian' with 'International' and renamed the institute as International Institute of Information Technology.

Around the same time when IIIT was being conceived in Hyderabad, India's top business leaders were planning a new business school to train the next generation of business leaders. Their dream was to create a business school of international standard. International companies that came to India after 1991 found that Indian management graduates (MBAs) lacked a global perspective. Most management graduates did not have industry experience, unlike the West where management courses were meant for those who had worked in industry for some time.

Rajat Gupta, a Harvard Business School graduate who became the managing director of McKinsey & Company in 1994, was behind the idea of a new business school. He discussed it with Anil Ambani, Adi Godrej, Kaki Dadiseth, Lakshmi Mittal, Kumar Mangalam Birla and others. In early 1996, this group formed an Executive Board to pursue the creation of 'a private, independent, international business school' in India.[30] Rahul Bajaj, Anand Mahindra and Deepak Parekh joined the group subsequently. Each member of the group agreed to contribute USD 1 million to seed-fund the project. By the end of 1996, they had raised USD 15 million. It was decided to enlist Kellogg, Wharton and London Business School as academic partners to launch one-year MBA programme in India.

Mumbai being the financial capital was the first choice to locate the school. A 'land and development committee' chaired by Adi Godrej identified a 100 acre site in Navi Mumbai. At that time, a coalition of Shiv Sena and BJP was in power. To speed up government clearances, committee members called on Shiv Sena leader Balasaheb Thackeray. The meeting boomeranged. Thackeray demanded that Indian School of Business (ISB) set aside seats for Maharashtrian students and give preference to hiring local people.[31] This was not acceptable to the promoters of the business school as it would have meant diluting the quality of teaching and education. The Board then formed another committee to search for an alternate site. The panel checked out over fifty locations, including Hyderabad, and found many states ready to host the school.

A business daily reported about the trouble ISB faced in Maharashtra. It caught the attention of officials in Naidu's office and they convinced the chief minister that he should seize the opportunity. The same day, Naidu wrote a personal letter to all the board members and followed up with a telephone call.[32] The executive board decided to send a delegation to Hyderabad. 'Leaving no stone unturned, I sent two of my cabinet ministers to receive them at the airport. Breaking the protocol, I served breakfast to them (at my residence),' Naidu later recalled.[33] 'I told them they will have unbridled access to me, directly. They were startled. This never happened in the India of the 1990s,' he added. ISB was given 250 acres of land in Gachibowli in 1998 at 'an extremely favourable rate of Rs 25,000 per acre'. Management professors from the universities of Yale, Stanford, Chicago and Texas, besides Wharton and Kellogg, were invited to serve as visiting faculty.

Naidu's hope that ISB would work as a magnet for investment in Gachibowli was fulfilled early. Microsoft, which was operating its development centre from Cyber Towers, decided to build its campus on a plot next to ISB in 2004. Many others—Novartis, Wipro, Infosys, Sierra Atlantic, Polaris, Cap Gemini, Bank of America and Franklin Templeton Investments—set up their offices in the area.[34]

The presence of a business school backed by Wharton and Kellogg became an additional selling point for Cyberabad. 'Every time we went abroad for road shows or had visitors or whenever the chief minister made a presentation about Andhra Pradesh, there always used to be a slide about ISB,' recalled Sudan.[35]

Success of Cyberabad

Several domestic and external factors contributed to the shaping of the technology business in Hyderabad during the 1990s and the success of Cyberabad in later decades. While outsourcing as a business strategy had existed for a long time in sectors like manufacturing, it expanded to information technology services, software development and business processes prominently in the 1990s. Traditionally, companies outsourced their non-core functions for financial reasons like cost reduction, generating additional profits and cutting down capital outlays. Manufacturing companies began contract manufacturing to take advantage of the easy availability of experienced vendors and to achieve economies of scale.

A new driver for outsourcing—shortage of skilled manpower in the West—emerged in the 1990s, along with the advent of new technologies in telecom as well as the internet, and the need to shift existing computer systems to new technology platforms. The changes in the visa rules introduced in 1993 made it difficult for foreign nationals to come and work in businesses in America. If American companies wanted to hire foreign professionals to work in America, the visa rules stipulated that they should be paid market wages prevailing locally and given social security benefits. All this restricted the ability of the US corporations to directly employ foreign technical workers. Indian IT companies then devised a new model under which a part of the work would be done at the client site in America while the rest would be executed offshore, meaning in India. The model gradually became a success with more and more service companies in Bangalore and Hyderabad working for American and European clients. Most of them operated from STPs.

Then hit the so-called Millennium Bug or the Y2K problem. It was a problem ingrained in COBOL, one of the oldest programming languages in use until the 1990s. The language was designed for large mainframe computers that had limited memory. Programmers used standardised dates with two digits each for day, month and year. For example, 28 January 1992 would be denoted by 012892 (month–day–year). They left out 19 in the year field. So, for 1 January 2000, all these programmes would show the date as 010100. Computer programmers realised that computers might interpret 00 as 1900 and not 2000. This, banks and insurance companies feared, could impact interest calculations and repayment schedules. So, they began to fix it from the mid-1990s onward. It was a laborious task to scan all the software, identify the date fields and rewrite them. Western companies needed to hire thousands of workers to fix this problem. The US government was forced to ease visa rules for software professionals, while corporations started shipping work to India for cost and technical advantage (familiarity of Indian professionals with the mainframe technology and COBOL).

Y2K opened new opportunities in Hyderabad. The city became the Y2K hub in India. Satyam formed a subsidiary, Dr Millennium, to offer a web-based solution for the Y2K problem to clients in America. It developed a software-fix called Cure2000 which could diagnose and repair basic input/output system (BIOS), operating system and application software. Telugu software entrepreneurs in America formed small companies and farmed out Y2K-related work to units in Hyderabad. Training centres cropped up and thousands of youngsters got trained in COBOL and mainframe systems. 'A few months of training would have made a fresh graduate saleable. A fresher could suddenly dream of his first foreign junket. The scarcity of human resources was so severe that managers would not know whether a particular employee would turn up the next morning,' recalled A.S. Murthy, who joined Satyam Computer Services when the Y2K scare was just spreading.[36]

The Y2K boom opened the doors to a larger IT market for companies in Hyderabad. They hired graduates from non-IT streams and trained them. As the business expanded in the post-Y2K years, they used the domain knowledge of such workers for software development work. American and European companies who outsourced Y2K work to India got a taste of the model and saw the benefits. Meanwhile, other opportunities in new areas kept the business flowing. 'It was not just Y2K. Then you had the internet boom, technology boom, and telecom boom. And we also had a lot of platform shifts—SAP, CRM and ERP and so forth,' explained Saurabh Srivastava, industry analyst and angel investor.[37] Each such shift generated more opportunities for software services companies.

Competitive pressures and the need for better financial performance altered the nature and scale of outsourcing in the 2000s. Almost every function started getting outsourced. On one end, corporations outsourced basic processes like human resources management and customer relations, and on the other end, they outsourced certain core functions like engineering and R&D. With the requisite infrastructure, technical manpower and favourable government policies, Cyberabad could take advantage of the full spectrum of outsourcing.

12

A Party Drug, Diazepam and Reverse Engineering

∽

A NALGESICS AND ANTIBIOTICS WERE THE TWO DRUG classes that engaged the attention of scientists and pharmaceutical companies in the middle of the twentieth century. Antibiotics saved millions of lives during the Second World War, while new types of analgesics helped relieve pain of injured soldiers. After the War, drug companies in Europe and America were in a race to develop newer analgesics and antibiotics, and patent them quickly so that they could reap the profits. Dr Yellapragada Subbarow, a biochemist working with Lederle Laboratories in America, developed several new drugs, including tetracycline in the 1940s. He was born in Bhimavaram in coastal Andhra, then a part of Madras Presidency. People in his homeland, however, could not benefit from his discoveries as the drugs were all patented by the American company. Indian drug companies were too small and lacked the resources for research and development.

At that time, a few research groups got interested in developing effective painkillers. They were looking for synthetic alternatives for existing drugs that were mostly based on opioids like morphine (derived from the opium poppy). As a young chemist at Lucknow University in 1944, Syed Husain Zaheer came across reports about pethidine that the German chemist Otto Eisleb had synthesised in 1939. It was claimed to be an efficient analgesic but was not habit-forming like morphine. Zaheer asked two of his research students—Gurbachan Singh Sidhu and Indra Kishore Kacker—to synthesise the drug as it was not available outside Germany. The research group explored heterocyclic organic compounds like piperidine and quinazoline, which were similar to the structure of pethidine.

Scientific research in an Indian university at that time was difficult. The supply of even ordinary chemicals was scarce due to the Second World War. 'We had to synthesize ethylene chlorohydrin for which even ethylene had to be prepared by us,' Zaheer recalled.[1] The lack of chemicals was compensated with a good library to keep students abreast about the latest developments in chemistry, particularly in Germany which was considered a leader in the field. 'In spite of the War, the library was rich in German literature and the textbook sections were also well stocked,' remembered Kacker.[2] 'In the beginning, Dr Zaheer used to painstakingly read the German journals to me, after which I joined German language classes. In order to read the German literature, we were required to take a German course examination, especially if you were a research student.' Three of the faculty members, including Zaheer, were trained in chemistry in Germany. One of them, A.C. Chatterjee, also took German language classes.

Meanwhile, Zaheer shifted to Hyderabad in 1946 as the principal of the City Science College and Kacker joined the chemical laboratories of CSIR (then located in the University of Delhi) to work under Dr Salimuzzaman Siddiqui—a leading organic chemist who later became the founding head of Pakistan CSIR. Sidhu continued the work on synthesising derivatives of piperidine and quinazoline in Lucknow. From the City Science College, Zaheer shifted to CLSIR in 1948 as its director. Here he recruited Kacker to work with him while Sidhu remained in Lucknow to complete his PhD.

Piperidine was a hot subject of research globally because its structure was similar to that of morphine, and pethidine was one of its derivatives. Nathan B. Eddy, a leading expert on opiate analgesics, had postulated that 'the presence of a tertiary nitrogen group in beta relationship to a quaternary carbon carrying a phenyl group' in piperidine was an optimal condition for analgesic activity as seen in morphine and pethidine.

The structure of the quinazoline derivatives that Zaheer's group synthesised had 'two nitrogen atoms with one of them in beta relationship with the tertiary carbon atom at 4 although the chain separating these is –N-C- instead of –C-C-'. This means it was similar in many ways to the conditions described by Eddy. The group synthesised seventeen new quinazolines, which, Zaheer proposed, could be 'intermediaries in the preparation of substituted 4-quinazolines and their esters for testing their analgesic activity'. In effect, they could yield a potential analgesic.

A research note on the experiments, co-authored by Kacker and Zaheer, was submitted for publication to *Journal of Indian Chemical Society* in October 1950 and it was published in mid-1951.[3] The two acknowledged the role of Dr A.C. Chatterji who offered the research facilities at Lucknow University and Dr G.S. Sidhu for his help in conducting the experiments. The research paper did not contain data on the biological activity of the potential analgesic.

Zaheer subsequently sent the synthesised compounds for investigating their pharmacological activity to Professor Gujral at King George's Medical College, Lucknow. The screening did not find any analgesic activity in any of the starting materials but one of the resulting compounds, 2-methyl-3-orthotone-4(3h) or methaqualone, was found to be a potential hypnotic drug. After testing it in animals, it was tested clinically in medical and surgical patients as well as a set of healthy volunteers. It was found to be 'a hypnotic of lesser toxicity and greater duration of activity' than diallyl-barbituric acid, another classic sedative.

Meanwhile, the 1951 research paper of Kacker and Zaheer attracted the attention of drug companies and laboratories globally and they synthesised several compounds based on the leads provided in the paper. Multinational drug companies also launched new analgesics based on the findings of the research done in Lucknow and Hyderabad. It was suspected that pharmacological information about the potential hypnotic was deliberately leaked from Lucknow University. Zaheer's colleagues, according to some accounts, blame a mole in the Pharmacology department at K.G. Medical College who secretly contacted an American company after he found one of Zaheer's compounds to be a potent analgesic.[4] It was only in 1959 that Zaheer and Kacker got an Indian patent for 'a process for the manufacture of 2-methyl-3 orthotolyl- 4-(3H), or quinazoline, and its salts'.[5]

Boots Pure Drug Company Limited was the first one to commercialise methaqualone as a drug (branding it Melsedin), followed by Standard Pharmaceuticals which sold it under the brand name Hypnodine. A German company, Grunenthal, obtained a patent on methaqualone as a muscular relaxant. The US FDA approved methaqualone as a sedative-hypnotic sold under the brand name Quaalude. Indians discovered a new molecule but others took the critical steps necessary to convert it into a drug.

Methaqualone attained global blockbuster status as a 'sleeping pill'. The wide popularity of this drug in Europe, America and elsewhere also brought it infamy. It was addictive and began to be misused and gained notoriety as a 'party drug' in the 1960s. Some countries restricted its sale, while others prohibited its use fully. The widespread concern over its abuse forced its listing in the schedules of the UN Convention on Psychotropic Drugs in 1971. Eventually, methaqualone faced a full ban in many countries.[6] It was listed among banned narcotics substances in India but available in some countries under the brand name Mandrax and Quaalude.

The methaqualone experience left a bitter taste in Zaheer's mouth. He realised the need both for the protection of intellectual property and the infrastructure crucial for converting a discovered molecule into a commercial drug. After a few years, Kacker left CSIR and joined IDPL in Delhi. He then started his own company, K Methaqualone and Chemicals Private Limited, in Lucknow to manufacture drug intermediary chemicals. 'He was so attached with his discovery that he named the company after it although it did not manufacture methaqualone and had nothing to do with it,' said Anuj Kacker, his son.[7]

In later years, Zaheer's group, working on derivatives of tetra hydroquinolines used for malaria treatment, discovered another analgesic that was found to produce 'sedation and loss of aggressive behaviour' in dogs and cats. For pharmacological evaluation, the samples were sent this time to a lab in America—Riker Laboratories. Clinical studies in America suggested it could be a potential tranquilliser. Another American firm, Strassenburgh Laboratories, was willing to collaborate for screening the compounds synthesised at RRL. It requested 5 to 10 grams of substances for preliminary screening and sent certain required chemicals as a gift.

The approach to drug discovery at RRL was still empirical, as Zaheer noted, because 'the chemist who synthesizes new potential drugs according to certain hypotheses is never certain that the compound planned will prove to be biologically active.'[8] Moreover, the mode of action of these drugs on the central nervous system was never clear in the early stages. Therefore, he suggested, 'frequent meeting of minds of chemists, pharmacologists, biologists and others connected with this subject'.[9]

In 1964, RRL's Medicinal Chemistry Division synthesised another new molecule, N-phenethyl anthranilic acid or mefenamic acid, as a potential anti-inflammatory agent, after screening hundreds of compounds. With the methaqualone experience at the back of their mind, this time round researchers moved with caution. The chemical structure of the molecule was kept under wraps. It was code-named RH-8, after the initials of S. Riaz Hashim, one of the two discoverers, the other being Prahlad Balwantrao Sattur. The duo experimented with the drug for almost a decade and obtained two patents in 1974 for the analgesic, anti-inflammatory and antipyretic properties of their discovery. This was the first synthetic drug to be developed in India.

A postgraduate in chemistry from Aligarh Muslim University, Hashim joined RRL in 1963 and started working in stereochemistry. 'We synthesized several compounds and used to send them for testing to a laboratory in Bombay. The compounds were code-named after my name's initials, RH. The eighth one produced a good result. We synthesized more of it and contacted one Dr Sisodia who was a professor of pharmacology at Osmania Medical College and Gandhi Medical College. It was tested on rats and dogs,' Hashim recounted.[10]

In 1977, RRL tied up with Unichem Laboratories, a Bombay-based pharmaceutical company, for the next steps, which involved conducting clinical studies for safety and toxicity. The company paid Rs 25 lakh for these studies and agreed to pay a 9 per cent royalty to RRL on the annual turnover, while the patents remained with RRL.[11] Unichem launched the drug Tromaril in 1980. It was marketed by the firm for several years, but it lost its market due to the subsequent introduction of more effective drugs in this area.[12]

In the early 1960s and 1970s, foreign firms still dominated the Indian pharmaceuticals market. This was because they could get Indian patents for formulations sold under different brand names under the provisions of the Patents and Design Act of 1911. In addition, Indian companies could not compete because they hardly invested in R&D and lacked the financial and marketing resources of their foreign counterparts. After nearly two decades of debate in and outside the Parliament, the Patents Act was amended in 1970. Instead of brands or products, the new law allowed only process patents for drugs and that too only for a single method or process of manufacture. This meant that if an existing drug was made with a new process, it qualified for a new patent.

The law, which came into force in 1972, was to encourage the 'production of process-patented drugs by alternative methods' and to 'crack patents of items not patented in India' to produce less expensive drugs.[13] In addition, the government capped prices of essential drugs and foreign firms were told to reduce overseas holding to 26 per cent. Simultaneously, the government identified drugs and intermediates considered essential to serve the health needs of India. States were told to boost manufacturing

units in industrially 'backward areas' and float joint ventures with
the private sector for bulk drug manufacture. Units for making
aluminium foil for strip-packing of tablets, glass ampoules and
glass containers were established.[14] These steps gave birth to an
indigenous drugs and pharmaceutical industry.

Taking advantage of the new patent law and enabling policies,
the public sector firm Indian Drugs and Pharmaceuticals
Limited (IDPL) decided to make formulations for retail
markets, in addition to bulk drugs. It identified thirty-four
new drugs including Vitamin B6, sulphadiazine, metronidazole
and diazepam, for making formulations using the bulk drugs
it produced.[15] The company was issued a 'letter of intent' for
the manufacture of diazepam (5 mg and 10 mg tablets) and
metronidazole (200 mg tablet) and was permitted to import
bulk drugs for the production of these two formulations.[16] At
that time, diazepam, a tranquilliser, was being manufactured by
Roche while metronidazole, used for treatment of dysentery,
was marketed by Rhone-Poulenc.

*The library at RRL Hyderabad where researcher M.F. Rahman
worked out a new process for diazepam which became a blockbuster
drug (courtesy: Nehru Memorial Museum and Library)*

In the 1960s, diazepam (sold as Valium) was a top-selling drug for Roche but somehow it had not been patented in India. Most multinational firms introduced their new drugs in India only after they had reaped profits in the West and were at the end of their commercial lifecycle. Ranbaxy, a Delhi-based pharmaceutical firm, decided to take up the production of diazepam. It started procuring diazepam in bulk from a state-run company in Hungary where patented drugs could be manufactured because of lax regulation. Since Roche had no patent for it in India, Ranbaxy imported diazepam from Hungary and got a licence to sell it in retail. The drug was given a fancy brand name, Calmpose, and aggressively marketed in north India. It recorded a sales turnover of Rs 1 crore in 1969, making it a blockbuster.[17] But the situation changed soon as the government capped prices of essential medicines, including diazepam, and foreign exchange too became scarce.

Ranbaxy decided to focus on developing new processes for popular drugs, taking advantage of the new patent regime. Bhai Mohan Singh, managing director of Ranbaxy Laboratories, approached the director of RRL, G.S. Sidhu, while he was visiting Delhi, for help in developing new processes for popular drugs. The first project he entrusted to RRL was diazepam. Sidhu came back to Hyderabad and assigned the project to G. Thyagarajan. Thaygarajan, who had an active group of young chemists working with him, called a meeting and asked for volunteers to work on diazepam.

'I instantly offered to work though I knew nothing about diazepam,' recalled M.F. Rahman, who had joined RRL in 1965 as a junior scientific assistant under a PL-480 project after completing MSc in organic chemistry from Marathwada University.[18] 'The first thing I did was to head straight to the RRL library, which used to be well stacked with books and the latest journals and started looking for literature on diazepam. There were no computers, no photocopying machines, and, of course, no internet. I used to take copious notes in my notebook,' he recounted. He studied all the available literature and, within a few days, worked out a process that consisted of seven steps to make diazepam.

The next task was to translate the process developed on paper to the bench with actual chemicals and reactions to see if it yielded the desired compound. 'The reactions were lengthy and we had to do them very carefully because they involved some fuming compounds. I used to request lab assistants to stay through the night and give them the next day off. This way we could run the reaction continuously and save time,' said Rahman. Within a few months, the laboratory scale process for diazepam was ready and it was transferred to Ranbaxy.

Scaling up the laboratory process to a commercial scale was not a smooth affair. The technical personnel from Hyderabad were called to help Ranbaxy at its Mohali plant. K.W. Gopinath, a research scientist from RRL Jorhat who had joined Ranbaxy as the head of its fledgling R&D unit, helped stabilise the process.[19] His team included M. Sivakumaran, who had done his doctorate under him in Jorhat. In 1974, Ranbaxy started manufacturing Calmpose at its Mohali plant using the RRL process.

Since the know-how for making Calmpose had been indigenously developed, Bhai Mohan Singh sought duty protection for this product and got the government to ban its import. This helped Ranbaxy gain a monopoly of the market. Even Roche was forced to buy diazepam in bulk form from Ranbaxy to make Valium in India. As a result, Ranbaxy made a killing. It sold the drug worth Rs 40.16 crore till 1987.[20] 'Developing a new process for diazepam was not such a great thing. If not me, somebody else could have done it,' Rahman said modestly.

In a way, Rahman was right because far away in Pune, unknown to him, another young organic chemist at the National Chemical Laboratory (NCL), A.V. Rama Rao, was engaged in developing a process for the same drug. The director of NCL, B.D. Tilak received a letter from Prime Minister Indira Gandhi, also the president of CSIR, asking him to help Indian companies take advantage of the new patent law. Tilak, in turn, directed senior scientists to identify processes that the industry could take up.

The response was lukewarm. Senior scientists were reluctant to take up projects for the industry, remembered Rama Rao, who attended the meeting on behalf of Venkataraman, former director of NCL with whom he was working then.[21] The meeting set young Rama Rao thinking. While going through trade magazines and journals, he found that Valium of Roche was making more money than antibiotics. It was a tranquilliser and a mood-elevating drug, so he decided to work on it.

He developed a process to make the compound and synthesised a few grams of it in the lab. Since it was not a sponsored project, he kept the information about the diazepam process to himself. During a visit to Bombay in early 1972, an acquaintance took Rama Rao to visit the R&D centre of Cipla where he happened to meet Yusuf Hamied, son of Cipla founder Khwaja Abdul Hamied. Yusuf Hamied was a doctorate in natural products chemistry from the University of Cambridge, where he had an opportunity to work with Alexander Todd, who later received the Nobel Prize.[22] The two young men got talking, and Hamied was surprised when Rama Rao casually mentioned that he had developed a process to make diazepam. At that time, Cipla was planning to manufacture the same molecule. The two exchanged notes, and Cipla formally approached NCL for the know-how.

After this exchange, Hamied and Rama Rao became lifelong associates—a friendship that was to pitchfork India into a leading destination globally of life-saving drugs in the decades to come. In 1975, Rama Rao proceeded on a two-year stint to Harvard in the laboratory of the Nobel laureate E.J. Corey and worked on anti-cancer compounds. 'When I came back, Hamied asked me to join Cipla. He said, "You can build a lab, and even do fundamental work up to 50 percent of strength." Ranbaxy also offered to pay a salary equalling ten times my CSIR package,' Rama Rao recalled.[23] But he chose to continue in NCL, becoming the head of the Organic Chemistry division.

In a project funded by the Maharashtra government, he developed an anti-cancer agent, vincristine, derived from the leaves of *Vinca Rosea*. Cipla commercialised it, pricing it 75 per cent lower than the imported equivalent. Over the next decade, the partnership between Rama Rao and Hamied resulted in the production of copies of several key drugs at affordable prices. This included ibuprofen, ketoprofen, salbutamol, vitamin B6 and so on. But the best out of this unique partnership was yet to come.

In July 1985, Rama Rao was appointed the director of RRL. He moved to Hyderabad, with some reluctance and trepidation. 'By this time, I was already an established expert in drug copying, working with Cipla and others. I went to them for projects and did not bother about funds from CSIR headquarters,' said Rama Rao. As a review panel headed by senior bureaucrat Abid Husain was scrutinising the work of CSIR laboratories, Rama Rao argued that RRL should be renamed as National Institute of Chemical Technology because 'there was nothing regional about it'. It was eventually named as Indian Institute of Chemical Technology (IICT) in April 1989. Later on, a prefix was added to make it CSIR-IICT. This was the third name change for the laboratory that started as CLSIR in 1944.

IICT developed cheaper processes for many drugs for Indian companies. The list included anti-cancer drugs (etoposide and mitoxantrone), antibiotics (norfloxacin and ciprofloxacin), omeprazole, astemizole, flurbiprofen, gemfibrozole, imipenam, ketorolac, ketotifen, mefloquin, sulbactam and so on. Around this time, HIV was emerging as an epidemic in many Western countries as well as in Africa. Scientists at the US National Cancer Institute (NCI) initiated work on developing therapies for HIV/AIDS, working with some compounds having potential antiviral activity. Virologists at Burroughs–Wellcome & Co. identified a set of compounds and sent them to NCI for further testing. In early 1985, one of them, AZT, was found to be potentially effective against HIV. After clinical trials, the company filed a patent and the US FDA approved AZT in 1987 as the only known therapy for HIV.

Rama Rao, who was closely following these developments, set his eyes on AZT. By 1990, when the drug received approvals for use in HIV-affected children, he was already working on a new process to make AZT. 'I proposed the idea to Hamied in 1990, but he was not fully convinced. He said there aren't enough (HIV) patients. I forced him to take it up and told him there would be enough of them in future,' Rama Rao recalled.[24] And AZT turned out to be a landmark development, for both IICT and Cipla, and also for India in its journey to gain global recognition as the 'pharmacy of the world'. Cipla came out with its version of AZT in 1993 and marketed a 100 mg capsule at one-sixth of the prevailing international price.

Three years later, scientists found that AZT, in combination with two other retrovirals, abacavir and lamivudine, had a dramatic impact on HIV treatment. Combination antiretroviral therapy (ART) became the new standard treatment but it came with a price tag of USD 14,000 per patient per year. Cipla once again took up the challenge. Working with scientists at IICT and NCL, it developed a single drug cocktail, Triomune. In September 2000, Hamied made a dramatic announcement at a meeting of the European Union (EU) health ministers and pharmaceutical company heads that Cipla was going to make ART available for USD 800 per person per year. The move caught the pharma giants by surprise. Cipla eventually supplied the combination to ninety countries at a much lower price of a dollar a day, virtually changing the course of the global HIV epidemic.

Other Indian companies followed suit and started manufacturing generic versions of HIV drugs. This was a moment of glory for the pharma industry and India, seeds for which were sown in government-run labs in India in the 1970s. The new Patents Act of 1971 was specifically designed to trigger the development of an indigenous drugs and pharmaceuticals industry in the private sector so that drugs could become affordable. In this task, the national research laboratories were made a partner and given an industry orientation. Private sector and government laboratories forged a unique partnership to develop processes for patented and patent-expired drugs. This, together with the availability of trained manpower from Indian universities, resulted in a vibrant industry that produced affordable medicines not just for the India market but also for other poor countries in Asia and Africa.

'The secrets of pharma industry are in the city's air. The learning and spreading of skills and capability happens seamlessly when national laboratories, industries and academia are present together in a city. And that's what happened in Hyderabad in the 1970s and 1980s. Developing new processes requires domain knowledge, instruments and a lot of ingenuity. Research–academia linkage and then its linkage with industry was the most critical aspect of circulation of knowledge to industry,' explained Dinesh Abrol, former scientist at CSIR-National Institute of Science, Technology and Development Studies.[25]

How this process helped Hyderabad emerge as a key player in the pharmaceutical sector in India as well as globally is elaborated in the next chapter.

13

A Catalyst and a Chain Reaction

∽

IDPL was where I gained the experience and the confidence to become an entrepreneur in the bulk drug industry. No other institution could have prepared me better.

—Dr K. Anji Reddy,
founder, Dr Reddy's Laboratories (DRL), Hyderabad[1]

IN 2023, HYDERABAD RANKED FIRST IN BULK DRUG manufacturing in India and was placed third in the production of formulations.[2] It accounted for nearly half of the bulk drugs exported from India. So, when India is called the 'pharmacy of the world', most of the credit should go to Hyderabad. The city's journey of becoming the pharmaceutical hub in the 1990s was long and intertwined with the story of India's drug industry, beginning in the 1940s.

In the 1940s, the pharmaceutical industry was a monopoly of a handful of British and European companies. Most of them either imported finished formulations or imported formulations in bulk and repackaged them to market in India. Under pressure from the government in post-Independence India, multinational firms began importing bulk drugs and got them processed into formulations by

Indian companies on a 'jobwork basis'. This approach helped avoid investing in building factories or hiring technical personnel in India, even though they earned huge amounts from the Indian market.

Of the 1,600 drug companies operating in India in 1956, as many as 1,550 accounted for only 20 per cent of the total production. They were tiny, primitively equipped and employed only six or seven people—and could hardly be called industrial units.[3] In the 1950s, foreign companies introduced antibiotics, synthetic drugs and steroids under international brand names and captured the market through aggressive marketing to doctors.

Indian companies either marketed formulations of foreign companies or manufactured simple products like tinctures, syrups, vitamins and so on. In Hyderabad, Karkhana Zinda Tilismath and J&J DeChane typified these companies. Both of them began the business around the First World War and were engaged in making proprietary Unani and Ayurvedic formulations. Karkhana Zinda Tilismath was founded in 1920 by Hakeem Mohammed Moizuddin Farooqui who had studied Unani medicine in Delhi. Zinda Tilismath, a remedy for everything from a cold to body pain, became an iconic brand that still survives in 2024. Its tagline 'har marz ki dawa' (a cure for all ailments) says it all. J&J DeChane was founded by Durante F. de Souza, a Goan medical practitioner in Hyderabad, in 1917 to make herbal formulations. DeChane sold a kit of eight bottles to treat common and chronic ailments like cough, cold, indigestion, headache, etc.

Another firm, Hyderabad Chemicals and Pharmaceuticals, came into the business in the 1930s, producing medicines to treat blood pressure as well as medicinal and vitamin tablets and injectables. Among its popular products were Infantone ('the best and safest medicine for babies'), Pepsinal ('useful in gastritis, hyperacidity and dyspepsia'), Gastronal ('a remedy for indigestion and stomach') and Vitatone ('an ideal tonic in all kinds of debility, nervousness and exhaustion').[4] Imported medicines were sold in Hyderabad, like in other parts of the country, and there was little local production up to the mid-1960s. In the 1970s, Warner-Hindustan and Biological Evans emerged as big pharmaceutical companies in Hyderabad.

As antibiotics became available in Indian markets in the years following the Second World War, leading companies in western and eastern India began importing essential drugs in bulk or in the form of penultimate compounds that could be converted into a final product using simple and easy processes. Till 1956, almost all antibiotics and essential drugs were imported.[5] Foreign companies were not interested in manufacturing bulk drugs. They used the Indian market to reap profits through formulations and non-medical products like cosmetics and chewing gums. The production of drugs entirely from indigenous raw materials was done only when technological processes were simple or they did not require large manufacturing facilities. Such a skewed market structure led to exorbitant pricing. For instance, the prices in India of broad-spectrum antibiotics were among the highest in the world.[6]

In the face of intense lobbying by multinational firms for high royalty and patent protection, Prime Minister Nehru decided in favour of setting up a penicillin factory in the public sector with help from the World Health Organization (WHO), United Nations International Children's Emergency Fund (UNICEF) and the UN Technical Assistance Fund. The factory took the shape of Hindustan Antibiotics Limited in 1952, symbolising India's resolve to end foreign monopolies in pharmaceuticals. Nehru then sought help from the Soviet Union, which was already involved in building steel plants and large dams in India. In 1958, Hindustan Organic Chemicals was established with technical know-how from the Soviet Union.

An expert panel led by Dr G.P. Kane, head of Chemical Engineering at the University of Bombay, was sent to the USSR in 1956 to explore further collaboration. Kane recommended India could save time in setting up drug factories if it opted for Soviet help as drawings and technical details were readily available from similar plants that the Soviets had built in Eastern Europe and China.[7] The government went ahead with Soviet collaboration for the manufacture of antibiotics, synthetic drugs and surgical instruments. Based on project reports prepared by the Soviet firm Technoexpert, IDPL was established in 1961. Hyderabad was selected for the synthetic drugs project while the antibiotics unit went to Rishikesh and Madras got the surgical instruments plant.

Hyderabad was found suitable because of the 'availability of water, closeness to research laboratories, possibilities of supply of raw materials and market for finished goods, climatic conditions etc.'[8] IDPL was the first large manufacturing industry to come up in Hyderabad. The funds for the unit were sanctioned in 1962, trial production began in 1967-68 and commercial production started in 1972. The unit was designed to produce 851 tonnes of vitamins, sulpha drugs, anthelmintics, analgesics, antipyretics, diuretics and anti-tubercular drugs every year.

A number of Soviet consultants were based in Hyderabad and several Indian engineers were sent to the USSR for training. This had an unexpected fallout—an increased demand for Russian language courses offered at Osmania University as the requirement for translators and interpreters increased. Hyderabad had other collaborative projects as well with the Soviet Union. The importance of the city went up and it was included in the itinerary of visiting dignitaries. Pioneering Soviet cosmonauts Yuri Gagarin and Valentina Tereshkova visited Hyderabad on goodwill missions.

The construction work of the IDPL factory was hampered due to the national emergency during the 1965 war. Moreover, the unit faced multiple technical challenges before its commissioning. The project report, it appeared, did not provide basic and vital information about the plants and their working results.[9] For instance, even after five years into the project, the Soviets kept on modifying the process to make tetracycline. 'The reason was that Russians had no patents of their own and they had to bypass the existing patents and evolve a new procedure. The collaborators were experimenting with the particular project of IDPL to get around the patents,' an official told a parliamentary committee.[10] The Soviet processes for sodium sulfacetamide and analgin had to be modified because they did not give satisfactory yields and purity.

The process of production of ribose, an intermediate for making vitamin B, involved the use of metallic sodium and mercury for amalgamation. A parliamentary investigation revealed that IDPL imported 5,000 kg of mercury as against the projected requirement of 400 kg.[11] It turned out that the Soviet process was defective and resulted in the splashing of mercury as well as the release of mercury vapour. The Soviets knew about this problem but did not alert engineers in Hyderabad about the possibility of mishaps. 'When I was in the Soviet Union, I found that the process they had given to us was quite different from what they were following. They had given us stainless steel pipes, whereas they were using glass pipes. When they gave us the design, it was at an experimental stage in their own country,' an engineer confided.[12]

Commercialising the Soviet processes was not easy. The R&D team of IDPL had to tackle many technical problems before production could begin. The unit was originally formed to develop new processes and products, besides finding locally available alternatives for imported raw materials. But in the initial years it had to mainly focus on production problems to achieve the desired quality and efficiencies of reactions. A new process for making para-Nitro benzoyl-glutamic acid—an intermediate for the synthesis of folic acid—was developed to economise on raw materials. Another project was on developing an economic method to make nikethamide, a cardiac stimulant.[13]

Atluri Raja Rao, who headed the R&D unit, was a brilliant chemist. He was 'extraordinarily good at making processes work' and in overcoming glitches while scaling up lab processes that typically yielded a few grams of chemicals to commercial scale.[14] Hailing from an agriculturist family from Vanapamula village in Krishna district, Raja Rao was a postgraduate in chemistry from Andhra University. In his modest research team were youngsters who could work under the difficult circumstances typical of a public sector unit. They were a motivated lot, driven by the national goals of self-reliance and import substitution.

One such member of the team was Kallam Anji Reddy who was pursuing his PhD at NCL after post-graduation in chemical engineering from the University Department of Chemical Technology (UDCT) in Bombay. He joined IDPL in 1967. Son of a turmeric farmer from Tadepalli near Vijayawada, Anji Reddy was a bright chemist. Along with his mentor at NCL, Dr L.K. Doraiswamy, Reddy made a fundamental theoretical contribution, which is known as the Reddy–Doraiswamy Equation. The equation is still used for estimation of liquid diffusivity. One of Anji Reddy's contemporaries from Andhra Christian College, Guntur, was G. Alfred who was already employed with IDPL. He encouraged Anji Reddy to apply for a job. After his selection for IDPL, NCL allowed him to complete the doctoral work from Hyderabad. For this, Anji Reddy used to consult the library at RRL and use the mainframe computer there for data analysis.

Raja Rao deployed Anji Reddy in the pilot plant where chemicals were produced in commercial quantities. The glitches identified during the trials had to be ironed out. Often young research workers like Anji Reddy would tinker with processes to get the desired quality and yield of the end product. Anji Reddy's exposure to industrial processes at UDCT and NCL—both had pilot plant facilities—helped him in this work. 'A group of four of us, who were reporting to the Chief Technologist, were asked to go to the research lab and verify the R&D process at the ground level scale. It was our responsibility to take this to the manufacturing scale,' recalled Anji Reddy.[15] 'Raja Rao used to say, "Let one or two batches fail; it does not matter. But why should we waste time?" He was a go-getter. So, all four of us would come in shifts. It was a 24-hour job.' Such challenging work environment in an emerging field like bulk drug manufacturing was a great learning for the team.

'Translating the laboratory process into a manufacturing process was all that was required for me to become an entrepreneur,' said Anji Reddy.[16] 'He (Raja Rao) taught me the tricks of the trade, for which I am enormously grateful.'[17] It was not just Anji Reddy who learnt these tricks at IDPL or from Raja Rao. 'He mentored so many youngsters. He is the one who opened the pharma window in Hyderabad. Aspiring entrepreneurs would go to him, and he would freely share information and knowledge. He prompted many to the opportunities in this sector and guided budding entrepreneurs,' remembers Dr N. Bhaskara Rao, a former member of the Board of Directors at IDPL.[18] Raja Rao left IDPL in 1985 after serving the company right from its inception. He was disappointed and felt isolated due to internal politics. Raja Rao then floated a consulting firm, R.R. Consultants, but it did not become a great success.

A Catalyst Called Anji Reddy

As discussed in the preceding chapter, leading pharmaceutical companies, mostly based in Bombay, Gujarat and Delhi, were knocking at the doors of government research laboratories to help them develop copies of popular drugs, taking advantage of the new patent law enacted in 1971. At the same time, something else was happening in Hyderabad. Several ancillary units were established to serve the raw material requirements of IDPL. Young chemists who had learnt the ropes of bulk drug manufacturing at the public sector unit turned into technocrat–entrepreneurs. Anji Reddy quit IDPL in 1973 and became one such entrepreneur. He carefully studied the market and decided to manufacture metronidazole (an anti-dysentery drug), one of the thirty-four drugs in IDPL's production plan.

The drug Reddy chose was in great demand and it was being imported. 'My first step was to set up a laboratory to develop the process for manufacturing metronidazole from basic raw materials. I finalized the process sitting in the library of RRL,' Reddy recalled.[19] He established the laboratory in the city, in Narayanguda, and a modest production facility in an industrial area, Nacharam. Anji Reddy floated the firm, Uniloids, with five partners—A. Krishnaswamy, Damidi Kamlakar Reddy, Pulasani Venkat Krishna Reddy, V. Lakshminarayana Rao and P.V.N. Raju.[20]

Uniloids, however, did not begin bulk drug production till 1977 for various reasons. Instead, it established a small-scale unit to make formulations using imported bulk drugs. In November 1976, it applied for a 'carry on business' licence which was refused. In May 1977, Uniloids sought to get a full industrial licence to manufacture formulations (seventeen drugs like tetracycline, analgin, etc., syrups, capsules and ointments). Bulk drug manufacturers were allowed to use their production capacity to manufacture formulations provided the ratio of bulk drug to formulation was maintained at 1:10. The licence issued in December 1977 stipulated that the ratio of imported and indigenous raw materials should be 1:2.[21]

While Uniloids was grappling with licencing and production problems, three promoters (Kamalakar Reddy, P.V. Krishna Reddy and Anji Reddy) teamed up with a new partner, Majety Rama Koteswara Rao, to float another company in May 1977. The new company, Standard Organics Limited (SOL), applied for a licence to manufacture raw material for bulk drugs. M.R.K. Rao was a chemical engineer with experience in production of organic chemicals. He developed a process to manufacture 2-Methyl Imidazole, an intermediate chemical needed to make metronidazole.[22] SOL's factory was built in Patancheru in Medak district, a notified backward area, to avail of government concessions. It raised finance from the Industrial Development Bank of India, AP Industrial Development Corporation and AP State Financial Corporation. The company, incorporated on 27 March 1978, employed 136 people.

Meanwhile, differences cropped up among the partners, most of whom were common to both Uniloids and SOL. Anji Reddy proposed a settlement deal to Kamlakar Reddy and Krishna Reddy— they would get to keep Uniloids, which was already in business, and he would get full ownership of SOL. He then got a new investor–partner—C. Chandrasekhar Reddy—who had studied chemical technology with him at UDCT and was dealing in textile chemicals in Nigeria.

Although SOL already had a licence to manufacture 2-Methyl Imidazole, Anji Reddy chose another bulk drug with a large potential market—sulfamethoxazole. Though IDPL was making major sulpha drugs but sulfamethoxazole was a relatively new addition. Anji Reddy developed a process to make sulfamethoxazole but it is unclear where he did so. In an interview recorded in 2009, Reddy told the interviewer categorically, 'I was involved in making sulfamethoxazole at IDPL and it was profitable. We made profits in IDPL, we stopped imports of sulfamethoxazole and we saved foreign exchange.'[23] But in his autobiography (published in 2015, after his death), he says he had set up a laboratory in Dwarkapuri locality in Hyderabad while he was in Uniloids and that's where he 'developed sulfamethoxazole from basic raw materials for the first time in the country.'[24]

An October 1973 note of the Ministry of Chemicals and Fertilisers supports Reddy's 2009 assertion that the process for sulfamethoxazole was developed at IDPL. It was among thirty-four drugs for which IDPL had developed process know-how and was licensed to manufacture both in bulk form and formulations.[25] Whatever may be the case, sulfamethoxazole became a grand success for SOL. Even Burroughs–Wellcome & Co. procured it from SOL for making formulations.

Having tasted success with two drugs in high demand, Anji Reddy was now ready to take the next step—formulations. Given that this market was dominated by established players like Ranbaxy, Cipla, Cadila and Lupin, Reddy thought he should make new molecules based on research. The promoters of SOL had earlier floated several small firms to work in different segments of the market and took over a sick manufacturing unit, Cheminor. Anji Reddy was a partner in another firm, Dexo Pharma, along with Chandrasekhar Reddy (who was also a partner in SOL) and Ramachandra Reddy. As differences cropped up among SOL and Dexo partners, Anji Reddy offered to exit both companies. In return for his stakes in SOL and Dexo, he received a substantial amount of money. He used this money to buy shares of Cheminor held by the other partners and take full control of the company.

SOL Works Manager M. Purushottam Chary also walked out with Anji Reddy. Chary was an old hand in pharma manufacturing, having worked with Reddy in IDPL, Uniloids and SOL. He was not a chemical engineer but had 'an amazing capability to get production up and running once a process came out of the lab'.[26] Another SOL employee who joined Anji Reddy was Murali Krishna Prasad Divi, a doctorate in pharmaceutical sciences from Kakatiya University. Divi had worked in Uniloids before going to the US where he was employed with Fike Chemical. After some years, he came back and joined SOL. Thus, Anji Reddy had in his team two long-time colleagues who excelled in chemistry and production processes.

Along with managing Cheminor, Anji Reddy began offering consultancy to Indian and foreign customers. Once a customer from Thailand came asking to develop a process for making sulfamethoxyl. Reddy tried to dissuade him as the market for this drug was highly competitive. 'He said, "No, no, I want it. Tell me how much you want." I quietly said, "Give me 100,000 dollars,"' recalled Reddy. The Thai firm agreed to pay the amount and Reddy proclaimed to his colleagues, 'We have a company. Let's call it Dr Reddy's Consultancy Services Private Limited.'[27] He appointed Chary the managing director of the consulting firm and made Divi incharge of Cheminor. At the suggestion of Chary, Anji Reddy registered the new company as Dr Reddy's Laboratories Limited (DRL) in 1984.

Yet again, Anji Reddy dug into the repertoire of failed or shelved drugs at IDPL and chose methyldopa, a drug for the treatment of high blood pressure, as the first project for DRL. IDPL had got an industrial licence to manufacture the drug in September 1973 but was facing problems in its production process. 'I thought it was a good commercial opportunity as there would be a vacuum in the market if IDPL discontinued the product and Merck would be happy to source the bulk drug from a domestic manufacturer in the private sector,' Anji Reddy reasoned.[28] DRL had its methyldopa production up within a year—by July 1985. Simultaneously, Cheminor started the production of a painkiller—ibuprofen—using a process Anji Reddy and A.V. Ram Rao of RRL had developed. Patents of both methyldopa and ibuprofen had expired many years ago. Both generics performed very well in the market.

The success of Anji Reddy in the difficult market of bulk drugs set a chain reaction in Hyderabad that soon impacted the fortunes of DRL too. Anji Reddy inducted his son-in-law, Prasad, as managing director of Cheminor, replacing his once-trusted lieutenant Divi. This followed complaints against Divi relating to the functioning of the Cheminor plant in Visakhapatnam. Prasad, who had studied chemical engineering at the Illinois Institute of Technology, had a small firm, Benzex Labs. Anji Reddy's son, Satish, who had studied medicinal chemistry at Purdue University, also joined DRL. Even before Prasad could settle down at Cheminor, Divi resigned with a bulk of the workers (nearly 200), bringing the production to a grinding halt.[29]

Divi launched Divi's Research Centre as a consulting firm in 1990 and later Divi's Laboratories to manufacture bulk drugs. The company carved out a niche for itself as a contract manufacturing company for international firms. Ramesh Babu Potluri, a chemist who worked with Divi on the ibuprofen project at Cheminor, also branched out and founded SMS Pharma.

The next major exit from DRL was that of Bandi Partha Saradhi Reddy (B.P.S. Reddy) who had been heading the R&D unit for a long time. A doctorate in synthetic organic chemistry from Osmania University, B.P.S. Reddy resigned along with twenty researchers, which included Ramaprasad Reddy, Alla Venkata Reddy and Nata Reddy. In 1993, they launched a new company. They were all engaged at DRL in developing a cheaper process for making omeprazole, a potentially profitable drug, but decided to walk out with the know-how to upstage DRL.[30] To its credit, DRL reworked the process on a war footing and could launch omeprazole before B.P.S. Reddy could do so. B.P.S. Reddy's company, Hetero Drugs, became a big name in the generics market very soon.

Alla Venkata Reddy, a postgraduate in economics who started his career with DRL and was a co-promoter of Hetero, left it in 1996 to start Lee Pharma.

M. Satyanarayana Reddy (M.S.N. Reddy), a PhD in organic chemistry from Osmania University, also left DRL and floated MSN Laboratories in 2003.

P.V. Ram Prasad Reddy, who looked after the stores in SOL, developed an interest in chemistry though he was a commerce graduate. A couple of years after Anji Reddy and others left SOL, Ram Prasad Reddy followed suit. He floated Aurobindo Pharma Limited in 1986, along with K. Nityanand Reddy, a postgraduate in chemistry. The company established its factories in Pondicherry to avail the tax benefits given in the union territory. Aurobindo started by manufacturing semi-synthetic penicillin—the first company to do so in India. It followed up with a bulk drug plant in Hyderabad.

Around the same time, Venkaiah Chowdary Nannapaneni, a pharmacy postgraduate from Andhra University, returned from America and founded Natco Fine Pharmaceuticals. He started with formulations and diversified into bulk drugs as well as research-based products. The company was subsequently renamed Natco Pharma. It introduced the 'sustained release pellet' technology in India in 1988. Next year, Targof Pure Drugs, floated by Harish C. Pandey and Asit K. Mukherjee, established a plant for making pellets. Pandey and Mukherjee were pharmaceutical graduates from Banaras Hindu University (BHU) and had worked in Africa before settling down in Hyderabad. Mukherjee began his career in Warner–Hindustan in 1977 while Pandey started with IDPL.

Between 1989 and 1995, both bulk and formulation manufacturing exploded in Hyderabad. Many companies got into the business, some merged, some closed down and a few marched ahead. Many of them had their lineage in IDPL, Uniloids, SOL and DRL. The first-generation entrepreneurs who founded them were all educated, efficient, ambitious, resourceful, daring and far-sighted. A majority of them hailed from the coastal Andhra region.

External Drivers

Several domestic and external factors facilitated the exponential growth in pharmaceutical manufacturing in Hyderabad. Companies in Europe and America were under pressure to bring down prices. In the early 1990s, the total per capita expenditure on pharmaceuticals in several OECD countries was rising faster than the rate of inflation and the rate of growth of total health expenses. In the US Congress, three bills were introduced during 1993-94 to control the prices of prescription drugs.[31] While prices were going up, the demand for medicines was projected to rise due to the ageing population in many European countries. The only solution they had was to outsource manufacturing to save costs. The period also saw a significant wave of mergers and acquisitions in the pharmaceutical industry in the West. All these factors gave rise to a market for generics significantly.

At that time, the production of pharmaceuticals was concentrated in six countries—America, Japan, France, Germany, Switzerland and the UK. Several countries adopted policies that allowed manufacturers of generics to conduct limited trials to establish the 'bioequivalence' of their drugs.[32] Since generics were copies of patent-expired drugs, they were priced much lower and could thus induce competition in the market. This prompted large pharmaceutical companies to sign contracts for manufacturing deals with generics manufacturers.

These external market and regulatory factors benefited the pharmaceutical industry in Hyderabad. Companies started exporting bulk drugs to several countries in Europe and Asia, and soon entered the global markets with their own brands. Many firms signed export deals, joint ventures and marketing arrangements in foreign markets. In the early 1990s, DRL made a breakthrough in exports with Russia, followed by joint ventures in South Africa and France. The economic liberalisation unleashed in 1991 catalysed this process.

The rapid expansion of the bulk drug and formulation industry gave rise to several other business opportunities such as contract research, contract manufacturing, custom synthesis, clinical research and so on.

Custom synthesis involves synthesising a molecule in small quantities according to the needs of the customer. The customer provides the process information and specifies the level of purity needed. Drugs in small quantities (typically a few kilos) are often required for experimental work, clinical trials and so on. For this, the use of large-scale manufacturing plants is neither feasible nor affordable. For custom synthesis, small reactors are used. Since environmental laws and regulations were very stringent in Europe and North America, many customers would reach out to Hyderabad for custom synthesis.

In the 1980s and 1990s, custom synthesis became almost a cottage industry in and around industrial areas like Bollaram, Gandhinagar, Kukkatpally and Patancheru. Organic chemists working in research-based firms like DRL would often moonlight and undertake custom synthesis work in their home labs. 'Such people would work through the night and synthesize molecules for foreign customers. They were adept in refining molecules by adding functional groups. People had 5-litre, all-glass reactors installed in their kitchens and bedrooms, and resulting solvents were just drained in sewers. Sometimes, for a half kg of crystals, they would charge 100,000 dollars. It was a lucrative business. No license, no pollution control, nothing,' Asit Mukherjee recalled.[33] They could also develop alternate processes. 'If a good organic chemist gets a process to develop, then he can play around with functional groups—as they say in Urdu "*Nukte ke pher me Khuda juda*"—and can come up with a new and different process. Organic chemistry runs in the bone marrow of chemistry graduates here,' explained Mukherjee. (In Urdu, just interchanging diacritic mark can change the meaning of a word, like khuda can become juda).

This laid the foundation of a new line of organised business— outsourcing of chemistry services. In the early 1990s, several non-resident Indian professionals in America and Europe were in top positions in the chemical and pharmaceutical industries there. Many of them launched entrepreneurial research and manufacturing firms or were suppliers of services to big pharma companies. They were fully aware of the technical skills and capabilities of organic chemists back home and could easily drive the custom synthesis market in Hyderabad. Custom synthesis, in a way, opened a critical window of opportunity for small companies. American and European customers who initially came for custom synthesis saw the potential of outsourcing research, clinical trials and contract manufacturing to firms in Hyderabad.

———•———

An indigenous drug and pharmaceutical industry took roots with the objective of achieving self-reliance and making medicines available to the Indian people at affordable prices. This was achieved through the new patent law, process development in national laboratories and the rise of entrepreneurial firms as a result of the opportunities created by the public sector units. By the mid-1990s, Hyderabad became the bulk drug capital of India, accounting for more than a third of the national production. In the next phase, the industry took up the export of bulk drugs and eventually started supplying life-saving medicines to countries globally. Gradually, Western markets became heavily dependent on genetics made in Hyderabad. For instance, in 2022, Aurobindo Pharma was the largest generics supplier in America by the number of prescriptions. Laurus Labs was a major supplier of bulk drugs to make Anti-Retroviral (ARVs) for HIV/AIDS treatment, hepatitis C and cancer drugs globally. Hetero alone catered to 40 per cent of the global demand for ARVs in bulk drug and finished dosage forms. In December 2022, the company launched a generic version of an oral drug developed by Pfizer to treat COVID-19—nirmatrelvir.

While the generics business has grown a great deal, India lost its edge in the bulk drugs segment with the rise of China in the API market after 2000. Many drug manufacturers, including several in India, became dependent on China for the supply of bulk drugs (or active pharmaceutical ingredients—APIs) even for essential formulations. Before the COVID-19 pandemic, China accounted for nearly 30 per cent of the global API market. The pandemic disrupted API supplies from China, which in turn affected the pharma manufacturing in Hyderabad and other pharma clusters in India. To avoid a similar situation in the future, the effort is to regain the ground lost to China in APIs. The Central government announced policies to boost API production, while the Telangana government in 2021 began developing a massive Hyderabad Pharma City for API manufacturing. Once completed, it is projected to be the largest single pharmaceutical cluster anywhere in the world.

14

Vaccine Wars and Genome Valley

❧

At this (WHO) meeting I heard about hepatitis B, for the first time in my life. Some speakers made disparaging comments about developing countries—'they come with begging bowls for subsidized vaccines', 'How long should the world carry this burden', etc. I felt very uneasy. This got into my head and I started thinking about doing something to change this situation of poor countries not being able to afford available vaccines due to high prices.

–K.I. Varaprasad Reddy,
founder of Shantha Biotechnics,
on why he thought of making a Hepatitis B vaccine[1]

HYDERABAD SHOT TO INTERNATIONAL PROMINENCE during the COVID-19 pandemic as it emerged as the site for the development and production of several vaccines against the virus. With a clutch of developers and suppliers of these vaccines located in one geographic area, the city claimed its position as the vaccine capital of India. Like the journey in bulk drugs and pharmaceuticals, Hyderabad's path to success in vaccine production too has been unsteady.

The widely deployed methods to make vaccines involve either the use of attenuated organisms or inactivated organisms. By exposing pathogens to air or chemicals they can be attenuated. Louis Pasteur discovered that such attenuated organisms can be used for vaccination. Viruses can be inactivated by removing their disease-causing genetic material and then used in vaccines because they are still capable of evoking the desired immune responses from the human body. Such vaccines are referred as 'killed vaccines' as they don't make use of the whole organism but are based on inactivated toxins, virus particles or conjugates. For several decades, life-saving vaccines for children were based on these two technologies.

At the time of Independence, India had several British-era laboratories like the Haffkine Institute, the Pasteur Institute and the Central Research Institute at Kasauli that made vaccines for smallpox, plague, cholera and typhoid. The vaccines produced were used in the event of epidemics and outbreaks. India did not have any routine immunisation programmes and there were no production facilities to make vaccines at a commercial scale. The BCG Laboratory at Guindy was established in 1948. BCG (Bacillus Calmette-Guerin) vaccine against tuberculosis was introduced in the health programme on a limited scale in 1948, with technical help from UNICEF.

Mass vaccination for smallpox began in 1962 with the launch of the national smallpox eradication programme under World Health Organization (WHO). The successful eradication of smallpox achieved in 1977 spurred the start of the Expanded Programme of Immunisation to immunise infants with life-saving vaccines like DPT (Diphtheria, Pertussis and Tetanus). Universal immunisation became a national programme in 1985.

All these efforts boosted the demand for children's vaccines and the need for indigenous production on a mass scale. Among the suppliers of DPT vaccines was Biological E. in Hyderabad. It was the first vaccine manufacturer in the private sector. It began its journey as Biological Products Private Limited in 1953 in Bombay. It was founded by Dr Datla Venkata Krishnam Raju (D.V.K. Raju) and G.A. Narasimha Raju (G.A.N. Raju) to manufacture liver extracts and anti-coagulants. The Rajus hailed from the West Godavari district and were distantly related. While G.A.N. Raju was an agriculturist, D.V.K. Raju was a chemistry postgraduate from Andhra University and a doctorate from the University of Edinburgh. Upon his return from the UK, D.V.K. Raju worked for some time with Sarabhai Merck, which was a part of the Ambalal Sarabhai group based in Baroda. Subsequently, D.V.K. Raju joined hands with G.A.N. Raju to make drugs under franchise from the foreign firms Philips-Duphur and Crookes Laboratories.

In 1963, the Rajus shifted their operations to Hyderabad where the state government was developing an industrial estate and offering incentives. Here Biological Products started manufacturing anti-snake venom serum, tetanus vaccines and DPT vaccines. Retired and abandoned horses were procured from the army, the police and race courses to produce the serum required for making anti-snake venom serum. A year later, the company entered into collaboration with a British firm, Evans Medicals, and renamed itself as Biological Evans. Following the acquisition of Evans by GlaxoSmithKline, its shareholding in Biological Evans got transferred to the new owners. When Glaxo exited in 1995, the company was renamed Biological E.

Meanwhile, the partnership between the two Rajus was cemented with the marriage of G.A.N. Raju's daughter, Dr Renuka, with D.V.K. Raju's son, Dr Vijay Kumar Datla, in 1967. Renuka was working as a professor of clinical pharmacology at Nizam's Institute of Medical Sciences. Two years after her wedding with Vijay, her father passed away and Vijay was appointed managing director while she was named medical director and later executive director. After Vijay died in 2013, the family-run business landed in a bitter courtroom battle, with Renuka dragging her three daughters to the court to retain control over the company. In its tumultuous journey over the decades, the company pioneered several products and established itself as a leader in the production of children's vaccines.

After inactivated and attenuated vaccines, the next big development in vaccine technology came from cell culture by using a kind of re-assortment of viral genetic material to make vaccines. Genetic engineering made it possible to clone or replicate a 'foreign' DNA in a host or a living cell. This came to be known as recombinant DNA or rDNA. With this technology, antigens could be produced outside an infectious agent, eliminating the risk associated with using live pathogens or their parts. This resulted in the development of recombinant vaccines. The first one was a hepatitis B vaccine announced in 1988.[2] A specific protein of the hepatitis B virus was produced by inserting its genetic code into yeast cells and then using them as a vaccine. This eliminated the use of any viral DNA in the vaccine. The path-breaking technology was commercialised by the new-age biotechnology firms Genentech and Chiron.

A young Indian biochemist working at the University of California at San Francisco, Ramareddy Guntaka, found himself surrounded by such exciting developments. 'On one floor, we had Herbert Boyer setting up Genentech and on another floor, William Rutter founded Chiron. In the same building, I was working with J.M. Bishop and Harold Varmus in the team that discovered the proto-oncogenes which eventually won the Nobel for the two in 1989,' said Ramareddy.[3] As a research scientist, he identified fundamental steps in the lifecycle of retroviruses that cause cancers and HIV. He molecularly cloned the whole genome of a retrovirus— *Rous Sarcoma Virus*. A decade later, Ramareddy played a pivotal role in the development of the biotech industry in his home state.

Ramareddy had his early education in Mudnuru in coastal Andhra and then pursued microbiology at Uttar Pradesh Agriculture University in Pantnagar established with American help. For his doctoral study, he went to Kansas State University and stayed on to take up research and teaching at American universities. He remained in touch with research institutes back home, like the CCMB and the Centre for Plant and Molecular Biology at Osmania University.

Biotechnology was a relatively new academic stream in India in the early 1990s and thinking of starting a biotechnology-based company like Genentech was a pipedream. Yet Koduru Ishwara Varaprasad Reddy, the son of a farmer from Nellore in Andhra Pradesh, did so. He had a degree in electronics and communication engineering. He turned to entrepreneurship under strange circumstances after having worked as a research scientist (in Defence Electronics Research Laboratory), government industrial promotion officer and a partner in private industry in the pre-liberalisation decades.

While looking for new opportunities after quitting Hyderabad Batteries Limited under acrimonious circumstances in 1992, Varaprasad landed in America at the invitation of his cousin, Varada Reddy, who was working in the US Environment Protection Agency (EPA). Varada Reddy earlier worked in the Biochemistry division of NIN in Hyderabad. When Varaprasad reached America, Varada was proceeding to Geneva to participate in a WHO conference on immunisation. He asked Varaprasad to come along. The meeting was to include a new hepatitis B vaccine in universal immunisation programmes. Genentech had developed the vaccine using rDNA technology and licensed it to SmithKline Beecham and Merck, but it was prohibitively costly at USD 23 a dose. Low-income countries could not afford it despite hepatitis B being a major health challenge. Varaprasad heard all this from the sidelines of the meeting and sensed a great business potential in an affordable hepatitis B vaccine.

On return to Hyderabad, Varaprasad met Anji Reddy of Dr Reddy's Laboratories and unsuccessfully tried to convince him to take up biotechnology-based vaccine production. 'He told me "rDNA is an unknown area for us, it will take us a long time to develop it, so it is foolish to enter this area. Don't be emotional, take it easy." But I decided to proceed on my own. Perhaps because I did not know anything about rDNA, I took the plunge,' says Varaprasad.[4]

Having decided to make an rDNA vaccine from scratch, Varaprasad needed everything to fulfil his audacious dream: a laboratory, technology, trained scientists, investors and the capital, know-how for large-scale vaccine production, industrial licence, regulatory approvals and, of course, buyers. Isanaka Ramakrishna Reddy, another cousin of Varaprasad who was working with the City of New York, offered to help. He hailed from a farming family in Nellore and had migrated to the US in 1970 with a degree in civil engineering from Sri Venkateswara University. He was an active member of the Telugu Association of North America (TANA) and the American Telugu Association (ATA). This gave him easy access to visiting political leaders from Andhra Pradesh. Isanaka became a co-promoter of the proposed venture of Varaprasad, providing 'moral, financial and technical support to ensure that the venture succeeded'.[5]

Back in Hyderabad, Varaprasad registered his company as Shantha Biotechnics, in his mother's name, in March 1993. Through social contacts, he approached Osmania University for some laboratory space till a permanent facility was built. While the concept of incubation did not exist with the university, vice chancellor G. Malla Reddy provided a room in the Department of Microbiology. He deputed Geeta Sharma, an associate professor in the department, to work with Shantha. Venkat Ramana, a specialist in fermentation, was the third member of the team. For one year, this small team of Shantha tried to develop a vaccine but couldn't make any headway.

Varaprasad turned to Isanaka and Varada for help. They approached biotechnology firms for getting the technology but no one showed any interest in partnering with a novice firm founded by an electronics engineer. Varada then proposed a meeting with Guntaka Ramareddy, with whom he was already familiar having spent a few weeks in Ramareddy's lab to study molecular biology techniques. Isanaka also knew Guntaka due to his TANA connections. In early 1993, Isanaka, Varaprasad and Varada drove to Missouri–Columbia to see Ramareddy.

The meeting proved to be fruitful. Guntaka agreed to come on board as the scientific advisor and guide the vaccine development. 'Varaprasad's emphasis on affordability touched me. At the same time, I knew it was a complicated technology. From my regular visits to institutions in India, I was aware that the development work in India would be difficult. Even basic reagents were not available, trained people were not there. Considering all this, I said, "Give me five years and you can launch the vaccine,"' recalled Ramareddy.[6] After obtaining a formal permission from his employer, the University of Missouri–Columbia, Ramareddy became a consultant to Shantha. Subsequently, Varaprasad sent Geeta Sharma for training at Ramareddy's laboratory.

The first genetically engineered hepatitis B vaccine in the world was launched in 1986. It was based on the surface antigen (HBsAg) 'expressed' or encoded in genetically engineered yeast. When injected, the antigen reassembled itself into virus-like particles and produced immunity in the human body. The vaccine was protected by over ninety patents relating to the core technology and manufacturing processes like isolation and purification.

Ramareddy chose to develop a new process for making a similar hepatitis B vaccine since that would not be an infringement of the patented vaccine under Indian patent law. The law permitted new processes for already patented medicines. Instead of *Saccharomyces cerevisiae* (known as Baker's yeast), which was used by the original inventors, Ramareddy selected a yeast strain called *Pichia pastoris* to develop the vaccine. The *Pichia* 'expression' system was developed by James Cregg at the Salk Institute Biotechnology/Industrial Associates Inc. in the 1980s for Phillips Petroleum.[7] The *Pichia* 'expression' technology was later licensed to Invitrogen and Research Corporation Technologies (RTC) for use by researchers.[8]

'The DNA sequence of the surface antigen was already known. From the sequence, I designed the primer and amplified the viral genome. Then I cloned it in *Pichia pastoris* in my lab. The cloning and expression work I did myself because I love working on the bench. The primer and the whole DNA which I had cloned in 1993 are still stored in the freezer of my lab. By the time Geeta Sharma came to my lab in August 1993, I had already cloned the surface antigen,' recounted Ramareddy.[9] He directed the development work at Shantha, exchanging notes and data via fax messages since email had not become commercially available in India.

Meanwhile, the group faced problems at Osmania University, like frequent power cuts, lack of instruments, departmental politics and so on. The company needed a laboratory facility until its building got ready in the upcoming industrial area, Medchal. CCMB director D. Balasubramanian agreed to provide laboratory space to Shantha on a monthly rental of Rs 1.25 lakh and permitted access to instruments like the electron microscope and DNA sequencing machines. CCMB provided scientific ambience and facilities to

Shantha though it was not involved institutionally in the vaccine project. During his visits to Hyderabad, Ramareddy used to bring reagents, salts, enzymes and primers as cabin baggage, sneaking them through customs. Shantha's hepatitis B vaccine was a process innovation, but the company also had to develop novel production methods and the purification process.[10]

Scaling up the R&D project to industrial production needed technical expertise and substantial capital. Banks and financial institutions refused to lend any money for a research-based project. Government agencies were lukewarm. The Department of Biotechnology (DBT), formed a decade ago to promote biotechnology, had no mechanism to support projects of a commercial nature. Shantha came to know about the Technology Development Board (TDB), which had been established by the Department of Science and Technology (DST) in September 1996. The company applied for financial support for its project immediately.

TDB was formed to fund private companies engaged in research-based projects. It was funded from the proceeds of the R&D cess on technology imports introduced in 1986. The government wanted to use this money for encouraging technology development in the private sector. 'We were told you can give loans, grants, take a risk and support new ideas to develop indigenous technology or to adapt foreign technology by Indian companies,' recalled V. Ramamurthy, DST secretary and TDB chairman in 1996.[11] Shantha became the first beneficiary in 1997, receiving a grant of Rs 3 crore out of the total project cost of Rs 15 crore to produce hepatitis B vaccine.

The company faced serious challenges in erecting a manufacturing plant. Once again, help came from Telugu networks in America. In one of the review meetings with TDB, Varaprasad was asked to explain how he could achieve certain technical milestones so fast and at such a low cost. 'He smiled and said "When you set up a laboratory of this kind, someone must design it, you procure equipment from somewhere else and a third person puts everything together to make it functional. For each of these steps, I can find one Andhra fellow somewhere in America. I invite him here and take him to Tirupati for a darshan, he gives me all the information and points to people or companies who can do it at a lower price." The committee members said if this is the way you are cutting costs, we have no objection,' said a member of TDB at the time of approval of Shantha's application.[12]

Shantha's vaccine—Shanvac-B—was launched in 1997 at a selling price of USD 1 a dose as against the prevailing price of USD 23 in international markets. Shell-shocked MNCs reacted by drastically slashing their prices, intending to destabilise Shantha. They threatened a hostile takeover. Some mischievous stories that raised doubts about the safety and efficacy of the vaccine started appearing in media. Apparently, these had been planted by foreign companies and local competitors. The company stood its ground and, backed with assured government purchase orders, it could survive the MNC onslaught.

Shanvac-B was the first commercially available recombinant DNA product in India. The development coincided with the golden jubilee of India's independence. The Central government hailed it as a major achievement as it made India the fourth 'genetically capable nation' in the world. Prime Minister Inder Kumar Gujral agreed to unveil the product as it fitted well with his emphasis on swadeshi. The date fixed for the launch in Hyderabad was 18 August 1997. But the office of Andhra Pradesh chief minister Chandrababu Naidu played spoilsport. It did not send a formal request to the Prime Minister's Office. So, the prime minister did not come and the vaccine was launched by the Union Minister of State for Health and Family Welfare Renuka Chaudhury.

In the first year of its production, Shantha sold 22 million doses of the vaccine. It started exporting and began supplies through international vaccine networks after WHO prequalified the vaccine in 2002.

Even as Shantha was working on the vaccine, another Hyderabad startup, Bharat Biotech, approached TDB for funding a similar hepatitis B vaccine. Happy with its experience with Shantha, TDB readily agreed to release a grant of Rs 3.25 crore to the new venture. The promoters of Bharat Biotech, Dr Krishna Ella and his wife Suchitra Ella, returned from America to start the company in Hyderabad in 1996. Coming from a farming family, studying agriculture was Krishna Ella's first choice. After a short stint with an agrochemical firm, Krishna proceeded to study plant pathology in the US on a fellowship. He drifted towards vaccinology while pursuing a doctorate in molecular biology at the University of Wisconsin–Madison. 'I did not want to come back, but my wife wanted to. My mother also requested me to come back,' Krishna Ella told journalist Raj Chengappa in December 2021.[13]

For developing the vaccine, Bharat Biotech took advantage of another government initiative—Technology Development Mission (TDM). TDM was launched in 1994 to boost academia–industry collaboration, and IISc was among the participating institutions. IISc researchers took the same approach that Ramareddy had taken a couple of years earlier for Shantha—using *Pichai pistoris* instead of *S.cerevisiae* used in the Energix B vaccine of SmithKline. 'The technology for the vaccine was already available, but what we did was indigenization of this technology,' said P.N. Rangarajan, who led the development work at IISc.[14] He had joined the institute in 1993 as an assistant professor in biochemistry after completing his postdoctoral research at the Salk Institute of Biological Studies in America.

The IISc technology helped Bharat Biotech launch its hepatitis B vaccine in October 1998, just a few months after Shantha did. Named Revac-B+, the vaccine was formally unveiled in the presence of A.P.J. Abdul Kalam, then principal scientific advisor to the Government of India, and the director of IISc, G. Padmanabhan. Newspaper reports described Padmanabhan (he was the mentor of Rangarajan) as 'the guiding spirit behind the vaccine'[15] but Bharat Biotech did not formally acknowledge the contributions of IISc.[17]

The availability of two hepatitis B vaccines and the vast potential in domestic and export markets led to a war for market share. Shantha and Bharat fought battles in the media, courts and regulatory agencies, with the conflict taking a political hue at times amidst allegations that one company was being favoured by the chief minister Naidu. Bharat Biotech alleged that Shanvac-B had toxic elements since Shantha's process made use of a caesium chloride gradient. 'There were no traces of caesium in the product. SmithKline also tested it. Shanvac gave the highest immunogenicity among all available hepatitis B vaccines. We published the data in *Vaccines*,' Ramareddy recounted.[17] 'Later I heard it was a motivated campaign backed by some politicians.'

The resounding success of Shantha initiated the era of biotechnology-based industry in Hyderabad and India. The credit for kick-starting this industry, to a large extent, goes to a government body—TDB—which seed-funded hepatitis B vaccine projects of Shantha and Bharat. It acted like a selfless venture capitalist since it did not insist on equity participation while taking all the risk. Its grants were generous. For the interferon development project, TDB funded Shantha to the extent of Rs 12 crore in 1999, while Bharat Biotech was given Rs 11 crore for developing streptokinase in the same year. Two more grants of Rs 9 crore and Rs 15 crore were sanctioned for Shantha for DPT-HepB combivalent vaccine and Hib and other vaccines, respectively, by 2005. In 2009, Bharat Biotech received Rs 10.9 crore for a 'liquid adsorbed Rabies vaccine'. The Board helped the two firms build a national profile by bestowing on them National Technology Award, first to Shantha and then to Bharat Biotech.

It was as if TDB had opened the floodgates for grants to biotech and pharma companies in Hyderabad. The list of Hyderabad companies that received TDB assistance between 1997 and 2014 includes Matrix Laboratories (Rs 4.5 crore), Gland Pharma (Rs 3.5 crore, Rs 4.5 crore and Rs 8.6 crore), Issar Pharmaceuticals (Rs 2.75 crore), Biological E. (Rs 7.92 crore), Virchow Biotech (Rs 2.5 crore), Sudershan Biotech (Rs 2.5 crore), Zenotech Laboratories (Rs 6 crore), Avra Laboratories (Rs 4.75 crore and Rs 3 crore), Vimta Labs (Rs 4.85 crore), Ocimum Biosolutions (Rs 4 crore), Shri Biotech Laboratories (Rs 3.75 crore), BioGenex Life Science (Rs 9.99 crore), Sanzyme Limited (Rs 5 crore) and Sparsh Pharma (Rs 8 crore).[18]

One of the largest funding of TDB went to Biological E. in 2016 as 'loan assistance' of Rs 100 crore out of the project cost of Rs 320 crore for the development and commercialisation of the pneumococcal conjugate vaccine. 'TDB funding for the development of life-saving vaccines has helped manufacturers target large-scale production and keep the costs of vaccines low,' pointed out Mahima Datla, chief executive officer of Biological E.[19]

The hepatitis vaccines Shanvac-B and Revac-B+ became commercial successes, but their developers (Ramareddy and Rangarajan) became disenchanted with their respective companies. Ramareddy Guntaka parted ways with Shantha and started a new firm, Sudarshan Biotech. He cloned and sequenced the whole genome of the Indian strain of hepatitis C virus in 2001 with a plan to make a vaccine. Isanaka, a co-promoter of Shantha, decided to go on his own, forming Issar Pharmaceuticals to make peptide-based therapeutics—another new segment of the industry.

After his experience with Bharat Biotech, which did not acknowledge IISc as the developer of the hepatitis B vaccine technology, Rangarajan transferred the technology to two other Hyderabad firms—Biological E. and Indian Immunologicals. Armed with the recombinant *P pastoris* yeast strain from IISc, the two companies carried out necessary clinical trials, went through regulatory approvals and launched their respective hepatitis B vaccines—BEVAC and Elevac-B—in 2004 and 2006. The two companies acknowledged the contribution of IISc and paid it 1 per cent royalty on total sales. Thus, in less than a decade, four companies from Hyderabad were making hepatitis B vaccines, facilitating the inclusion of the hepatitis B vaccine in the Universal Programme of Immunisation.

Dreaming Big with Genome Valley

The success of Shantha and Bharat Biotech drew the attention of policymakers in Delhi and Hyderabad to the huge potential of the biotechnology industry and spurred the formulation of new policies to boost the biotechnology-based industry. The Vision 2020 document adopted by the unified Andhra Pradesh government spoke about the potential of developing a 'Knowledge

Corridor' to promote knowledge-based services in sectors such as biotechnology, advanced materials, industrial technologies and so on.[20] It cited examples of successful corridors like the Research Triangle Park in North Carolina and the Hsinchu Science-Based Industrial Park in Taiwan. Andhra Pradesh, it said, could achieve similar success by creating world-class educational institutions and linking them with R&D centres and business estates where 'new enterprises can start up and flourish as has happened with Stanford University and MIT'.[21]

The chief minister Chandrababu Naidu asked the Industries secretary Sheela Bhide to promote the biotechnology sector in a big way. An IAS officer with a doctorate in international trade, Bhide was appointed the Industries secretary in January 1995. She knew little about biotechnology. She proceeded to Bangalore to meet the best-known person in this sector—Kiran Mazumdar Shaw, founder of Biocon. After the meeting, Bhide said, 'I told her "We want to set up a biotech park in Hyderabad." She shot back, "Are you crazy? A biotech park in Hyderabad? There is nothing there. Do it in Bangalore. I will give you full support."'[22]

Not to be disappointed, Bhide conducted a situation analysis herself. She found that the biotechnology industry had not grown in Hyderabad in spite of having several obvious advantages: a well-developed drugs and pharmaceuticals industry, rich bio-resources, availability of healthcare and medical facilities, and the presence of several research centres engaged in biotechnology-related work. Besides, biotechnology was a key strength of Telugu NRIs. At the advice of the chief minister, she toured biotechnology clusters in America, Europe and Singapore including the Research Triangle Park to gain firsthand knowledge.

Bhide found that all these technology parks had grown around either a research university or an R&D institution and none of them were driven by a government. 'Here we (the government) were trying to force the development of a cluster,' Bhide commented.[23] Another crucial difference was that a close link between R&D and industry was missing in Hyderabad.

Bhide approached Osmania University and the University of Hyderabad with a proposal that they host a biotechnology cluster on the lines of what she had seen at Cambridge, Oxford and Harvard. The two universities had huge land banks, research facilities and good science faculties. To her surprise, both the universities rejected the idea saying that they were forbidden from using the land for any non-academic purpose and they were not engaged in industry-oriented research.

Meanwhile, help came from an unexpected quarter. Krishna Ella, who had founded Bharat Biotech and was building his factory at Turkapally village in Shamirpet, walked into Bhide's office one day and invited her to see his upcoming unit while promising help in developing the proposed park. Shamirpet was a barren and rocky area with little habitation. It was about a ninety minute-drive from Hyderabad. 'I thought it was a good site for a biotech park. Krishna Ella was already building his unit there. Still, the missing piece in the puzzle was the link to an R&D centre,' recalled Bhide. A chance meeting with Narayanan Vaghul, the chairman of ICICI, on the sidelines of a conference of the Confederation of Indian Industry (CII) in Hyderabad helped Bhide find the missing piece.

Vaghul mentioned that ICICI had borrowed funds from KfW Development Bank and lent them in the Indian market at higher interest rates. The differential was kept separately in a fund to be used for long-term development projects. His brother, S. Manian Bala, who was a serial entrepreneur based in California, suggested the money could be utilised to promote R&D in life sciences. His suggestion was to create a high-quality research facility for companies interested in doing innovative R&D. This was like music to Bhide's ears. She told Vaghul that this was what the Andhra Pradesh government was looking for—an R&D facility in the biotech park.

Vaghul was surprised, 'Are you sure? The state government is going to invest in R&D?' He could not believe when he heard a 'Yes!' from Bhide and also that the land for the proposed park had already been identified. Vaghul and others in the group present there wanted to see the site right away, skipping the conference sessions. A visit to Turkapally was promptly arranged with the help of local officials in the afternoon. Vaghul liked the area but wanted a large chunk of 200 acres for building a life sciences R&D park.

Vaghul and others went back to the CII conference, while Bhide went to brief the chief minister. According to her, this is what happened at this meeting, 'CM was looking at some files. He did not look up. He asked me three questions: Is it going to be for R&D for life sciences, will it be non-profit, and will it have spinoff effects on the industry in Hyderabad? I said "Yes" to all the three questions, and he sanctioned 200 acres of land for what was to be India's first life sciences park.'[24]

The first block of the ICICI Knowledge Park (later renamed as IKP Knowledge Park) building was ready in nine months. It had ready-to-use modular wet laboratory blocks with research infrastructure like DNA sequencers, protein synthesisers, NMR spectroscopes, liquid chromatography–mass spectrometry machines, high performance liquid chromatography, Fourier-transform infrared spectroscopy and so on. The park also provided administrative and statutory support like customs clearance, environmental approvals, legal and patent counselling, access to venture funding and so on.

'The idea was to help mid-sized companies, provide them facilities so that they can do R&D without investing in any research infrastructure. Once they succeeded, they could move out and build their corporate R&D,' explained Deepanwita Chattopadhyay, founding CEO of IKP.[25] With the addition of the Life Science Incubator, the park evolved from a space-and-rental model to an incubation and ecosystem development model.

By mid-2000, Turkapally had two buildings—the Bharat Biotech building and the IKP Knowledge Park. 'One day I was driving to Shamirpet from Hyderabad. There is the Shamirpet Lake on the way and the area around it is at a higher elevation. To reach the Biotech Park one had to go a little downward. It looked like a valley to me. In the morning newspapers I had read a news story about the Human

Genome Project which was in the headlines those days. It suddenly struck me, why not call it Genome Valley? That's how Shamirpet became the Genome Valley,' Bhide recounted.[26]

While the IKP Knowledge Park became the R&D arm of Genome Valley, there was only one firm, Bharat Biotech, on the manufacturing side. Instead of following the existing model of developing industrial parks and giving away land to individual companies, a step that was bound to attract political criticism, the government came up with the idea of developing a biotechnology park with a private partner. Since the idea was new, consultancy firm Ernst & Young was commissioned to prepare a feasibility report. It suggested that the task of developing the infrastructure could be farmed out to a private company and the state government could provide land as its share of equity in the proposed joint venture company (to run the biotechnology park), which could then lease out space to individual units. A few companies responded to the call for 'expression of interest'. Of them, two were shortlisted—the Bombay-based firm Shapoorji Pallonji (SP) and the Hyderabad-based IVRCL Infrastructure and Projects Limited (formerly Iragavarapu Venkata Reddy Construction Limited).

As part of the selection process, government officials met officials of the shortlisted firms to explain the project to them and to clear their doubts. Cyrus Mistry, who had just returned after graduating from Imperial College to join the family business at SP, was apprehensive about the proposed venture because of factors like lack of dedicated water pipelines in the proposed park site. 'His grandfather was the producer of *Mughal-e-Azam*. I cited that example and told him that, "You are from a family that takes risks." Hyderabad also had a strong Parsi connection—Shapoorwadi. Incidentally, Zafar Iqbal, an ex-IAS officer who was the CEO of SP then, had family links with Hyderabad. We used all such connections to get SP on board,' remembered Bibhu Acharya, who succeeded Bhide as the Industries secretary in March 2001.[27] SP was finally selected and it formed the SP Biotech Park Limited. The first phase of the biotech park was ready by the end of 2003 with basic infrastructure needed for setting up of manufacturing units.

The next task was to attract companies and other players to the Genome Valley. Big names like Dr Reddy's Laboratory and Biological E. refused to relocate or open new facilities in the Valley. (Later, Biological E. did come in.) The Indian Council of Medical Research (ICMR) agreed to develop a national animal facility—crucial for biomedical research—but the proposal got up caught in red tape for many years. The facility eventually became functional in 2022.

The Valley faced rough weather on other fronts too. 'Our biotech policy was being criticized by a former director of CCMB in newspapers. The two biotech pioneers, Krishna Ella of Bharat Biotech and Varaprasad Reddy of Shantha Biotech, were not on the same page. They were publicly blaming each other. All this generated negative publicity,' recalled Acharya.[28]

The state government came up with a biotechnology policy euphemistically titled 'Beyond Tomorrow (BT)' with the same abbreviation as biotechnology. The document was prepared by consultants from Ernst & Young, with inputs from the Biotechnology Advisory Board constituted by Naidu. 'We were hired since we had a strong footprint in life biotech globally. We used to bring out an annual report on biotechnology, Beyond Borders. We started releasing it in Hyderabad. We would take CEOs attending our annual conclave to visit the biotech park. We did everything that would bring attention to Hyderabad,' summed up Utkarsh Palnitkar, who was then office managing partner and leader (life sciences) in the consulting firm.[29] The All-India Biotech Association led by Dr B.S. Bajaj joined hands with the state government to create buzz using promotional and networking events. Companies operating in the park were offered speedy approvals, tax and fiscal incentives, relaxation from labour laws, access to venture capital funds and uninterrupted power supply. Bioinformatics companies were given a financial incentive of Rs 30,000 for every job created.

Global Positioning of the Genome Valley

With a promotional policy in hand and an upcoming biotech park, government officials actively started marketing Genome Valley at industry events such as Biotechnology Innovation Organisation (BIO) conventions in America and India. This yielded some good results.

Close competitor Karnataka, meanwhile, started to host a local version of the event, BIO Bangalore, and had a public face of the industry in Kiran Mazumdar Shaw. Hyderabad responded with BIO Asia in 2004 and 'tried to project Mahima Datla (of Biological E.) as industry ambassador at our show'. In 2002, the chief minister toured the USA, Ireland and Dubai to market the Genome Valley.

Among the early movers to IKP were Medicorp Technologies, Bijam Biosciences, Krebs Biochemicals, Optiwave Photonics, GVK Bio-Pharma, Maanya Biotech, Bioserve Biotechnologies, Helvetica Industries and Medifil Pharma. Medicorp was acquired by Matrix Laboratories in 2002, which in turn got acquired by American pharma major Mylan in 2007. This automatically brought a global player to IKP and made Mylan a leading generics manufacturer globally with Matrix under its fold.

Around the same time, senior Matrix executive Satyanaryana Chava, a doctorate in organic chemistry from Andhra University, branched out and founded Laurus Labs. Incubated in IKP, the firm developed APIs for anti-retroviral, hepatitis C and oncology drugs, and became the first anchor company of IKP. Laurus received 200 patents for processes it developed. The United States Pharmacopeia, a nonprofit organisation working on standards of medicines, opened its first centre outside America in 2006 at IKP, bringing Hyderabad to the radar of international research and pharma companies. Meanwhile, SP Biotech Park was acquired by a US-based firm, Alexandria Real Estate Equities, in 2018.

By 2022, Genome Valley had 3 million square feet of multi-tenanted laboratory space—more than all other clusters in India put together. It became a home to over 200 Indian and foreign companies in multi-tenanted and standalone spaces, including the facilities of the three large vaccine makers: Bharat Biotech, Biological E. and Indian Immunologicals. Among international firms present in the Valley by 2022 were Novartis, GlaxoSmithKline, Ferring Pharma, Chemo, DuPont, Ashland and Lonza. The companies in the Valley engaged in drug research, biological manufacturing (vaccines, injectables and monoclonal antibodies), pharmaceutical formulations and provided clinical research support. The life science sector in Telangana was worth USD 80 billion in 2022, according to Shakthi Nagappan, director (life sciences and pharma).

The COVID-19 pandemic proved to be a golden moment for the Genome Valley. Early in the pandemic, in June 2020, Bharat Biotech announced India's first COVID-19 vaccine, COVAXIN, developed in collaboration with the National Institute of Virology, Pune. The company already had several vaccines to its credit—vaccines for H1N1, Rotavirus, Japanese Encephalitis, Rabies, Chikungunya, Zika, a conjugated vaccine for Typhoid—and delivered over 4 billion doses of vaccines globally. COVAXIN brought an unprecedented focus on Bharat Biotech and Genome Valley, given the uncertainties connected with the novel virus.

Biological E. followed with the manufacturing of Corbevax, a receptor-binding domain protein subunit vaccine, developed at Baylor College of Medicine. Bharat Biotech also developed a second COVID-19 vaccine—an intra-nasal vaccine—in 2022. The technology for making COVAXIN was transferred to Indian Immunologicals, another manufacturer in the Valley. A delegation of about a hundred diplomats visited the vaccine manufacturers at the Genome Valley and observed its research and manufacturing capacity.

The emergence of Genome Valley as India's first biotechnology cluster benefited from pre-existing resources of knowledge creation (universities, public research laboratories), production (pharmaceutical and vaccine manufacturers) in Hyderabad and the availability of a large domestic market in the country. The policy interventions aimed at infrastructural development helped shape the Valley further. The industrial investment promotion policies of Andhra Pradesh (during 2005–10) specifically emphasised aggressive R&D activities, industry-academia linkages, export promotion and incentives for FDI investments. Cluster development was conceived as a strategy for industrial growth. The broad policy direction remained the same despite political changes and the formation of Telangana in 2014.

The success of the biotechnology sector in Hyderabad is often portrayed as a story of innovation and private entrepreneurship, but private firms could not have achieved success without the helping hand from the state agencies. The benevolent hand of the state was present at all crucial stages, even in the post-liberalisation era. In the initial phase, TDB extended liberal grants to vaccine companies in Hyderabad and wrote off the risk of failure, while another state-funded institution, IISc, helped companies in technology development.

During the COVID-19 pandemic, state-funded agencies actively collaborated with private companies. DBT provided access to its facilities which was necessary for vaccine development (assay labs, animal facilities and clinical trial sites) and extended financial grants for manufacturing. Biological E. received Rs 112 crore while Bharat Biotech was given Rs 100 crore for the intra-nasal vaccine development. Among the beneficiaries of Rs 250 crore manufacturing grants given to vaccine firms was Indian Immunologicals Limited, based in the Genome Valley.

———•———

External factors like the changing nature of the pharma and biotech industries in the early 2000s attracted American and European firms to Hyderabad. The concentration of a large number of USFDA-approved and WHO–pre-qualified facilities provided assurance of quality supplies. The supply chain disruptions caused during the pandemic due to the overdependence on China for pharmaceutical ingredients and APIs forced Western countries to look for alternate sources like India with a large pharma manufacturing base. Hyderabad was a beneficiary of this shift.

15

The Price of Development

We have destroyed everything—lakes, hills, rocks, parks, open spaces, heritage—in the name of development. Cyberabad is also unplanned and unscientific, not following any municipal rules, they don't have lakes, open spaces, or rocks, only concrete buildings. Flooding happens there all the time.

—P. Anuradha Reddy,
heritage conservationist, March 2022[1]

WITH THE CHANGING ECONOMIC AND POLITICAL realities over the decades, the spatial expansion of Hyderabad took place as new housing colonies, industrial estates and institutional areas were developed. The change was quite rapid from the 1990s onward. In the process, the natural, ecological and geological structure of the city was damaged. Once known as Bagh Nagar or the City of Gardens, Hyderabad lost much of its green spaces, lakes, tanks, baolis and, most importantly, its unique rock formations. Civic amenities in the older parts of the city did not keep pace with the rapid expansion of economic activity and the increased population.

In the initial decades after 1948, several monuments and heritage buildings were either demolished to make way for new structures or were left to decay. The mansions and palaces, which were state-owned and whose ownership was transferred to the Government of Hyderabad after 1948, were repurposed as government offices, guest houses, educational institutions and the Raj Bhavan.

Andhra Pradesh was formed in 1956. Most of the political elites who came to power belonged to coastal Andhra and had little affinity with the city and its immediate past. Heritage buildings were either neglected or simply razed. One of the buildings that was targeted was the magnificent High Court building on the riverfront. 'Some influential politicians from Andhra proposed a new building for the High Court and they wanted to convert this beautiful building into a five-star hotel. When this was attempted, the Chief Justice firmly said no,' recalled A. Pulla Reddy, who started his practice in the High Court in 1953.[2] The pretext was that the building had become unsafe after a mysterious fire that gutted several volumes of the *Deccan Law Report*. 'Many people felt It was an intentional fire,' according to Reddy.

Many mansions including the King Kothi Palace, categorised as the personal property of the Nizam, were caught in legal battles among the direct descendants of the Nizam and his extended family. 'Other Indian princely states joined the Union by agreement and discussion, while Hyderabad was taken by force. The nobility, jagirdars and descendants of Nizam were left with no income. So, they sold whatever properties they had for survival,' pointed out P. Anuradha Reddy, a heritage activist and descendant of the house of Hindu nobility, Sirnapalli Samsthan.[3] Moreover, she said, 'The power, from 1956 onward, was in the hands of people who had little sense of history, heritage or aesthetics. It became politically expedient for them to blame the Nizam but they did not realise that heritage also has economic value.' In the 1990s, Chandrababu Naidu gave the city a facelift but some scholars see this phase of transformation more as a 'visual process' in which the role of the government was to show that 'something was happening'.[4]

After the formation of Telangana in 2014, the preservation of heritage structures received some attention. The Moazzam Jahi Market, an all-stone shopping plaza built during the Nizam era, was one of the old structures that were renovated. The government, however, took a controversial decision in 2023 to demolish the Osmania General Hospital building on the riverfront on the grounds that years of neglect had made it unsafe for patients and doctors.[5]

Built heritage apart, the fast-paced expansion of the city has adversely affected the city's environment. While the development of the pharmaceutical industry had put Hyderabad on the global map, it came at a huge ecological cost to the city surroundings. The water bodies were particularly affected as were the communities living around the manufacturing units. The problem of pollution is as old as the pharma industry itself. Soviet experts, who prepared the project report for IDPL, originally recommended that the synthetic drug plant should be located at the seashore as had been done in the case of some chemical plants in India 'so that effluent could be released in the sea after they were "naturalized"'.[6]

The Location Committee of the Planning Commission overlooked this caution and selected Hyderabad as the Andhra Pradesh government suggested that effluents could be pre-treated and channelled into River Musi. As construction progressed, officials realised that effluent disposal in Musi was not feasible since it was not a perennial river. They suggested the disposal of effluents containing hazardous chemicals by evaporation.[7] The state government did not pay for effluent treatment as promised and failed to provide an assured water supply for plant operations. This made a later parliamentary panel conclude that the choice of Hyderabad for locating the unit was not a 'happy one'.[8]

Hardly any pollution control norms existed in the 1970s when private drug units were given industrial licences. The licences were issued by the Central government solely based on the state government certifying that the plant would be 'non-polluting'.

Pollution control found casual mention in licence applications, such as this one in the application of a bulk drug unit submitted in 1974: 'A part of the effluent is acidic in nature; this is diverted to soak pits dug adjacent to factory in the company's premises and are treated thereon.'[9] While issuing the licence, the Central government would ask companies to ensure that 'adequate steps shall be taken to avoid pollution of water, air and soil.'[10]

As a result of lax regulation, factories located in the Patancheru–Bollaram industrial area were found to be releasing hazardous waste with little or no treatment into Nakkavagu, a tributary of River Manjira. The effluents contaminated drinking water sources in surrounding villages and caused the death of livestock. 'It was common knowledge that every bulk drug factory had a *pokka* (hole) in its boundary wall which would be quietly opened during the monsoons to let effluents mix with water flowing into storm water drains. Every nallah, canal, wetland and lake around industrial areas was filled with toxic waste. It will not be an understatement to say that if pollution control was enforced at that time, Hyderabad would not have become the pharma capital,' summarised an industry insider.[11]

The matter landed in the courts in 1989 in the form of a letter from Advocate C. Pratap Reddy to the Chief Justice of India, citing a news report published in the Telugu daily *Eenadu*. The Chief Justice passed on the letter to the Andhra Pradesh High Court, asking it to treat it as a writ petition. After a long legal battle, Patancheru was eventually declared a 'critically polluted area' and a moratorium on new units was imposed.

Disappearing Rocks

In the 1990s, government officials chose Madhapur for the development of an IT park because they found that it had very little habitation and had vast areas available for future expansion. 'There were just rocks and some thorny bushes around, and virtually no human habitation,' recalled an official involved in the process.[12] The government planners overlooked the cultural and geological heritage of the region. Villages like Madhapur, Masjid Banda, Nanakramguda, Khajaguda, Raidurgam, Kothaguda, Tellapur and so on—all subsumed in Cyberabad—had a rich cultural history dating back to medieval times. They are also home to a unique geological heritage—granite rocks that are 2.5 billion years old. The region extending beyond Jubilee Hills exemplified the granitic landscape of the Deccan with boulders, tors, inselbergs and rocky outcrop.

The hard crystalline rocks seen in the Deccan Plateau, of which Hyderabad is a part, have been formed through crystallisation and consolidation of molten magma that was pushed upwards when the earth's crust solidified. Geologists date this process to some 2,500 million to 2,800 million years ago. This places Hyderabad granites among the oldest rock types in India, much older than the dinosaurs and the Himalayas. The rocks that were exposed on the surface had weathered over millions of years to take the shape of myriad, interesting formations.

At several places, intriguing formations look as if huge rocks are precariously perched on each other while some are like layers in a hamburger. The weathering and sedimentation process facilitated rocks to nurture flora and fauna such as diverse species of birds, lizards and butterflies. Several medicinal plants and herbs grow around rocks. In addition, the rocks have subterranean passages that allow water to seep through them, thus helping recharge groundwater, besides generating waterfalls, springs and streams during the monsoon months.

For centuries, Hyderabadis have lived in harmony with all the rocks, boulders and rocky hillocks. They have been a part of culture, folklore, art and crafts and local history, as well as modern urban fabric. Dozens of localities are still known after their rocks and hillocks: Shah Ali Banda, Bora Banda, Phisal Banda, Allah Banda, Ghazi Banda, Hanumak Tekdi, Keshav Giri Tekdi, Moosaram Tekdi, Chandrayan Gutta, Panja Gutta, Gagan Pahad and so on. Rocks and hillocks are home to holy shrines, dargahs and temples: Daragah Pahad-E-Shareef, Moulali Dargah, Dattatreya Mandir, Gangabowli-ka-Pahad, Baba Fakhruddin

Aulia Dargah, Darghaghar-e-Mubarak, Birla Mandir (Naubat Pahad) and so on. Rocks have been integrated with built structures like private houses and institutional buildings. The tony residential areas of Banjara Hills and Jubilee Hills once had houses built around rocks without cutting them down, for example, the house of author Narendra Luther. Lamakaan, an open cultural space, is another such bungalow. Some famous single rock formations found in the campuses of the University of Hyderabad (mushroom rock), Maulana Azad National Urdu University (Pathar-Dil, United-We-Stand) and National Institute of Tourism and Hospitality Management (hamburger rock) are well protected. A civil society group, Society to Save Rocks, founded in 1996 by Frauke Qauder, Laxma Goud and other concerned citizens, has highlighted the need for preserving the rocks. These efforts have resulted in scientific studies, risk mapping and systematic documentation of rock formations in Telangana, and in getting twenty-five of them, located in and around the city, declared as heritage rocks.

Revival of Water Bodies

The expansion of the urban sprawl put pressure on the city's water bodies, which mainly consisted of lakes and tanks built during the Qutub Shahi and Asaf Jahi periods, such as the Hussain Sagar, Durgam Cheruvu, Saroornagar Lake, Shamirpet Lake, Talab Katta, Mir Alam tank, Ma-Saheba tank, Osman Sagar, Himayat Sager and so on. In the 1970s, water bodies and lakes in and around Hyderabad numbered over 800. Many of them have either shrunk in size or disappeared completely. Over the centuries, natural and artificial water bodies served as sources of drinking water, irrigation, groundwater recharge and micro-climate moderation. As the demand for housing, and commercial areas went up, lakes were encroached upon to develop large building complexes and roads. Concretisation hampered the natural drainage systems and catchment areas of lakes, streams and wells.

In recent years, voluntary efforts to protect lakes and revive disued step wells in the city have yielded some good results. The revival and restoration of a large step well at the Bansilalpet area that was completed in 2022 is a good example. The motivation for this project came from the personal experience of the designer and architect Kalpana Ramesh who moved to Hyderabad after a stint in America and Singapore.

'I found that water was being supplied by tankers in many localities. It was of poor quality and I discovered that it was being sourced from illegal borewells in which groundwater was polluted. This got me thinking, and I installed a rainwater harvesting and greywater recycling system when I built a house in 2010. In 2016, when there was a drought-like situation and water was being rationed, I did not have to buy water from any tanker,' recalled Kalpana Ramesh.[13] She then founded an NGO to spread the ideas of rainwater harvesting and wastewater treatment to communities around her, and incorporated a for-profit social entrepreneurship startup, The Rainwater Project, in 2020. It was incubated at IIIT Hyderabad and takes up zero-discharge projects for corporates.

The revived Bansilalpet stepwell has a capacity of 2.2 million litres of water. It has led to the recharge of borewells in the nearby areas and prevented flooding of low-lying areas during the monsoon. Kalpana raised money for this project through crowdfunding and corporate social responsibility (CSR) funds from the industry, and the government paid for the construction of the walking paths, interpretation centres and so on. The stepwell has become a tourist attraction while yielding ecological benefits to the community around it. 'There are many localities in Hyderabad named after baolis like Gachibaoli, Doodhbaoli, Moosabaoli, etc. All these wells have either been used as waste dumps or have been fully encroached. We are trying to locate them and revive them as we have done with Gachibaoli where much of the IT corridor is located,' Kalpana added.

The stepwell at Bansilalpet in Secunderabad revived by architect and designer Kalpana Ramesh (courtesy: The Rainwater Project)

Along with concerns relating to natural, human-built and ecological heritage, old Hyderabadis are worried about the likely extinction of something intangible—Hyderabadi tehzeeb. The Persian descent of Qutub Shahi rulers who founded Hyderabad had a tremendous impact on the art, culture, architecture, literature and food habits of the people for nearly two centuries.[14] At the same time, different communities from north and south India migrated to Hyderabad. Then there were the French and the British who left their imprint on the city during the colonial period.

The ethnic Telugu-speaking people of the region intermingled and amalgamated with all of these people over centuries. Hyderabad thus developed into a culturally heterogeneous society with people of diverse ethnic, racial, religious and social backgrounds. People of Hyderabad were influenced by multiple cultures, and it is this influence which has shaped the Hyderabadi tehzeeb or Ganga–Jamuni tehzeeb, according to historian Sheela Raj.[15] The composite culture is reflected prominently in Dakhani boli and Hyderabadi cuisine.

'Hyderabadi Tehzeeb for decades has identified itself with not only its cuisine, rehen-sehen, lingo, attire but also with wit and humour so typical of Hyderabad. While the coming of migrants as IT professionals and the advent of social media has resulted in exchange of cultural ideas, the process is restricted to the newer parts of the city and the old city seems largely unaffected,' felt Vinay Varma, actor and founder of the theatre group Sutradhar.[16] The Hyderabadi tehzeeb, however, has failed to attain a pan-Indian status like Punjabi or Rajasthani cultures. According to Varma, this is primarily because of the overemphasis on the typical Hyderabadi lingo and making it a source of humour.

The changing geography of the city, with the addition of Cyberabad and new living styles typified by apartment blocks, gated communities, malls and pubs in the recent decades has not only changed the look and feel of Hyderabad but also influenced its cultural ethos. 'For a visitor, Hyderabad may present a very satisfactory picture but for those residents who see Hyderabad changing at such a high pace, the change is not always welcome,' notes sociologist Vinita Pandey. 'In the winds of these changes, the basic nuances of Hyderabadi tehzeeb are gradually missing.'[17]

The map of the city has shifted to accommodate the movement of capital, the aggregations of workplace and workforce, along with some deeper secondary level changes that need greater attention, say University of Hyderabad researchers Usha Raman and Aditya Deshbandhu who conducted a rapid ethnographic study in three parts of the city in 2022.[18] Most people they spoke to mentioned 'difficulties of crossing the figurative divide between Hyderabad and Cyberabad as part of their everyday lives.' Those residing and working in Cyberabad were keen to point out the lack of necessity to engage with areas of the old city, while people from the old city showcased their capabilities of navigating the digital and thereby minimising their need to travel beyond the vicinities of their places of work and residence.

The Hyderabadi culture survives only in some pockets of Hyderabad and with some Hyderabadis spread across the world, feels Anuradha Reddy. 'Hyderabadis speak many languages.

That is what makes them Hyderabadis. Languages were a means of understanding, cooperating, and bringing people together. After 1956, we got another (type of) Telugu into Hyderabad, that Telugu never understood our Telugu,' she said.[19] 'People from Cyberabad don't visit the Old City. When I ask them why, they say, "People there don't speak our language." We need the city to be a shared space for all. Hyderabad today exists only in the minds of Hyderabadis. We must remember that there is no future without the past. You just look around, everything you see in today's Hyderabad is connected to the past.' As Kalpana Markandey, former professor of geography at Osmania University, aptly summarises, 'The Old City, New City and Secunderabad, and the upcoming IT and technology hub Cyberabad, represent the separation as well as blend of three generations: the medieval, the modern and the postmodern.'[20]

Conclusion: Dreams of a Globalised City

∽

We are not only going to compete with Silicon Valley but might even surpass it in the future.

—Mahankali Srinivas Rao,
CEO of T-Hub, May 2022[1]

EVERY TIME YOU KEY IN A WORD TO SEARCH ON GOOGLE, launch a Microsoft product on your laptop or mobile phone, click on Amazon to buy a product, post a picture on Facebook, book an airline ticket on a travel website, use a map to navigate through city traffic, take a taxi ride using Uber or Ola, make a financial transaction on an app or through a leading bank, scan a QR code to make a micropayment through UPI, watch an animation film on your favourite OTT platform, pop a pill or vaccinate your child, you are most likely either using a technology partly or fully developed in Hyderabad, getting connected with a data centre or a business processing office located there or using a medical product manufactured there.

Since Microsoft inaugurated its largest development centre outside its US headquarters in Hyderabad in 2008, the city has seen several other tech giants do the same. In May 2022, the foundation was laid for a new facility of Google that will have a built-up area of 3.3 million square feet, in the same area where Amazon has its 3 million square feet facility. There is hardly any Fortune 500 firm or major global technology company that does not have a presence in Hyderabad in the form of a development centre, R&D unit, data centre or a backroom.

At the beginning of the twentieth century, an influx of British officers and those from northern and western India opened a crucial window for the winds of modernisation to blow into Hyderabad. A flood protection plan prepared by one of British India's ablest engineers, M. Visvesvaraya, effectively became the blueprint for urban renewal, triggering a wave of institution building. Mir Osman Ali Khan, who was on shaky political ground when he was anointed the seventh Nizam, opted for administrative reforms and took direct control of the administration. He wished to see Hyderabad at par with the best cities in Europe. The vision of Osman Ali Khan got translated in new institutions like the City Improvement Board, Osmania General Hospital and Osmania University, as well as the renewal of existing ones.

The First World War provided the stimulus for industrial research. Early industrial activity was modest, focusing on the utilisation of raw materials available in the state. In this period, technical skills and knowledge were acquired through several means, such as higher education in England and Europe, direct training at relevant institutions in British India or England, an invitation to experts to work in institutions in Hyderabad, and through networking with technical institutions elsewhere. This was similar to what other progressive princely states like Baroda and Mysore did.

While princely Hyderabad benefited greatly from ideas and expertise from all over, some of its home-grown ideas contributed to the making of modern India post 1947. The Urdu-medium Osmania University triggered a pan-Indian debate on technical education in Indian languages, and its formula for translation of technical terms was widely accepted in other parts of India. The participation of the Nizamiah Observatory in a prestigious global project brought international recognition to Indian astronomy. The industrial research model of Hyderabad that focused on the industrial use of locally available raw materials was adopted in independent India by CSIR which established several regional research laboratories on the lines of RRL Hyderabad. Such contributions of princely states to modern India are often overlooked in the mainstream history of the colonial and postcolonial periods.

Once Hyderabad came out of isolation in 1948, it became a part of the larger project of nation-building in the 1950s. By this time, Hyderabad was the capital of a new Telugu state, the unified Andhra Pradesh. As a part of the planned development approach, large industries, steel plants, fertiliser factories, heavy machinery plants and power generation plants were established in different parts of India. Hyderabad received special attention as it was felt that the state had lagged under the Nizam's rule, particularly in industrial development. CLSIR was made a central institution under CSIR; it was renamed Regional Research Laboratory and its research agenda was overhauled. It attracted highly qualified foreign-trained scientists as well as competent technologists from all over India. Over the years, it became the nucleus for developing more scientific institutions, and its technical expertise was used for industrial development in the region and the rest of India.

A major technological and industrial push came in the form of two public sector units, IDPL and ECIL. Their goal was to make India self-reliant in critical areas through R&D and technology absorption. ECIL was supposed to achieve self-reliance in strategic electronics, computers, communications and consumer products through R&D. The two public sector units (PSUs) developed a large pool of technical manpower, which, in turn, prepared the ground for entrepreneurs to foray into new sectors.

The first crop of entrepreneurs who floated start-ups in bulk drugs, electronics, software and so on were byproducts of PSUs (ECIL, IDPL, CMC) as well as research establishments like ASCI and NRSA. The presence of well-funded technical institutions stimulated the growth of technology-based entrepreneurial firms in the 1970s and 1980s. As the Telangana region lacked traditional mercantile communities, most of the new businesses in Hyderabad were floated by first-generation entrepreneurs belonging to cash-rich agriculture families from coastal Andhra. The younger generation from the coastal districts diversified from traditional industries like sugar, tobacco and rice milling and ventured into new areas like IT, pharmaceuticals and healthcare.[2] The change coincided with the rise of TDP, which represented peasant castes like Kammas, on the political front.

The next phase of the modernisation process began when new opportunities opened in 1991 due to policies of economic liberalisation and an end of the Licence Raj. The STPI scheme was specifically to boost small entrepreneurial firms in the technology sector. It was formulated before 1991 but came to fruition only after the liberalisation process was set in motion. It assured units of single-window clearances, handsome tax concessions and provided shared computing and data communication facilities. From being a regulator and licenser, the state donned the role of a facilitator and promotional agent. The Bangalore STPI was located in the Electronics City established in 1977. In addition, in 1993 the Karnataka government roped in the Tata group and a consortium of Singapore-based companies to form the Information Technology Park Limited in Whitefield as the second technology enclave. Hyderabad did not have such an enclave.

The politically dramatic entry of N. Chandrababu Naidu as chief minister in 1995 proved to be equally dramatic for the fledgling technology sector in Hyderabad. His brief to his team was 'beat Bangalore in information technology'. Hyderabad had almost everything needed for it: a good base of technical manpower, a functional STP, central PSUs engaged in technology-related areas and a string of research institutes and entrepreneurs willing to take the plunge. But it lacked the basic infrastructure like a technology enclave, dependable power supply, good road infrastructure, international airport and a social infrastructure conducive for young professionals. Naidu's government worked on each of these elements simultaneously and marketed the city aggressively to investors in India and abroad.

Much like Osman Ali Khan who took to developmental projects and administrative reforms in the right earnest to carve out a niche for himself as the maker of a modern Hyderabad in the 1920s, Naidu wanted to create an identity for himself as the maker of a globalised Hyderabad by aggressively pushing economic reforms and focusing on knowledge industries. The Nizam's aides dreamt of Hyderabad as an 'intellectual capital' like Baghdad while drawing inspiration from the Japanese models of educational and technical development. Naidu and his team looked east to Singapore, Malaysia and Japan for models of city-centric technology clusters.

Naidu adopted the science park model, which had been tried successfully in the West as well as in East Asian countries like South Korea, Taiwan and Malaysia as a vehicle for technology-based economic growth and development. The HITEC City and Genome Valley developed quickly as catalysts for boosting economic growth and exports. They could take a shape and yield results due to several domestic and external factors, not solely due to the political will and aggressive marketing as is often projected.

The Y2K problem, the internet and dotcom booms, and platform shifts were among the demand-side factors that made economic sense for American and European corporations to outsource. They found Hyderabad an attractive option due to a good supply of skilled people. In the same way, the process patent regime helped pharma companies in Hyderabad cater to the growing demand for generic medicines in several countries. The Genome Valley attracted foreign companies as the change in the patent regime after 2005 created demand for contract research, R&D outsourcing and third-party clinical research business.

Among the biggest domestic factors that favoured Naidu was the emergence of coalition politics at the centre. The support of Naidu's TDP was crucial for the survival of successive political formations that ruled in Delhi after the Congress party lost power in 1996. This turned a regional leader like Naidu into a kingmaker on the national stage. It meant he could swing policy decisions of the Central government in favour of Andhra Pradesh at will. Naidu faced no hurdles in getting the Centre's approvals whenever needed, including for his frequent foreign trips to market Hyderabad. He engaged in what has been called 'economic para-diplomacy' that saw him holding bilateral talks during his business trips and getting heads of state flying straight to Hyderabad.[3]

In both information technology and biotechnology sectors, the Telugu diaspora in North America proved to be a critical link. 'Coastal Andhra had a well-developed educational system for a long time. Engineering and medicine graduates from there went straight to America in the 1960s and 1970s. When P.V. Narasimha Rao, a Telugu, became prime minister in 1991 and announced liberalisation policies, many of them decided to come back. They preferred to return to Hyderabad, and not go to Vijayawada, Vizag or Guntur. Several Reddys, Rajus and Kammas from coastal Andhra started new businesses in Hyderabad,' explained Sanjaya Baru, economist and author.[4]

Yet another major factor that aided the ascent of Hyderabad from the 1960s onward was the availability of large chunks of government land in and around the city. The land was made available freely for developing PSUs, research laboratories, and national and international institutions in earlier decades and for major projects like Cyberabad and Genome Valley in the 1990s. For instance, DAE officials came to Hyderabad in 1965 looking for a site to locate their electronics unit but decided to locate three units instead when they found the state government ready to part with a large tract of land in one place. The availability of land near RRL made it easy for other labs like NGRI and NIN to locate them in the same area. The ICRISAT was another classic case in which 3,500 acres were allocated within five months of the project being approved. The same was the case with new projects in the 1990s—HITEC City, Genome Valley, ISB and so on. In every case, the state government was generous with the land and quick to take decisions.

The accessibility of large tracts of government land with little or no inhabitants around Hyderabad was a legacy of the Nizam era. Land during the Asaf Jahi period was classified as Diwani (revenue land) and non-Diwani. Nearly half of the land in the state was classified as non-Diwani whose administration was with Paigah nobles, jagirdars (people who received land grants) and Samsthandars (Hindu nobles). A significant part of the non-Diwani area was classified as Sirf-i-khas Mubarak (Crown lands). This was the property of the Nizam and revenue from it (about Rs 1 crore annually) went to his Privy Purse and the maintenance of the royal household.

The Sirf-i-khas Board managed the Crown lands which constituted about 10 per cent of the total area of the state—an area larger than the entire (princely) state of Travancore.[5] A major chunk of the Sirf-i-khas lands—a full district called Atraf-i-Balda made of seven talukas (932 villages)—surrounded Hyderabad.[6] As a part of the Central government's decision to abolish the jagirdari system in all the former princely states, in 1949 the Government of Hyderabad took over the Sirf-i-khas lands and fixed a Privy Purse of Rs 50 lakh for the former Nizam.[7] As the state government became the new owner of the land, it could easily transfer it to PSUs and national institutions without much trouble. After 1991, the state government used the concept of 'land as equity' to develop projects like the HITEC City with private participation. The concept was borrowed from the highly successful model of the IFSC.

Barring a short period during 2014-15 when there was uncertainty about the future of Hyderabad as Andhra Pradesh was bifurcated to form Telangana, there has been continuous political support for the development of the technology sector in the state. A broad consensus about the need to promote information technology since 1991 created a favourable atmosphere for attracting domestic and foreign investments. Naidu won the 1999 state assembly elections but lost the next one in 2004 with political rivals accusing him of being elitist, anti-poor and pro-market. Yet, analysts don't attribute his defeat solely to his single-minded focus on IT; they also point at several other political factors including the rise of Telangana Rashtra Samithi (TRS), which was later renamed as Bharat Rashtra Samithi (BRS).[8]

The reform policies and focus on IT continued under Y.S. Rajasekhar Reddy of the Congress party, who succeeded Naidu. Similarly, K. Chandrasekhara Rao of TRS, who came to power after the formation of Telangana state in 2014, not only continued the support to this sector but further increased it. He inducted his son K.T. Rama Rao, a former management professional, as the minister for IT. A postgraduate in biotechnology and MBA in marketing, Rama Rao aggressively marketed the new state to investors in IT, biotechnology, as well as other emerging areas. There was no change in the policies for the IT and biotechnology sectors after the assembly elections in December 2023 which saw the Congress party elected to power.

The Future

From being the backroom of large corporations providing IT-enabled services in the late 1990s, Hyderabad is moving up the value chain. The Y2K problem, coupled with a shortage of skilled manpower in the West, laid the foundation of the technology business in Hyderabad. The outsourcing of labour-intensive tasks and routine work helped Indian service companies scale up their operations. In the next phase, companies moved up the value chain in niche areas like engineering R&D, semiconductor design and so on. International companies set up their R&D centres to develop products. All this created high-paying jobs and earned foreign exchange for the country. The COVID-19 pandemic proved to be another Y2K moment as it accelerated the adoption of digital technologies, creating newer opportunities for businesses in Hyderabad.[9]

The new ICT policy announced in 2021 envisages doubling the annual exports of the IT and ITES sector to Rs 3 lakh crore by 2026 while increasing the total direct employment to 1 million in five years. The policy goal is to establish Telangana as 'the global hub for product development, engineering and R&D'. It also seeks to grow the IT sector in Hyderabad. In addition, emerging technologies—blockchain, additive manufacturing, space technology, robotics, and digital twins (creating virtual replicas)—will get institutional support with plans to develop the Telangana Emerging Technologies corridor to boost them.

The startup ecosystem in the city is looking up, with several of the companies working in niche areas like space, electric mobility, artificial intelligence, the Internet of Things, machine learning, etc. For instance, Skyroot Aerospace started by Pawan Kumar Chandana and Naga Bharat Daka in 2018 is developing a satellite launch vehicle series called Vikram to be powered by a cryogenic engine.

The startup scene received a further boost with the opening of T-Hub, a massive incubation centre, in mid-2022. The Rs 400 crore, ten-storeyed building has everything—from mentorship to venture capital—that a startup needs to incubate, scale up and corporatise. Built on the lines of Station F in Paris and spread over half a million square feet, it is claimed to be the world's largest innovation campus. 'We are not only going to compete with Silicon Valley but might even surpass it in future,' says Mahankali Srinivas Rao, CEO of T-Hub.[10]

During the COVID-19 pandemic, vaccine manufacturers in Genome Valley demonstrated their capabilities to a global audience with fast-track development and manufacture of new vaccines. This helped attract more companies to the valley. In 2022, Hyderabad had 800 pharmaceuticals, med tech and biotech companies, with Genome Valley having six of the world's top R&D companies in life sciences and three of India's largest vaccine manufacturers. As the next step, the state government has plans to develop a separate Pharma City spread over 19,000 acres as the 'world's largest integrated eco-system for life sciences.'[11]

Yet Hyderabad companies lag in product development and intellectual property creation. Of the top fifty software export companies in Hyderabad in 2020, only two had their entrepreneurial origins in Hyderabad.[12] In terms and size and revenue, the software business in Hyderabad is still small. For instance, the total software export from Hyderabad (about USD 23 billion) is lower than the annual revenue of India's largest software company TCS (USD 25 billion). The software exports from Bangalore are estimated at USD

65 billion in 2022. In the startup segment, the city has produced just a couple of Unicorns compared with other clusters like Bangalore which had some thirty startups in this category.

'Hyderabad has everything—technical expertise, number of institutions, industrial base and the entrepreneurial spirit. One gap is a robust funding ecosystem for startups compared with Bangalore. That is what T-Hub is trying to address. Hyderabad is catching up with Bangalore,' feels Rashmi Pimpale, CEO of Research and Innovation Circle of Hyderabad (RICH) which acts as a bridge between research institutions and industry to promote innovation.[13] 'Bengaluru had an early start and positioned itself as the Silicon Valley of India. Instead of competing with Bengaluru, we need to find our own niche. I think Hyderabad is well poised to become the innovation capital of India,' adds Manisha Saboo, president of the Hyderabad Software Enterprises Association.[14]

Innovation and product development are the basic requirements of the technology business and that's where Hyderabad needs to focus on to sustain the growth momentum. At the same time, public policies are needed to reduce income disparities and ensure affordable access to technology for citizens. The use of technological tools for governance and public services is critical, but it must respect citizens' right to privacy and basic human rights. The infrastructure development should be even across the city and the state, and basic amenities like transport, health and water need to be ensured for all. A globalised Hyderabad should not remain an elitist enclave within the city and a mere aspiration for the rest of the citizenry. As the city continues to transform, expand and reinvent itself, driven by the focus on knowledge-based industries and infrastructure development, it can serve as a working model for other cities and states in India and elsewhere.

Notes and References

Introduction: Biryani and Backroom

1. Pratibha Karan, *Biryani* (Penguin, 2009).
2. 'Creative Cities Network: Hyderabad', UNESCO, https://en.unesco. org/creative-cities/hyderabad, accessed on 10 November 2022.
3. 'Hyderabad Haleem Gets Geographical Indication Certification', ICAR website, https://icar.org.in/node/543, accessed on 10 November 2022.
4. 'Swiggy Reveals Indians Placed 7.6 Crore Biryani Orders in Last 12 Months', *Business Today*, 1 July 2023, https://www.businesstoday.in/latest/trends/ story/swiggy-reveals-indians-placed-76-crore-biryani-orders-in-last-12-months-387844-2023-07-01, accessed on 6 October 2023.
5. 'Paradise Launches Fiery Biryani and Kebab for All Spice Lovers', *Devdiscourse*, 2 July 2022, https://www.devdiscourse.com/article/ business/2118360-paradise-launches-fiery-biryani-and-kebab-for-all-spice-lovers, accessed on 10 November 2022.
6. https://telangana.gov.in/wp-content/uploads/2023/12/Telangana-Economy-2023.pdf.

7.   Serish Nanisetti, *Golconda/Bagnagar/Hyderabad: Rise and Fall of a Global Metropolis in Medieval India* (Self published, 2019), pp. 78–79.

8.   Nanisetti, *Golconda/Bagnagar/Hyderabad*, p. 68.

9.   Nanisetti, *Golconda/Bagnagar/Hyderabad*, p. 75.

10. Shah Manzoor Alam, *Hyderabad–Secunderabad, Twin Cities: A Study in Urban Geography* (Allied Publishers, 1965), pp. 7–9.

11. Tazia is wooden replica of the tomb of Husain—martyred grandson of Muhammad—and carried in processions during observance of Muharram by Shia Muslims.

12. Nanisetti, *Golconda/Bagnagar/Hyderabad*, p. 76.

13. Narendra Luther, *Hyderabad: A Biography* (Oxford University Press, New Delhi, 2006), p. 15.

14. Luther, *Hyderabad*.

15. Nanisetti, *Golconda/Bagnagar/Hyderabad*, pp. 82–84.

16. Muhammad A. Nayeem, *The Splendour of Hyderabad: The Last Phase of an Oriental Culture, 1591-1948 AD* (Hyderabad Publishers, 2002), p. 16.

17. Nayeem, *The Splendour of Hyderabad*, p. 25.

18. Nanisetti, *Golconda/Bagnagar/Hyderabad*, pp. 104–105.

19. Nanisetti, *Golconda/Bagnagar/Hyderabad*, p. 44.

20. Nayeem, *The Splendour of Hyderabad*, pp. 84–86.

21. Nayeem, *The Splendour of Hyderabad*, p. 96.

22. For a fuller explanation, see Vasant K. Bawa, *The Last Nizam: The Life and Times of Mir Osman Ali Khan* (Viking, 1992).

23. Alam, *Hyderabad–Secunderabad*, pp. 7–9.

24. Bakhtiar K. Dadabhoy, *The Magnificent Diwan: The Life and Times of Sir Salar Jung I* (Penguin Random House, 2019), pp. 332–333.

25. Harriet Ronken Lynton and Mohini Rajan, *The Days of the Beloved* (University of California Press, 1974), pp. 243–244.

26. Bawa, *The Last Nizam*, p. 39.

27. Bawa, *The Last Nizam*.

Chapter 1: Chloroform, Malaria and Stargazing

1.   John G. McKendrick, Joseph Coats and David Newman, 'Remarks on the Report of the Second Hyderabad Chloroform Commission', *British Medical Journal* 1, no. 1537 (1890), p. 1345.

2.   Shiv Visvanathan, *Organizing for Science* (Oxford University Press, New Delhi, 1985), pp. 11–12.

3.   John Keay, *The Great Arc: The Dramatic Tale of How India Was Mapped and Everest Was Named* (HarperCollins, London, 2000), pp. 2–3.

4.   Keay, *The Great Arc*, p. 9.

5.   Rahul Devulapalli, 'Piece of History Arrives in Hyderabad', *The Hindu*, 24 January 2017, https://www.thehindu.com/news/cities/Hyderabad/ Piece-of-history-arrives-in-Hyderabad/article17083570.ece, accessed on 11 November 2022.

6.   Sir David Barr, *Hyderabad: Past and Present*, October 1905, p. 11. Syed Husain Bilgrami Collection, Nehru Memorial Museum and Library, New Delhi.

7.   B. Pati and M. Harrison (eds), 'Introduction', in *Health, Medicine and Empire: Perspectives on Colonial India* (Orient Longman, New Delhi, 2001), pp. 1–36.

8.   William Campbell Maclean, *Memories of a Long Life*, printed for private circulation, Edinburgh, 1895, p. 172.

9.   'Calcutta Review', reprinted in *Hyderabad Affairs*, 1849, pp. 164–165.

10. Report on the Administration of His Highness Nizam's Dominions, 1303 Fasli, published in 1895, Telangana State Archives and Research Institute, Hyderabad.

11. Maclean, *Memories of a Long Life*, p. 170.

12. D.V. Subba Rao, 'At Last, a Home!' Souvenir, *150 Years of Osmania Medical College*, 1996, p. 40.

13. George Smith, *The Hyderabad Medical School: Its Past History and Present Condition*, published at the request of The Nawab Mukhtar Ul Moolk Salar Jung Bahadoor, 1859, Madras, p. 23.

14. Smith, *The Hyderabad Medical School*, pp. 8–9.

15. Smith, *The Hyderabad Medical School*, pp. 8–9.

16. *Proceedings of Academy of Medical Sciences*, special number on medical history (Academy of Medical Sciences Hyderabad, 1962), pp. 68–69.

17. *Proceedings of Academy of Medical Sciences*, p. 69.

18. George Smith, *The Hyderabad Medical School*, pp. 24–25.

19. George Smith, *The Hyderabad Medical School*, pp. 33–34.

20. Sheela Raj, *Medievalism to Modernism: Socio-economic and Cultural History of Hyderabad—1869–1911* (South Asia Books, 1987), pp. 240–241.

21. George Smith, *The Hyderabad Medical School*, pp. 38–39.

22. *Report of the Hyderabad Chloroform Commission with a Preface by Sir Asman Jah* (Times of India Steam Press, Bombay, 1891).

23. A.H.B. Masson, J. Wilson and B.C. Hovell, 'Edward Lawrie of the Hyderabad Chloroform Commission', *British Journal of Anaesthesia* 41, no. 11 (1969), pp. 1002–1011.

24. 'Annotations', *The Lancet,* 2 March 1889, p. 438.

25. 'The Chloroform Commissions in India', *The Pioneer,* 6 November 1889.

26. 'Report of the Second Hyderabad Chloroform Commission', *The Lancet* 135, no. 3464 (18 January 1890), pp. 149–152.

27. 'Report of the Second Hyderabad Chloroform Commission'.

28. 'Report of the Second Hyderabad Chloroform Commission', pp. 12–13.

29. 'Report of the Second Hyderabad Chloroform Commission', p. 5.

30. K.B. Thomas, 'Chloroform: Commissions and Omissions', *Proceedings of the Royal Society of Medicine* 67, no. 8 (1974), p. 723.

31. Masson et al., 'Edward Lawrie of the Hyderabad Chloroform Commission'.

32. Masson et al., 'Edward Lawrie of the Hyderabad Chloroform Commission'.

33. Edwin Nye and Mary Gibson, *Ronald Ross: Malariologist and Polymath: A Biography* (Springer, 1997), p. 44.

34. Nye and Gibson, *Ronald Ross*, p. 68.

35. Naveed Hussain, *Dr Arastu Yar Jung (b. 1858–d. 1940)* (Self published, 2019).

36. Ronald Ross, 'On Some Peculiar Pigmented Cells Found in Two Mosquitoes Fed on Malarial Blood', *British Medical Journal*, ii (1897), pp. 1786–1788.

37. Speech by Maj. Gen. S.L. Bhatia, 25 May 1953, Hyderabad, B2P33, S.L. Bhatia Archives, Bangalore.

38. Bakhtiar K. Dadabhoy, *The Magnificent Diwan: The Life and Times of Sir Salar Jung I* (Penguin Random House, 2019), p. 165.

39. K. Krishnaswamy Mudiraj, *Pictorial Hyderabad Volume 2* (Chandrakanth Press, Hyderabad, 1929), pp. 84–85.

40. T.P. Prabhu, 'Notes for the Observer: 75 Years of the Nizamiah Observatory', *Bulletin of the Astronomical Society of India*, 16 (1988), pp. 53–55.

41. 'D.W.K. Barr to Maharaja Kishen Pershad, November 19, 1904, Hyderabad Deccan', Chowmahalla Collection, Hyderabad.

42. Michie Smith, 'Report on H.E. The Nawab Zafar Jung Bahadur's Telescopes', Chowmahalla Collection, Hyderabad.

43. George Casson Walker, 'Letter to Maharaja Kishen Pershad, March 9, 1907, Hyderabad Deccan', Chowmahalla Collection, Hyderabad.

44. H.H. Turner, 'Letter to His Highness the Nizam, Oxford, February 19, 1908', Chowmahalla Collection, Hyderabad.

45. T.P. Prabhu, 'Notes for the Observer', p. 2.

46. R.J. Pocock, *Astrographic Catalogue 1900-0: Hyderabad Section Dec. 16 to 21. From Photographs Taken and Measured at the Nizamiah Observatory, Hyderabad. Under the Direction of RJ Pocock* (Neill & Company, 1918), p. iv.

47. H.H. Turner, 'Letter to Amin Jung (Private Secretary to the HEH Nizam), Oxford, April 16, 1920', Chowmahalla Collection, Hyderabad.

48. 'List of Fellows and Associates (Volume 1895–1919)', Royal Astronomical Society, London, 1920, p. 20.

49. Rajesh Kochhar and Jayant Narlikar, *Astronomy in India: A Perspective* (Indian National Science Academy, New Delhi, 1995), Chapter 1, p. 20.

50. Jessica Ratcliff, 'Travancore's Magnetic Crusade: Geomagnetism and the Geography of Scientific Production in a Princely State', *The British Journal for the History of Science* 49, no. 3 (2016), pp. 325–352, http://www.jstor.org/stable/26350807, accessed on 28 August 2023.

51. Ala Narayana, K. Bharathi, P.K.J.P. Subhaktha, Manohar Gundeti and A. Ramachari, 'Dr. (Miss) Rupa Bai Furdoonji: World's First Qualified Lady Anaesthetist', *Indian Journal of Anaesthesia* 54, no. 3 (2010), p. 259.

52. 'Report of the Second Hyderabad Chloroform Commission', p. 274.

53. E. Lawrie, 'Chloroform', *The Indian Medical Gazette*, June 1900, pp. 201–209.

54. G.I.C. Glancy, 'Letter to the Resident O'Dwyer, July 1908, Hyderabad Deccan', Chowmahalla Collection, Hyderabad.

55. 'Obituary: Rao Saheb T.P. Bhaskara Sastry', *Current Science* 19, no. 10 (October 1950), p. 330.

56. J.C. Bhattacharyya, 'Manali Kallat Vainu Bappu (1927–1982) Elected Fellow 1968' (Indian National Science Academy, 1985), p. 18.

57. 'Cultural Activities: Hyderabad', *Islamic Culture* XXI, Hyderabad (April 1947), pp. 184–185.

58. Interview with Sanjar Ali Khan, Hyderabad, 21 August 2021.

59. A.S. Grewal, 'Letter to K. Vainu Bappu, Washington, July 13, 1949', Indian Institute of Astrophysics (IIA) Archives, Bangalore.

60. Fred Whipple, 'Letter to A S Grewal, July 26, 1949', Indian Institute of Astrophysics Archives, Bengaluru.

61. Bhattacharyya, 'Manali Kallat Vainu Bappu'; Interview with Sanjar Ali Khan.

Chapter 2: Mahua Flowers and the World Wars

1. 'Note on Industrial Potentialities of Hyderabad and a Few Connected Papers, Hyderabad-Deccan, 1916', Chowmahalla Collection, Hyderabad.

2. 'Report on the Manufacture of High Explosive Shell in India for the Ministry of Munitions by V. Bayley', Government, Central Branch Press, 1971, *Home Political 1917–04*, National Archives of India , p. 31.

3. 'Note on Industrial Potentialities'.

4. 'Note on Industrial Potentialities'.

5. 'Note on Industrial Potentialities'.

6. 'Notes Taken on London by G.E.C. Wakefield Esq., Director General of Revenue, in Connection with the Manufacture of Acetone from the Flowers of Mahua Tree, January 1, 1916', Chowmahalla Collection, Hyderabad.

7. 'Notes Taken on London'.

8. 'Note on Industrial Potentialities'.

9. 'Preliminary Memorandum Regarding Industrial Developments in the Dominions of His Highness the Nizam of Hyderabad, by Dr G.J. Fowler, Professor of Applied Chemistry, Indian Institute of Science, Bangalore, July 19, 1916', Chowmahalla Collection, Hyderabad.

10. *Annual Report (1917-18)* (Indian Institute of Science, Bangalore), p. 9.

11. *Annual Report (1917-18)*, pp. 17–18.

12. N.N. Inuganti, *The Manufacture of Glue*, Department of Industries and Commerce, HEH the Nizam's Government, Industrial Laboratory, June 1924 (The Government Central Press, Hyderabad-Deccan), p. 44.

13. *Annual Report (1922-23)* (Indian Institute of Science, Bangalore), p. 11.

14. G.A. Mahomadi, 'Annual Report of the Administration of Department of Industries & Commerce for the Year 1921, Hyderabad-Deccan', p. 7. Telangana State Archives and Research Institute, Hyderabad.

15. 'Report on the Working of the Commerce and Industries Department of HEH the Nizam's Government, Hyderabad Deccan for the Year Fasli

1337, 1927', pp. 6–7. Telangana State Archives and Research Institute, Hyderabad.

16. V.V. Krishna, 'Organization of Industrial Research: The Early History of CSIR, 1934–47.' *Science and Modern India: An Institutional History, c. 1784–1947* (2011), pp. 157–184.

17. Ghulam Mohammed migrated to Pakistan where he was appointed the finance minister and later the governor general.

18. Bharat Bhushan, *50 Eventful Years* (Indian Institute of Chemical Technology, Hyderabad, 1995), p. 5.

19. C.V. Subbarao, *Hyderabad: Social Context of Industrialization 1875 to 1948* (Orient Longman, Hyderabad, 2007), pp. 42–43.

Chapter 3: A Beautiful, Healthy and Efficient City

1. M. Visvesvaraya, 'City Improvements Schemes—Hyderabad Deccan' (Bombay, February 1930), Telangana State Archives and Research Institute, Hyderabad, pp. 47–48.

2. M. Visvesvaraya, 'City Improvements, Hyderabad (Preliminary Note)', May 1909, *Memoirs of Shri M. Visvesvaraya 1910–12*, Reel 2 (Nehru Memorial Museum and Library, New Delhi).

3. Visvesvaraya, 'City Improvements'.

4. K. Krishnaswamy Mudiraj, *Pictorial Hyderabad*, Volume 1 (Chandrakanth Press, Hyderabad, 1929), p. 7.

5. Transcript of Oral History Interview with Pannalal Bansilal Pitti, 1 August 1975, Nehru Memorial Museum and Library.

6. Interview with Shyam Tiwari, a descendant of Jhoomar Lal Tiwari, Hyderabad, 24 July 2020.

7. Interview with Shyam Tiwari; Harriet Ronken Lynton and Mohini Rajan, *The Days of the Beloved*, (University of California Press, USA, 1974), p. 16.

8. 'Minutes of the Meeting Held at the House of the Nawab Faridoon Jung Bahadur, on Tuesday, the 29th September 1908', *Faridoon Jung Papers* File 2 (Nehru Memorial Museum and Library, New Delhi).

9. 'Minutes of the Meeting Held at the House of the Nawab Faridoon Jung Bahadur'.

10. Mokshagundam Visvesvaraya, *Memoirs of My Working Life* (Publications Division, 1960), p. 32.

11.   Visvesvaraya, *Memoirs*.

12.   Visvesvaraya, 'City Improvements, Hyderabad (Preliminary Note)'.

13.   M. Visvesvaraya, 'The Flood of 1908 at Hyderabad: An Account of the Flood, Its Causes, Proposed Preventive Measures', Reel 2, Nehru Memorial Museum and Library.

14.   Visvesvaraya, 'The Flood of 1908'.

15.   Visvesvaraya, 'City Improvements, Hyderabad (Preliminary Note)'.

16.   Visvesvaraya, 'City Improvements, Hyderabad (Preliminary Note)'.

17.   Visvesvaraya, 'The Flood of 1908'.

18.   M. Visvesvaraya, 'Scheme for Flood Abatement in Hyderabad City and Irrigation in the Musi Valley, September 1909', *Memoirs of Shri M. Visvesvayara 1910–12*, Reel 2 (Nehru Memorial Museum and Library, New Delhi).

19.   John Law, *Modern Hyderabad (Deccan)*, (Thacker, Spink & Company, Calcutta, 1914), pp. 87–88.

20.   Law, *Modern Hyderabad (Deccan)*, p. 91.

21.   'Flood Protection for Hyderabad: New Dam Completed', *The Times of India*, 14 July 1927.

22.   'Report on Hyderabad Drainage, November 6, 1909', *Memoirs of Shri M. Visvesvayara 1910–12*, Reel 2 (Nehru Memorial Museum and Library, New Delhi).

23.   'Report on Hyderabad Drainage'.

24.   'Report on Hyderabad Drainage'.

25.   R.A.C. Cameron, 'Hyderabad Drainage Scheme: Details of a Big Project, Modern Installation in Nizam's Capital', *The Times of India*, 12 May 1927.

26.   'Hyderabad Drainage Project: Plague Retards Progress', *The Times of India*, 6 June 1928.

27.   Visvesvaraya, *Memoirs*, p. 36.

28.   'Progress Report of the Hyderabad City Improvement Board for Ten Years: From 1327 to 1336 Fasli' (HEH The Nizam's Government, Hyderabad, 1929).

29.   M.A. Husain, *Statistical Year Book 1348 Fasli (1939 A.D.)* (Government Central Press, Hyderabad, 1941), p. 479.

30.   S. Mallannah, 'The Glandular Extract from Immunized Animals as a Curative Agent in Plague', *The Lancet* 169, no. 4352 (1907), pp. 222–224.

31.   S. Mallannah, 'Tobacco as Flea Bane', *British Medical Journal*, March 1917.

32. S. Mallannah, 'Tobacco Fleas and Plague', *The Indian Medical Gazette*, February 1918.

33. S. Mallannah, 'Tobacco Fleas and Plague'.

34. The Urdu name for CIB was *Araish-e-Baldia*, which means 'embellishment of the city' and reflected the need for aesthetics along with health and sanitation. The riverfront or river district development, business district development, drainage and sanitation improvement, construction of concrete roads and residential colonies were major projects executed by CIB during its existence till 1948. The formation of the board was notified in 1912 but it became functional in 1914 with Nawab Wali-ud-Dowla Bahadur as its president. In later years, Mahdi Yar Jung Bahadur was CIB president until Prince Moazzam Jah Bahadur replaced him in August 1934. P.A. Bhavnani was superintending engineer for the first nine years.

35. 'Progress Report of the Hyderabad City Improvement Board for Ten Years—1327 to 1337/Fasli 1919 to 1928 A.D.' (Government Press, Hyderabad), p. 3.

36. 'Progress Report of the Hyderabad City Improvement Board for Ten Years'.

37. 'Report of the Progress of the Hyderabad City Improvement Board for the Year 1346 Fasli/1936 to 1937)', p. 22.

38. M. Visvesvaraya, 'City Improvement Schemes—Hyderabad (Deccan)' (Bombay, 1930), p. 2.

39. 'Drainage and Other Improvements Schemes in Hyderabad Deccan: Note Prepared for HEH Nizam's Government by Sir M. Visvesvaraya, 1932', *Memoirs of Shri M. Visvesvayara 1910–12* Reel 8 (Nehru Memorial Museum and Library, New Delhi).

40. 'Drainage and Other Improvements Schemes in Hyderabad Deccan'.

41. 'Drainage and Other Improvements Schemes in Hyderabad Deccan'.

42. 'Drainage and Other Improvements Schemes in Hyderabad Deccan'.

43. Manzoor Alam, 'The Growth of Hyderabad City: A Historical Perspective', in H.K. Sherwani (ed.), *Studies in Indian Culture: Dr. Ghulam Yazdani, Commemoration Volume* (Maulana Abul Kalam Azad Oriental Research Institute, Hyderabad, 1966).

44. Alison Mackenzie Shah, 'Constructing a Capital on the Edge of Empire: Urban Patronage and Politics in Asaf Jahi Hyderabad', PhD dissertation, University of Pennsylvania, 2005.

45. John Law, *Modern Hyderabad (Deccan)* (Thacker, Spink & Company, Calcutta, 1914), pp. 89–90.

Chapter 4: New Skyline on the Riverfront

1. M. Visvesvaraya, 'City Improvements, Hyderabad (Preliminary Note)', May 1909, *Memoirs of Shri M. Visvesvayara 1910–12*, Reel 2 (Nehru Memorial Museum and Library, New Delhi).
2. Visvesvaraya, 'City Improvements, Hyderabad (Preliminary Note)'.
3. Visvesvaraya, 'City Improvements, Hyderabad (Preliminary Note)'.
4. Visvesvaraya, 'City Improvements, Hyderabad (Preliminary Note)'.
5. M. Visvesvaraya, *Reconstructing India* (P.S. King & Son, London, 1920), pp. 222–223.
6. Visvesvaraya, *Reconstructing India*.
7. Bakhtiar K. Dadabhoy, *The Magnificent Diwan*, pp. 338–339.
8. 'A Note Prepared and Signed by R.I.R. Glancy, February 18, 1920', Chowmahalla Collection, Hyderabad.
9. 'Speech Delivered by HEH Nizam at Opening of the New High Court Building, April 14, 1920', Chowmahalla Collection, Hyderabad.
10. P. Jaganmohan Reddy, *The Judiciary I Served* (Orient Longman, Hyderabad, 1999), p. 142.
11. John Law, *Modern Hyderabad*, pp. 103–107.
12. 'Completion Report of the Construction of Osmania General Hospital', n.d., Chowmahalla Collection, Hyderabad.
13. 'Completion Report of the Construction of Osmania General Hospital'.
14. 'The Humble Petition of K.R. Chari & Son, Secunderabad to the Nizam of Hyderabad, March 2, 1926', Chowmahalla Collection, Hyderabad.
15. 'Completion Report of the Construction of Osmania General Hospital'.
16. 'Completion Report of the Construction of Osmania General Hospital'.
17. G.H.R. Tillotson, *Vincent J. Esch and the Architecture of Hyderabad, 1914–36, South Asian Studies* 9, no. 1 (1993), pp. 29–46.
18. Omar Khalidi, *A Guide to Architecture in Hyderabad, Deccan, India* (Aga Khan Program for Islamic Architecture and MIT Libraries, Cambridge, Massachusetts, 2009), p. 221.
19. Vincent J. Esch, 'Letter to the Chief Engineer (General Branch) and Joint Secretary, The HEH Nizam's PWD, Hyderabad Deccan, September 14, 1920', Chowmahalla Collection, Hyderabad.

20. Vincent J. Esch, 'Letter to the Chief Engineer'.

21. M.A. Husain, *Statistical Year Book 1348 Fasli (1939 A.D.)* (Government Press, Hyderabad, 1940), p. 446.

22. V.K. Bhatnagar, S.A. Hussain and Momin Ali, 'A Brief History of Ayurveda in Hyderabad', *Bulletin of the Indian Institute of History of Medicine (Hyderabad)* 24, no. 1 (1994), pp. 63–75.

23. M. Visvesvaraya, 'City Improvement Schemes—Hyderabad (Deccan)', p. 7

Chapter 5: India's First Vernacular University

1. *Eminent Musalmaans* (G.A. Natesan & Co., Madras, 1926), p. 502.

2. 'The Uplift of the Masses; Speech at a Public Meeting, September 25, Hyderabad', *Selected Works of Jawaharlal Nehru, Second Series,* Volume 19 (Jawaharlal Nehru Memorial Fund, 1996), p. 27.

3. 'New Members of the India Council', *The Times of India Illustrated Weekly,* Syed Hussain Bilgrami Collection (Nehru Memorial Museum and Library, New Delhi).

4. Sheela Raj, 'Progress of Education in Hyderabad State During 1911–1948', *Islamic Culture* 76, no. 2 (2002), pp. 115–136.

5. Wilfrid Scawen Blunt, *Ideas about India* (K. Paul, Trench, 1885), pp. 199–200.

6. Wilfrid Scawen Blunt, *India Under Ripon: A Private Diary* (T.F. Unwin, 1909), p. 197.

7. Dr H. Rajendra Prasad, 'Sunshine and Shadows: The Years of Direct Administration of the Nizam (1914–1919)', PhD dissertation, Osmania University, 1997.

8. V.K. Bawa, *The Last Nizam,* p. 78.

9. Bawa, *The Last Nizam,* pp. 48–49.

10. Margrit Pernau, *The Passing of Patrimonialism: Politics and Political Culture in Hyderabad 1911–1948* (Manohar, New Delhi, 2000), p. 106.

11. H.K. Sherwani (ed.), *Dr Gulam Yazdani: Commemoration* Volume', (Maulana Abul Kalam Azad Oriental Institute, Hyderabad, 1966), p. 240.

12. Michael O'Dwyer, 'Letter to R.I.R. Glancy, Lahore, February 3, 1917', Chowmahalla Collection, Hyderabad.

13. 'Mr Glancy's Opinion', n.d., Chowmahalla Collection, Hyderabad.

14. Akbar Hydari, '*Arzdasht* to HEH The Nizam, April 22, 1917', Telangana State Archives and Research Institute, Hyderabad.

15. Hydari, 'Arzdasht to HEH The Nizam'.

16. Sherwani (ed.), *Dr Gulam Yazdani*, pp. 241–242.

17. 'Firman Dated 4th Rajab, 1335 H/26th April 1917 AD Directing to Take Action for the Establishment of Osmania University', Telangana State Archives and Research Institute, Hyderabad.

18. 'The Curriculum of Intermediate Examination' (finally passed by the meeting on 4 July 1918), Telangana State Archives and Research Institute, Hyderabad.

19. Akbar Hydari, chairman, *Report of the Scientific Terminology Committee*, (Bureau of Education, India, 1941), p. 21.

20. Gulam Ahmed Khan, Census Commissioner, *Census of India, 1931, Volume XXIII, HEH the Nizam's Dominions (Hyderabad State) Part I* (Government Central Press, 1933), pp. 217–218.

21. 'Hyderabad—Papers and Correspondence Regarding Matters Relating to Education and Educational Reforms', Roll 00016, File number 114, National Archives of India.

22. 'A Short Account of the Work by the Compilation and Translation Bureau, Osmania University, 1917–46', Roll 00162, File No 865, National Archives of India.

23. Akbar Hydari, chairman, *Report of the Scientific Terminology Committee of the Central Advisory Board of Education in India, 1940 Together with the Decisions of the Board Thereon* (Manager of Publications, Delhi, 1941), pp. 82–84.

24. Sherwani (ed.), *Dr Gulam Yazdani*, p. 239.

25. Sushila Narasimhan (ed.), *India–Japan Narratives: Lesser Known Historical & Cultural Interactions* (Mombusho Scholars Association of India, New Delhi, 2021), pp. 206–227.

26. Narasimhan (ed.), *India–Japan Narratives*.

27. O'Dwyer, 'Letter to R.I.R. Glancy'.

28. Syed Ross Masood, *Japan and Its Educational System: Being a Report Compiled for the Government of His Exalted Highness the Nizam* (Government Central Press, Hyderabad, 1923), p. 341.

29. Masood, *Japan and Its Educational System*, pp. 342–347.

30. Syed Ross Masood, 'Letter to H.K. Shewani, Hyderabad, September 9, 1918, Papers of H.K. Sherwani, Ist Instalment' (Nehru Memorial Museum and Library, New Delhi).

31. Syed Ross Masood, 'Letter to H.K. Shewani, Hyderabad, September 25, 1919, Papers of H.K. Sherwani, Ist Instalment' (Nehru Memorial Museum and Library, New Delhi).

32. *Report of the Public Instruction in HEH The Nizam's Dominions for the Year 1328 Fasli* (Government Central Press, Hyderabad-Deccan, 1921), p. 3.

33. 'Note by Zoolcader Jung' (member of the Osmania University Construction Committee), n.d., Chowmahalla Collection, Hyderabad.

34. Akbar Nazar Hydari, 'Letter to Patrick Geddes, Hyderabad, June 22, 1918', Patrick Geddes Papers, GB 249 T-GED/9/1413, University of Strathclyde Archives and Special Collections.

35. Serish Nanisetty, 'How the Osmania University Came About,' *The Hindu*, 28 January 2019.

36. 'Report on the Progress of the Osmania University Building Project for the Year 1334 Fasli (1934–1935)', HEH The Nizam's Government, Hyderabad Deccan, Telangana State Archives and Research Institute, Hyderabad, p. 2.

37. 'Report on the Progress of the Osmania University Building Project', p. 68.

38. Akbar Hydari, 'Telegram to Akbar Yar Jung (Secretary, University Building Committee), London, October 2, 1931', Chowmahalla Collection, Hyderabad.

39. Serish Nanisetty, 'Arts College Building, a Hand-Me-Down Architectural Gem', *The Hindu*, 8 April 2017.

40. Dildar Husain, *Glimpses of an Engineer-Statesman of Hyderabad Deccan* (Institution of Engineers, Hyderabad, 1961), pp. 34–35).

41. 'Indian University Architecture', *Nature*, no. 3908, 23 September 1944, pp. 403–404.

42. 'Fortnightly Report on the Political Situation for the Month of October and November 1926', *Home Political* NA1926 F-112 IV PV, National Archives of India.

43. Akbar Hydari, '*Arzdasht* to HEH The Nizam'.

44. 'Hyderabad—Papers and Correspondence Regarding Matters Relating to Education and Educational Reforms', National Archives of India.

45. 'Hyderabad—Papers and Correspondence'.

46. 'Proceedings of the Twenty Fourth Indian Science Congress', Telangana State Archives and Research Institute, Hyderabad, pp. 13, 18.

47. 'Aide Memoire: Osmania University', File on 'Proposed Reconstitution of Osmania University as a Central Institution', Ministry of Education_G-III_1952_NA_F-29-73_52, PR_000003041693, National Archives of India.

48. Jawaharlal Nehru, 'Letter to N. Gopalaswamy Iyengar, September 23, 1951', *Selected Works of Jawaharlal Nehru Second Series, Volume 16 Part 2*, pp. 514–515.

49. 'Extracts from Chief Minister, Hyderabad (Deccan)'s DO Letter to Joint Secretary, Ministry of States, dated March 5, 1952', File on 'Proposed Reconstitution of Osmania University', National Archives of India.

50. Note on HEH's Endowment of Rs 3 Crore for the Osmania University Trust Fund (Confidential), 7 April 1952, Chowmahalla Collection, Hyderabad

51. 'Aide Memoire: Osmania University'.

52. 'Osmania University', Editorial, *The Hindu*, 18 May 1952.

53. Jawaharlal Nehru, 'Letter to B. Ramakrishna Rao', *Selected Works of Jawaharlal Nehru Second Series, Series 2, Volume 18*, pp. 131–134.

54. 'Reconstitution of Osmania University', *Selected Works of Jawaharlal Nehru Second Series, Series 2 Volume 18*, pp. 135–137.

55. 'Proposed Reconstitution of Osmania University as a Central Institution', National Archives of India.

56. Masood, *Japan and Its Educational System*.

57. Kavita Datla, 'A Worldly Vernacular: Urdu at Osmania University', *Modern Asian Studies* 43, no. 5 (September 2009), pp. 1117–1148.

58. Andrew McKinney Amstutz, 'Finding a Home for Urdu: Islam and Science in Modern South Asia', PhD dissertation, Cornell University, 2017, pp. 80–81.

59. Amstutz, 'Finding a Home for Urdu', p. 95.

60. Asma Rasheed, 'Subject Language: Preliminary Notes on Education Around Late Nineteenth Century Hyderabad State', *Language Policy and Education in India* (Routledge India, 2016), pp. 70–78.

61. Karen Leonard, 'Reassessing Indirect Rule in Hyderabad: Rule, Ruler, or Sons-in-Law of the State?' *Modern Asian Studies* 37, no. 2 (2003), pp. 363–379.

62. K. Srinivasulu, 'The Idea of University in a Princely State: Reflections on the Century-old Osmania University, Hyderabad 1', *The Idea of a University* (Routledge India, 2021), pp. 127–139.

63. Interview with M Chandrasekhar, Hyderabad, 1 August 1, 2020

Chapter 6: An Industrial Laboratory and a Culture of Science

1. V.V. Krishna, 'India@ 75: Science, Technology and Innovation Policies for Development', *Science, Technology and Society* 27, no. 1 (2022), pp. 113–146.

2. N.R. Rajagopal, *The CSIR Saga: Upto 1965* Vol. 1 (Publications and Information Directorate, New Delhi, 1991), pp. 53–54.

3. Indira Chowdhury, *Growing the Tree of Science: Homi Bhabha and the Tata Institute of Fundamental Research* (Oxford University Press, New Delhi, 2016), p. 30.

4. File relating to the recurring and non-recurring grant required by the CLSIR, Hyderabad Deccan, Ministry of N.R.&S.R., File PR_000003042347, National Archives of India, p. 72.

5. File relating to the recurring grant required by the CLSIR, p. 86.

6. M.H. Hasham Premji, 'Letter to Syed Husain Zaheer', Bombay, 3 January 1953.

7. File relating to recurring and non-recurring grant to CLSIR, Hyderabad Deccan, Ministry of Education and Scientific Research, 1953, PR_000003042393, National Archives of India, p. 17.

8. File relating to recurring and non-recurring grant to CLSIR, p. 15.

9. File relating to recurring and non-recurring grant to CLSIR, p. 13.

10. File relating to recurring and non-recurring grant to CLSIR, p. 18.

11. File relating to recurring and non-recurring grant to CLSIR, p. 68.

12. File relating to recurring and non-recurring grant to CLSIR, p. 20.

13. File relating to recurring and non-recurring grant to CLSIR, p. 21.

14. File relating to recurring and non-recurring grant to CLSIR, p. 30.

15. File relating to recurring and non-recurring grant to CLSIR, p. 215.

16. File relating to recurring and non-recurring grant to CLSIR, pp. 253–254.

17. N.R. Rajagopal, *The CSIR Saga: Upto 1965*, (Publications and Information Directorate, CSIR, New Delhi, 1991), p. 80.

18. Interview with Dr G. Thyagarajan, former director, RRL Hyderabad, Chennai, 18 July 2021.

19. Half Yearly Report—Entomology Section, January to June 1956, RRL Hyderabad.

20. File relating to the recurring and non-recurring grant required by the CLSIR, Hyderabad-Deccan, Ministry of N.R.&S.R., National Archives of India, p. 104.

21. File relating to the recurring and non-recurring grant required by the CLSIR, p. 105.

22. *CSIR-IICT: Celebrating Seven Decades of Service to the Nation* (IICT Hyderabad, 2014), pp. 78–79.

23. 'Annual Report', Regional Research Laboratory, Hyderabad, 1960-61, pp. 44–54.

24. 'Report on LTC Market Survey Carried Out in Hyderabad City', RRL Hyderabad.

25. Syed Husain Zaheer, 'The Problem of Domestic Fuels and Its Solution through Low Temperature Carbonisation', Presidential Address, Section of Chemistry, Forty-Third Indian Science Congress, Agra, 1956, pp. 14–15.

26. Syed Husain Zaheer, 'General Presidential Address, National Academy of Sciences' (National Academy of Sciences, Allahabad, October 1973), pp. 16–17.

27. 'Process Know-How Report for HCCL', February 1977, RRL Hyderabad.

28. IAEC (Industrial Development Division), Letter to NRDC, Bombay, 17 April 1958.

29. Syed Husain Zaheer, 'Letter to Karl Wolfram', Hyderabad, 5 May 1956.

30. Minutes of Group Meeting on Hand Made Paper Held on 8 March 1957, RRL Hyderabad.

31. Annual Report, 1960, RRL Hyderabad, pp. 63–65.

32. 'India Pushes mew Chemical projects, *Chemistry & Engineering News*, 14 January 1963.

33. Dr S. Husain Zaheer: A Short Biographical Note, RRL Hyderabad.

34. A. Rahman and S. Husain Zaheer, 'An Indian View', *Operational Research Quarterly* (1950–1952) 3, no. 4 (1952), pp. 57–59.

35. Rahman and Zaheer, 'An Indian View'.

36. 'High Acetyl Value Castor Oil: A Note from CLSIR', CLSIR Hyderabad, July 1952.

37. Dr S. Bhattacharji, Dr S.N. Ghatak, Dr S.S. Iyer (eds), *CSIR-Looking Back* (CSIR Pensioners Welfare Association, Lucknow, 1997), pp. 130–131.

38. Bhattacharji et al. (eds), *CSIR-Looking Back*.

Chapter 7: The Early Movers

1. Major General S.L. Bhatia, 31 March 1953, Bhatia B2P30 NRL, SL Bhatia Archives, Bangalore.

2. Interview with Sanjar Ali Khan, Hyderabad, 19 July and 21 August 2021.

3. Interview with Sanjar Ali Khan.

4. 'Atomic Research Institute for Hyderabad', *Daily News*, 27 March 1959.

5. V.N. Patwardhan, 'The Nutrition Research Laboratories, Indian Research Fund Association, Coonoor, South India', *Current Science* 16, no. 2 (1947), pp. 47–49.

6. B.S. Narasinga Rao, *Development of Nutritional Science in India* (Allied Publishers, New Delhi, 2005), p. 42.

7. Patwardhan, 'The Nutrition Research Laboratories'.

8. Narsinga Rao, *Development*, p. 50.

9. 'Progress of Nutrition Survey in Hyderabad', *Hyderabad Information*, March 1942, pp. 24–26.

10. Joseph Bhore, 'Report of the Health Survey and Development Committee Vol. II (Recommendations)' (Government of India, 1945), p. 427.

11. 'Nutrition Research Laboratories: Amrit Kaur Lays Foundation', *Deccan Chronicle*, 1 April 1953.

12. Oral Answers, Lok Sabha, 23 June 1952, pp. 1140–1141.

13. 'Nutrition Research Laboratories: Amrit Kaur Lays Foundation', *Deccan Chronicle*, 1 April 1953.

14. 'Advisory Committee for Coordinating Scientific Works–Meetings, Ministry of Education, File PR_000003042631', National Archives of India, pp. 64–65.

15. Dr S. Bhattacharji, Dr S. N. Ghatak, Dr S.S. Iyer (eds), *CSIR-Looking Back* (CSIR Pensioners Welfare Association, Lucknow, 1997), pp. 44–45.

16. Interview with Ali Hyder Naqvi (nephew of Sadequain), Ghaziabad, September 2021.

17. Interview with Dr Harsh Gupta, former director, NGRI, Hyderabad, 3 December 2021.

18. B.S.R. Murthy, 'Airborne Geophysics and the Indian Scenario', *Journal of Indian Geophysics Union* 11, no. 1 (2007), pp. 1–28.

19.   'Report of the Task Force on Aerial Surveys Constituted by the Planning Commission, Government of India, February 1972', p. 3.

20.   'Report of the Task Force on Aerial Surveys', p. 60.

21.   '10 Scientists Killed', *Indian Express*, 7 April 1977.

22.   'NRSA EFC Approval, Planning Commission (S&T Division), File PR_000002911786', National Archives of India, p. 132.

23.   'NRSA EFC Approval'.

24.   B.L. Deekshatulu, 'Satish Dhawan: Visionary, Humanitarian and Unparalleled Administrator', *Current Science* 119, no. 9 (2020), pp. 1440–1443.

25.   Deekshatulu, 'Satish Dhawan'.

Chapter 8: The Chemistry of Life

1.   'Yeast Fermentation and the Making of Beer and Wine', *Scitable*, Nature. com.

2.   'Annual Report 1960-61, RRL Hyderabad', pp. 34–41.

3.   'Report of Biochemistry Review Committee, University Grants Commission, New Delhi, 1959'.

4.   Bharat Bhushan, *50 Eventful Years* (Indian Institute of Chemical Technology, Hyderabad, 1995), pp. 43–48.

5.   P.M. Bhargava and Chandana Chakrabarti, *The Saga of Indian Science Since Independence: In a Nutshell* (Universities Press, 2003), pp. 59–60.

6.   D.P. Burma and Maharani Chakravorty (eds), *From Physiology and Chemistry to Biochemistry* (Pearson Education India, 2011), p. 153.

7.   National Biological Laboratory: A Plan, Council of Scientific and Industrial Research, New Delhi, 1965, P M Bhargava Collection, Azim Premji University Archives, Bangalore, pp. 2–3.

8.   'Regarding establishment of National Biological Laboratory by Council of Scientific and Industrial Research during Fourth Five Year Plan,' 17/1029/1970 PMS, National Archives of India.

9.   'Extract from the proceedings of the 71st Meeting of the Governing Body of CSIR held on 29 June, 1976', File 2 (1976–78), P M Bhargava Collection, Azim Premji University Archives, Bangalore.

10.   'New Molecular Biology Centre: Science and Beauty Together', *Press Trust of India*, 24 November 1987.

11.   Interview with Chandana Chakrabarti, Hyderabad, 28 July 2020.

12. Gauhar Raza, R. Gopichandran, Gurdeep S. Sappal and T.V. Venkateswaran (eds), *Moments of Eureka-Life & Works of Selected Indian Scientists* (CSIR-NISCAIR, Rajya Sabha TV and Vigyan Prasar), p. 125.
13. Interview with T. Thangaraj, director, CDFD, Hyderabad, 20 August 2021.
14. Interview with Lakshmi Rao Kandukuri, CCMB, Hyderabad, 8 February 2023.

Chapter 9: Electronics, Nuclear Fuel and Missiles

1. B.V. Sreekantan, 'Sixty Years of the Tata Institute of Fundamental Research 1945–2005: The Role of Young Men in the Creation and Development of this Institute', *Current Science* 90, no. 7 (2006), pp. 1012–1025.
2. Dinesh C. Sharma, *The Long Revolution: The Birth and Growth of India's IT Industry* (HarperCollins, New Delhi, 2009), p. 16.
3. Interviews with A.S. Rao, conducted by S.P.K. Gupta between December 1972 and June 1973, New Delhi and Hyderabad.
4. *Electronics in India: Report of the Electronics Committee* (Government of India, 1966).
5. C.V. Sundaram, L.V. Krishnan and T.S. Iyengar, *Atomic Energy in India: 50 Years* (Department of Atomic Energy, 1998), p. 80.
6. Sundaram et al., *Atomic Energy*, pp. 85–86.
7. S.R. Vijayakar, E.V.R. Rao and M.R. Parthasarathy (eds), 'A.S. Rao: Scientist, Visionary, Humanist—A Story of Self-reliance in Electronics* (Self published, Hyderabad, 2020), p. 24.
8. Vijayakar et al. (eds), *A.S. Rao*, p. 29.
9. Interview with Badrivishal Bajaj, former engineer, ECIL, Hyderabad, Hyderabad, 2 June 2020.
10. Interview with Yadaiah, former deputy general manager, ECIL, Hyderabad, Hyderabad, 29 July 2020.
11. Vijayakar et al. (eds), *A.S. Rao*, pp. 50–51.
12. Vijayakar et al. (eds), *A.S. Rao*.
13. S. Manikutty, 'Electronics Corporation of India (D): The Consumer Electronics Group' (Indian Institute of Management Ahmedabad 1996).
14. S. Srikantan, 'The Evolution of Minicomputer and the Scope of Its Use in India', *Electronics Today*, September 1974, pp. 46–48.
15. Vijayakar et al. (eds), *A.S. Rao*, p. 69.

16. Sridhar Mitta, 'Using Microprocessors in ECIL', *Itihaasa*, https://itihaasa. com/describe/orgartefact/001_001_0320?organisation=BARC, accessed on 29 August 2023.

17. Joseph Mathai, *Digital Republic: India's Rise to IT Power: History and Memoir* (Power Publishers, 2013), p. 143.

18. Tim Palmer, 'After IBM—An Indian Summer', *New Scientist*, 17 July 1978.

19. Manikutty, 'Electronics Corporation of India'.

20. Alok Shukla, *Electronic Voting Machine: The True Story* (Platinum Press, Mumbai, 2018).

21. Shukla, *Electronic Voting Machine*.

22. Shukla, *Electronic Voting Machine*.

23. Ramadas P. Shenoy, *Defence Research & Development Organisation, 1958–1982* (DRDO, New Delhi, 2006), p. 63.

24. Shenoy, *Defence Research & Development Organisation*, p. 85.

25. Shenoy, *Defence Research & Development Organisation*, p. 199.

26. V.S. Arunachalam, *From Temples to Turbines: An Adventure in Two World* (Defence Research and Development Organisation, New Delhi, 2019), p. 32.

27. Arunachalam, *From Temples to Turbines*, p. 32.

28. Shenoy, *Defence Research & Development Organisation*, p. 132.

29. Shenoy, *Defence Research & Development Organisation*, p. 36.

30. Vijayakar et al. (eds), *A.S. Rao*, p. 24.

31. *ICRISAT at 30: The Historic Journey to Semi-Arid Tropics* (ICRISAT, Hyderabad, December 2002), pp. 4, 8.

32. *ICRISAT at 30*, pp. 4, 8.

33. Vijayakar et al. (eds), *A.S. Rao*, p. 28.

34. Interview with Sanjaya Baru, economist and author, Hyderabad, 5 March 2022.

Chapter 10: Manna from Heaven

1. Interview with Ramesh P. Jhunjhunwala, former chairman and managing director, CMC Limited, Hyderabad, January 2007.

2. Interview with Sridhar Mitta, former head of R&D, Wipro, Bangalore, March 2007.

3. Interview with Arvind Sharma, former engineer, ASCI and CMC, Hyderabad, December 2006.

4. Interview with Arvind Sharma.

5. B.S.S. Gupta, 'The Computer Centre', *Retrospect: 25 Years of ASCI* (Administrative Staff College of India, Hyderabad, 1982).

6. *Origin and Growth of IT Industry in Hyderabad* (Dr Marri Chenna Reddy Human Resource Development Institute of Telangana, Hyderabad, July 2022), p. 39.

7. Dinesh C. Sharma, *The Long Revolution: The Birth and Growth of India's IT Industry* (HarperCollins, New Delhi, 2009), p. 96.

8. Interview with Prem Prakash Gupta, former CMD, CMC Limited, New Delhi, August 2003.

9. Syed Husain Zaheer, 'Letter to K S Krishnan (Director, NPL)', Hyderabad, April 1961.

10. Interview with Ramesh Jhunjhunwala.

11. Interview with Ramesh Jhunjhunwala.

12. Interview with Surendra Kapoor, former CMD, CMC Limited, Hyderabad, 29 May 2022.

13. Interview with Arvind Sharma.

14. Sharma, *The Long Revolution*, p. 148.

15. Interview with Arvind Sharma.

16. Interview with Prem Prakash Gupta.

17. Interview with Sridhar Mitta.

18. Interview with B.V.R. Mohan Reddy, founder chairman, Cyient, Hyderabad, Hyderabad, 2 December 2021.

19. Interview with Shakti Sagar, co-founder, Intergraph India, Hyderabad, 14 June 2022.

20. Interview with Shakti Sagar.

21. Bhupesh Bhandari, *The Satyam Saga* (Business Standard Books, 2009).

22. Sugata Srinivasaraju, 'Andhra's Very Own', *Outlook*, 3 February 2022, https://www.outlookindia.com/website/story/andhras-very-own/239523, accessed on 29 August 2023.

23. Ed Cohen, *Leadership Without Borders: Successful Strategies from World-class Leaders* (John Wiley, 2007).

24. Interview with B.V.R. Mohan Reddy.

25. *Software Directory* (Government of India, Department of Electronics, 1990).

26. Interview with Ashhar Farhan, co-founder, Daana Farmers Network, Hyderabad, 14 June 2022.

27. *Software Directory* (Government of India, Department of Electronics, 1990).

28. Interview with N. Vittal, former secretary, Department of Electronics, New Delhi, March 2004.

29. 'Stone for Rajiv Software Park to Be laid Today', *Deccan Chronicle*, 21 May 1992.

30. 'Achieving Rajiv's goals Is the best Tribute: CM', *Deccan Chronicle*, 22 May 1992.

31. Personal communication from Srinivas Chilakalapudi, chief strategy officer, Green Gold Animation, Hyderabad, September 2022.

32. Personal communication from Sandhya Khode, founder director, Motorola Software Center, Hyderabad, October 2022.

33. Interview with Anand Mariganti, Hyderabad Urban Laboratory, Hyderabad, March 2022.

Chapter 11: Two Coups and 20/20 Vision

1. Interview with J.A. Chowdary, former director, STPI Hyderabad, Hyderabad, 8 March 2022.

2. Video footage of the remarks made by President William Jefferson Clinton at the inauguration of HITEC City on 24 March 2000, available at Clinton Presidential Library.

3. N. Chandrababu Naidu with Sevanti Ninan, *Plain Speaking* (Penguin India, 2000), p. 47.

4. Naidu, *Plain Speaking*, p. 117.

5. Interview with Sheela Bhide, former secretary, Department of Industries—Andhra Pradesh, New Delhi, 18 May 2022.

6. Naidu, *Plain Speaking*, pp. 61–62.

7. Interview with Sheela Bhide.

8. 'APIIC Head Defends Selection of L&T', *Deccan Chronicle*, 1 November 1997.

9. Naidu, *Plain Speaking*, p. 76.

10. 'PM Praises "Cyber Pradesh"', *Deccan Chronicle*, 23 November 1998.

11. Interview with Randeep Sudan, former Special Secretary to Chief Minister Babu, Hyderabad/Singapore, March 2022.

12. Interview with Randeep Sudan.

13. Naidu, *Plain Speaking*, p. 8.

14. Syed Amin Jafri, 'Oracle to Invest Rs 600 Million in Hyderabad Facility', Rediff.com, 1 August 2002.

15. 'R&D in India: The Curtain Rises, the Play Has Begun', *Economic Times*, 24 August 2005.

16. 'Microsoft to Invest $50 Million in Hyderabad Centre', Rediff.com, 2 January 2002.

17. 'Talent Is Great in India', Rediff.com, 16 June 2006.

18. Interview with Sheela Bhide.

19. *Andhra Pradesh—Vision 2020* (Government of Andhra Pradesh, January 1999).

20. Naidu, *Plain Speaking*, p. 239.

21. *Andhra Pradesh—Vision 2020*, p. 283.

22. Digant Das, 'Hyderabad: Visioning, Restructuring and Making of a High-Tech City', *Cities* 43 (2015), pp. 48–58.

23. Naidu, *Plain Speaking*, p. 148.

24. *Andhra Pradesh—Vision 2020*, p. 45.

25. Interview with Randeep Sudan.

26. Interview with Sanjaya Baru.

27. Avvari V. Mohan, Haribabu Ejnavarzala and C. Naga Lakshmi, 'University Linkages in Technology Clusters of Emerging Economies—Exploratory Case Studies from Cyberjaya, Malaysia—a Greenfield Development and Cyberabad, India—a Brownfield Development', *World Technopolis Review* 1, no. 1 (2012), pp. 42–55.

28. Interview with M. Chandrasekhar.

29. 'Making of IIIT—How It All Started', video prepared by IIIT, *YouTube*, https://www.youtube.com/watch?v=-g_pQf_-s9s.

30. Pramath Raj Sinha, *An Idea Whose Time Has Come: The Story of the Indian School of Business* (Penguin India, 2011).

31. Sinha, *An Idea Whose Time Has Come*.

32. Sinha, *An Idea Whose Time Has Come*.

33. Naidu, Facebook post on Indian School of Business, 26 May 2022.

34. Sinha, *An Idea Whose Time Has Come*, p. 98.

35.   Sinha, *An Idea Whose Time Has Come*, p. 170.

36.   K.V. Kurmanath, 'Y2K: A Real Scare', *Hindu BusinessLine*, 28 September 2013.

37.   Interview with Saurabh Srivastava, founder, IIS, New Delhi, May 2006.

Chapter 12: A Party Drug, Diazepam and Reverse Engineering

1.   Syed Husain Zaheer, A Note on Methaqualone, n.d., RRL Hyderabad.

2.   Indra Kishore Kacker, 'My Early Life', unpublished, 2003 (provided by the Kacker family).

3.   I.K. Kacker and S.H. Zaheer, 'Potential Analgesics. 1. Synthesis of Substituted 4-Quinazolones', *Journal of Indian Chemical Society* 28, no. 6 (1951), pp. 344–346.

4.   Interview with Dr G. Thyagarajan, former Director, RRL Hyderabad, Chennai, 18 July 2021.

5.   Syed Husain Zaheer, 'A Note on Methaqualone' (RRL Hyderabad, n.d.).

6.   Etienne F. van Zyl, 'A Survey of Reported Synthesis of Methaqualone and Some Positional and Structural Isomers', *Forensic Science International* 122, no. 2–3 (2001), pp. 142–149.

7.   Interview with Anuj Kacker, CEO, Aptech Limited, Gurgaon, 15 July 2024.

8.   Presidential Address by Dr S. Husain Zaheer at the 43rd Annual General Meeting, Indian Chemical Society, 1967.

9.   Presidential Address by Dr S. Husain Zaheer at the 43rd Annual General Meeting, Indian Chemical Society, 1967.

10.   Interview with S. Riaz Hashim, former scientist, RRL Hyderabad, 20 June 2022.

11.   Amarnath Menon, 'Indian Scientists Achieve Major Breakthrough with Anti-inflammatory Drug Tromaril', *India Today*, 28 February 1981.

12.   'New Drug Developed by RRL Hyderabad', Lok Sabha Debates, English version, 13th Lok Sabha, 1989, p. 162.

13.   P.K. Ramachandran and B.V. Rangarao, 'The Pharmaceutical Industry in India', *Economic and Political Weekly* 7, no. 9 (26 February 1972), pp. M27–M36.

14.   'Report of the Committee on Drugs and Pharmaceuticals Industry' (Ministry of Petroleum and Chemicals, April 1975), p. 107.

15. Report of the Committee of Public Undertakings (1973-74), Fifth Lok Sabha, 56th Report, IDPL, pp. 226–227.

16. Bhupesh Bhandari, *The Ranbaxy Story: The Rise of an Indian Multinational* (Penguin Global, 2005), pp. 47–48.

17. Bhandari, *The Ranbaxy Story*, pp. 47–48.

18. Interview with M.F. Rahman, former scientist, RRL—Hyderabad, Hyderabad, 23 August 2021.

19. Bhandari, *The Ranbaxy Story*, p. 57.

20. Ranbaxy Laboratories Ltd. vs Dua Pharmaceuticals Pvt. Ltd, Delhi High Court Judgement on 22 July, 1988, AIR 1989 Delhi 44, 1988 (2) ARBLR 315 Delhi, 36 (1988) DLT, p. 133.

21. Interview with A.V. Rama Rao, former scientist, NCL and IICT, Hyderabad, 19 August 2021.

22. Richard Lane, 'Yusuf Hamied: Leader in the Indian Generic Drug Industry', *The Lancet* 386, no. 10011 (2015), p. 2385.

23. Interview with A.V. Rama Rao.

24. Interview with A.V. Rama Rao.

25. Interview with Dinesh Abrol, former Scientist, CSIR-NISTADS, New Delhi, April 2022.

Chapter 13: A Catalyst and a Chain Reaction

1.   K. Anji Reddy, *An Unfinished Agenda: My Life in the Pharmaceuticals Industry* (Penguin UK, 2015), p. 15.

2.   A bulk drug or active pharmaceutical ingredient (API) refers to the active chemical substances in powder form used as the main ingredient having therapeutic value. It is used for making pharmaceutical formulations (tablets, capsules, syrups, etc.).

3.   Report of Committee on Public Undertakings, Third Lok Sabha, March 1966, p. 3.

4.   Advertorial, Hyderabad Chemicals and Pharmaceuticals, published in a brochure of the Indian Academy of Science meeting, Hyderabad, December 1950.

5.   Report of Committee on Public Undertakings, Third Lok Sabha, p. 3.

6.   Report of Committee on Public Undertakings, Third Lok Sabha, p. 15.

7.   Report of Committee on Public Undertakings (1968-69), Fourth Lok Sabha, 46th Report, April 1969, pp. 6–7.

8. Report of Committee on Public Undertakings, Third Lok Sabha, pp. 35–36.
9. Report of Committee on Public Undertakings (1968-69), Fourth Lok Sabha, pp. 6–7.
10. Report of Committee on Public Undertakings (1968-69), Fourth Lok Sabha, p. 10.
11. Report of the Committee of Public Undertakings (1973-74), Fifth Lok Sabha, 56th Report, IDPL, pp. 194–195.
12. Report of the Committee of Public Undertakings (1973-74), Fifth Lok Sabha, p. 212.
13. Report of Committee on Public Undertakings (1968-69), Fourth Lok Sabha, 'Action Taken by Government on the Recommendations Contained in the 22nd Report of the Committee on Public Undertakings, Third Lok Sabha', February 1969, p. 44.
14. Reddy, *Unfinished Agenda*, p. 13.
15. Interview with K. Anji Reddy, DRL Archives.
16. Interview with K. Anji Reddy.
17. Reddy, *Unfinished Agenda*, p. 14.
18. Interview, with Dr N. Bhaskar Rao, former member of Board of Directors, IDPL, New Delhi, 30 June 2022.
19. Reddy, *Unfinished Agenda*, p. 22.
20. File relating to M/S Uniloids Limited, Secretariat for Industrial Approvals, 1976-1977, PR_000002842037, National Archives of India.
21. File relating to M/S Uniloids Limited.
22. File relating to M/S Standard Organics Ltd., Industrial Development, 1980, PR_000003009971, National Archives of India.
23. Interview with K. Anji Reddy.
24. Reddy, *Unfinished Agenda*, p. 29.
25. Report of the Committee of Public Undertakings (1973-74), Fifth Lok Sabha, pp. 227, 288.
26. Reddy, *Unfinished Agenda*, p. 41.
27. Interview with K. Anji Reddy.
28. Reddy, *Unfinished Agenda*, p. 43.
29. Reddy, *Unfinished Agenda*, p. 53.
30. Reddy, *Unfinished Agenda*, p. 56.
31. *Competition and Regulation Issues in the Pharmaceutical Industry* (OECD, 2001), p. 2.

32.   *Competition and Regulation Issues*, p. 37.

33.   Interview with Asit Mukherjee, founder, Targof Pure Drugs Private Limited, Hyderabad, 12 April 2022.

Chapter 14: Vaccine Wars and Genome Valley

1.   Interview with K.I. Varaprasad Reddy, founder, Shantha Biotechnics, Hyderabad, 4 August 2020.

2.   Stanley A. Plotkin, 'Six Revolutions in Vaccinology', *The Pediatric Infectious Disease Journal* 24, no. 1 (January 2005), pp. 1–9, doi: 10.1097/01.inf.0000148933.08301.02. PMID: 15665703.

3.   Interview with Ramareddy Guntaka, chief scientific advisor, Sudershan Biotech Limited—Hyderabad, Hyderabad, 5 March 2022, 29 April 2022.

4.   Interview, K.I. Varaprasad Reddy.

5.   Interview with Isanaka Ramakrishna Reddy, founder, Issar Pharmaceuticals Private Limited—Hyderabad, Hyderabad, 17 May 2022.

6.   Interview with Ramareddy Guntaka.

7.   James M. Cregg, Ilya Tolstorukov, Anasua Kusari, Jay Sunga, Knut Madden and Thomas Chappell, 'Expression in the Yeast Pichia Pastoris', *Methods in Enzymology* 463, (2009), pp. 169–189.

8.   Chandra Shekhar, 'Pichia Power: India's Biotech Industry Puts Unconventional Yeast to Work', *Chemistry & Biology* 15, no. 3 (2008), pp. 201–202.

9.   Interview, Ramareddy Guntaka.

10.   Justin Chakma, Hassan Masum, Kumar Perampaladas, Jennifer Heys and Peter A. Singer, 'Indian Vaccine Innovation: The Case of Shantha Biotechnics', *Globalization and Health* 7, no. 1 (2011), pp. 1–10.

11.   Interview with V. Ramamurthy, DST secretary and TDB chairman 1995–2006, Chennai, 5 May 2022.

12.   Interview with V. Ramamurthy.

13.   Raj Chengappa, Bharat Biotech's Chief Krishna Ella in an Exclusive Conversation, 7 January 2022, https://www.youtube.com/watch?v=gYyR0ZTC7Wk.

14.   Madhura Amdekar, 'How a Hepatitis B Vaccine Was Made in India', *Connect*, 19 March 2020.

15.   'Revac-B Vaccine Launched', *Hindu BusinessLine*, 24 October 1998.

16. Madhura Amdekar, 'How a Hepatitis B Vaccine Was Made in India'.
17. Interview with Ramareddy Guntaka.
18. 'TDB-Supported Healthcare Sector Projects—1997–1998 to 2013–2014', Technology Development Board website.
19. *Signature Companies & Technologies Funded by TDB for Commercialization* (Confederation of Indian Industry and TDB, 2021).
20. *Andhra Pradesh—Vision 2020*, p. 286.
21. *Andhra Pradesh—Vision 2020*, p. 289.
22. Interview with Sheela Bhide.
23. Interview with Sheela Bhide.
24. Interview with Sheela Bhide.
25. Interview with Deepanwita Chattopadhyay, CEO, IKP, Hyderabad, January 2023.
26. Interview with Sheela Bhide.
27. Interview with Bibhu P. Acharya, former secretary biotechnology, AP, Hyderabad, 25 May 2022.
28. Interview with Bibhu P. Acharya.
29. Interview with Utkarsh Palnitkar, former consultant Ernst & Young, Hyderabad, 3 October 2023.

Chapter 15: The Price of Development

1. Interview with P. Anuradha Reddy, convenor, INTACH—Hyderabad, Hyderabad, May 2022.
2. Interview with A. Pulla Reddy, senior advocate, Telangana High Court, Hyderabad, August 2020.
3. Interview with P. Anuradha Reddy, convenor, INTACH—Hyderabad, Hyderabad, May 2022.
4. Mirza, Isa, 'The Provision of Information Services in a New Political Economy: A Case Study from Hyderabad, India', *Journal of Contemporary Asia* 43, no. 1 (2013), pp. 148–172.
5. Ayesh Minhaz, 'Why Telangana Government Wants to Pull Down Osmania General Hospital', *The Hindu*, 24 August 2023.
6. Report of Committee on Public Undertakings (Third Lok Sabha), March 1966, 22nd report of the CPU on IDPL, p. 35.
7. Report of Committee on Public Undertakings (Third Lok Sabha), p. 35.
8. Report of Committee on Public Undertakings (Third Lok Sabha).

9.   File relating to M/S Uniloids Limited, National Archives of India, p. 49.

10. File relating to M/S Standard Organics Ltd., National Archives of India, pp. 10–17.

11. Interview with Asit Mukherjee.

12. Interview with Sheela Bhide.

13. Interview with Kalpna Ramesh, founder, The Rainwater Project, Hyderabad, 27 January 2023.

14. Vinita Pandey, 'Changing Facets of Hyderabadi Tehzeeb: Are We Missing Anything?' *Space and Culture, India* 3, no. 1 (2015), pp. 17–29.

15. Pandey, 'Changing Facets of Hyderabadi Tehzeeb'.

16. Interview with Vinay Varma, actor and theatre personality, Hyderabad, 19 July 2024.

17. Pandey, 'Changing Facets of Hyderabadi Tehzeeb'.

18. Raman, Usha, and Aditya Deshbandhu, 'The Digital Shaping of a City: A Biography of "Cyberabad" in Three Acts', in *The Palgrave Handbook of Everyday Digital Life* (Cham: Springer International Publishing, 2024), pp. 61–75.

19. Interview, P. Anuradha Reddy.

20. Kalpana Markandey, 'Hyderabad: From the Feudal City to a Hi-Tech Metropolis', in R.P. Misra (ed.), *Urbanisation in South Asia: Focus on Mega Cities* (Cambridge University Press, New Delhi, 2013), pp. 199–226.

Conclusion: Dreams of a Globalised City

1.   'We're Not Only Going to Compete with Silicon Valley, But Will Surpass It: T-Hub CEO', *Economic Times Online*, 6 July 2022.

2.   Harish Damodaran, *India's New Capitalists: Caste, Business, and Industry in a Modern Nation* (Hachette India, 2018), pp. 110–111.

3.   Tejaswini Pagadala, *India's Glocal Leader: Chandrababu Naidu* (Bloomsbury, 2018).

4.   Interview with Sanjaya Baru

5.   C.V. Subbarao, *Hyderabad: Social Context of Industrialization 1875 to 1948*, p. 145.

6.   Sheela Raj, *The Profile of Secular and Transparent Hyderabad Under Nizam VII* (Narahari Pershad Charitable Trust, Hyderabad, 2014), p. 51.

7.   Raj, *The Profile of Secular and Transparent Hyderabad*, p. 54.

8.   Tejaswini Pagadala, *India's Glocal Leader: Chandrababu Naidu.*

9.   *Telangana's Second ICT Policy (2021–2026)* (Government of Telangana, 2021), p. 4.

10.   'We're Not Only Going to Compete with Silicon Valley, But Will Surpass It: T-Hub CEO'.

11.   'Pharma – Invest Telangana', Official website of the Government of Telangana, https://invest.telangana.gov.in/pharma/ (accessed on 15 July 2024).

12.   *Origin and Growth of IT Industry in Hyderabad* (Dr Marri Chenna Reddy Institute of Telangana, Hyderabad, 2022), p. 126.

13.   Interview with Rashmi Pimpale, CEO, Research and Innovation Circle of Hyderabad, Hyderabad, January 2023.

14.   'Hyderabad Well Poised to Become India's Innovation Capital,' *The Times of India*, 26 July 2022.

Acknowledgements

WRITING THIS BOOK ON THE JOURNEY OF HYDERABAD has been a labour of love, and I would like to express my deepest gratitude to all those who have contributed to its completion. The research and exploration involved in unravelling the rich historical landscape of Hyderabad would not have been possible without the support and assistance of numerous individuals and institutions.

First and foremost, I thank the Jawaharlal Nehru Memorial Fund (JNMF) for its generous support in the form of the Jawaharlal Nehru Fellowship granted to me in 2020. I am grateful for the confidence that the Trustees and members of the Selection Committee placed in me and my proposal. Dr N. Balakrishnan, administrative secretary of the Fund, extended all necessary help despite the constraints placed by the COVID-19 pandemic. The Fund's commitment to promoting academic research, cultural understanding and historical scholarship is truly commendable.

Furthermore, I acknowledge the support I received from the International Centre Goa (ICG) which selected me as their Scholar-in-Residence for the year 2022-23. The residency in the tranquil environment, away from the humdrum of Hyderabad and New Delhi, helped me give a final shape to the book. I also benefited from my interactions with the Centre's director, Dr Pushkar.

A book that dwells into some important aspects of a city's history spanning over a century requires access to multiple sources—archives, institutions, libraries, interviews, newspaper records and field visits.

As a start, I dug into the material on Hyderabad I had collected over the years as a journalist, beginning with papers presented at a symposium to mark 400 years of Hyderabad organised by the Salar Jung Museum in 1991. I had a copy of the book on Hyderabad by Narendra Luther. I met him in 2015 and discussed with him my ideas. He is, unfortunately, no more but the inputs he gave were very useful. I would like to acknowledge authors, historians and scholars who have previously explored and documented different aspects of Hyderabad. Their meticulous research and insightful analyses proved inspiring to me to embark on this journey.

The archives serve as the guardians of our collective history, and without their meticulous preservation and organisation of documents, this project would not have been possible. The archival material I referred to came from the Nehru Memorial Museum and Library (NMML), National Archives of India (New Delhi), Telangana State Archives and Research Institute (Hyderabad), Indian Institute of Science Archives, Indian Institute of Astrophysics Archives, Major General S.L. Bhatia Museum for the History of Medicine, Azim Premji University Archives (all in Bangalore), Tata Institute of Fundamental Research Archives (Mumbai) and Dr Reddy's Laboratory (DRL) Archives, Hyderabad. I express my appreciation to the dedicated staff at these archives for their invaluable assistance. I am particularly thankful to Jyoti Luthra and Naveen Kumar at NMML and M.A. Raqeeb at Telangana Archives.

I am particularly grateful to Princess Esra Birgen for granting special permission to access the Asaf Jahi records preserved at the Chowmahalla Palace in Hyderabad, and to G. Kishan Rao, the director of Chowmahalla Palace, for facilitating the process. The staff led by Taqdees Habeeb, archivist and curator, was extremely helpful in letting me access relevant files and sharing their insights.

The second most important mode of research was oral history interviews with a diversified set of people—CEOs, senior scientists, bureaucrats, historians, economists, civil society activists and former employees of companies. Many of these fifty-odd interviews were conducted face-to-face, while others were over Zoom and phone given the pandemic-related restrictions. I am grateful to each one of them for sharing their views, memories and material like photographs and documents. These intimate glimpses into the past and the present have added depth and perspective to the narrative, which I hope will let readers connect with historical figures and events on a more personal level. In this regard, I am particularly grateful to Sanjar Ali Khan, J.A. Chowdhary, Randeep Sudan, K.I. Varaprasad Reddy, P. Anuradha Reddy, Dr N. Bhaskara Rao and Dr Indira Chowdhury.

In this book, I have also used some oral history interviews that were originally conducted for my book on the Indian information technology industry published in 2009, under a fellowship granted by the New India Foundation. I am indebted to the Foundation for its support and the guidance and encouragement I have received from Ramchandra Guha from time to time. I am truly fortunate to have had the opportunity to learn from his wealth of knowledge and experience.

I extend my heartfelt appreciation to my colleagues, friends and members of my extended family in Hyderabad and Delhi who have provided valuable insights and assistance. Mulugu Somasekhar, N.P. Chandrasekhar, Y. Mallikarjun, D. Ramakrishna Reddy, Parsa Venkateshwar Rao Jr, Dr Mohan Gupta, Dr Mahesh Sharma, Dr Subbarao M. Gavaravarapu and Badrivishal Bajaj were among those who shared contacts, information and ideas.

Scientists and officials at the Indian Institute of Chemical Technology, National Geophysical Research Institute, Centre for DNA Fingerprinting and other institutions in Hyderabad provided much-needed help. Their willingness to lend a helping hand was invaluable in shaping the ideas presented in this book. During the writing of the book, I gave three public lectures in Hyderabad on different aspects of the research work. I thank the Rajasthani Graduates Association, ICMR-National Institute of Nutrition (NIN) and Foundation for Advancing Science and Technology (FAST) for the opportunity to share my ideas with diverse audiences.

And a big thanks to Karthika V.K. at Westland Books for recognising the potential of this project and providing suggestions that greatly enhanced its quality. The commitment to excellence shown by the editor Sonia Madan, designer Saurabh Garge, and other members of the editing and marketing teams at Westland helped shape this book into its final form.

A time-consuming project like this one could not have reached fruition without constant love, patience and understanding from my family—Annu, Maanvi and Kushagr. Their support provided me with the motivation and inspiration to persevere.

www.ingramcontent.com/pod-product-compliance
Lightning Source LLC
Chambersburg PA
CBHW071136130626
46553CB00004B/1401